In Enemy Hands

In Enemy Hands
A Prisoner in
NORTH KOREA

LARRY ZELLERS

With a Foreword by John Toland

THE UNIVERSITY PRESS OF KENTUCKY

Publication of this volume was made possible in part
by a grant from the National Endowment for the Humanities.

Editorial and Sales Offices: The University Press of Kentucky
663 South Limestone Street, Lexington, Kentucky 40508-4008

03 02 01 00 99   5 4 3 2 1

Library of Congress Cataloging-in-Publication Data

Zellers, Larry, 1922-
   In enemy hands: a prisoner in North Korea / Larry Zellers ;
with a foreword by John Toland.
      p. cm.
   Includes bibliographical references and index.
   ISBN 0-8131-0976-0 (paper : alk. paper)
   1. Korean War, 1950-1953—Personal narratives, American.
2. Korean War, 1950-1953—Prisoners and prisons, North Korean.
3. Zellers, Larry, 1922-   I. Title.
DS921.6.Z45   1991
951.904'2—dc20   90-26375

To Frances, whose spirit supported me every step of the way and whose unflagging faith in my return never faltered.

Also to those who, in that unhappy land and for whatever reason, did not make it.

CONTENTS

FOREWORD

FOR most Americans, myself included, the emotional exhaustion left by World War II blocked out the three seemingly endless years of the Korean War. We were absorbed by the recovery of America and Europe rather than the perilous involvement in the Far East. We did not realize that this war was unique in our history. In fact, it wasn't even a war, only a police action—according to President Harry Truman. Yet fifteen of the United Nations had joined in fighting North Korea and China, and four million human beings perished in a brutal contest that eventually led to the tragedy of Vietnam.

Half of those who died in Korea were civilians and, although much has recently been written about the Korean War, too little has described the terrifying experiences of civilians trapped in the war. That is why *In Enemy Hands* by Larry Zellers, a Methodist missionary, is so important. His harrowing tale of western civilian prisoners of the North Koreans and Chinese is a fitting monument to the men, women, and children who endured starvation, beatings, humiliation, and privations for almost three years.

Zellers's detailed account of the Death March in North Korea in the winter of 1950 is an unforgettable saga of human tragedy and valor. During a journey of more than a hundred miles over rugged terrain in the bitter cold and snow, almost a hundred dead civilians and American soldiers were left along the way. Those who survived endured endless hardships until freedom at last came in 1953.

What makes Zellers's relentless chronicle so compelling is the moving portrayal of his comrades in the face of adversity. Unprepared and untrained for the rigors and terrors of imprisonment by an alien foe, they somehow managed to survive because of their indomitable spirit, their faith, and their common self-sacrifice. All this has allowed Zellers to make an unbearable tale inspirational.

John Toland

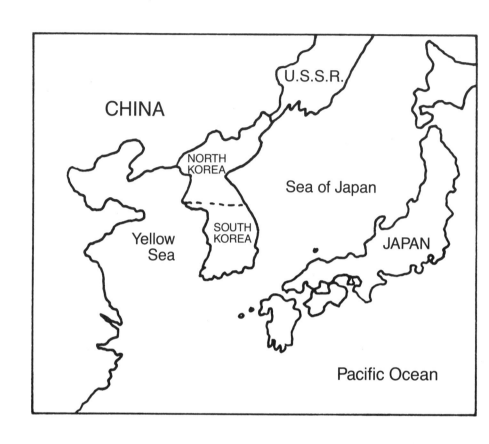

CHINA

U.S.S.R.

NORTH
KOREA

SOUTH
KOREA

Yellow
Sea

Sea of Japan

JAPAN

Pacific Ocean

PREFACE

WHEN I was released from North Korea in 1953, after three years in confinement, I discovered that I had more things to do than I could accomplish. I wrote down my experiences soon after I returned, but I never found time to arrange them for publication. I thought I might finish that task when I retired from the U.S. Air Force in 1975, but by that time the Korean War was ancient history, even to me.

I would never have undertaken it except for a chance meeting in 1987 in Seoul, Korea, with members of the United Nations Command Military Armistice Commission (UNCMAC). The Air Force had sent me to Korea in January 1987 to share my prison experiences with U.S. military personnel there. Following a speech at Camp Red Cloud near Seoul, I was interviewed by U.S. Armed Forces Korea Television. In response to a question, I mentioned the two neighboring North Korean villages of Hanjang-ni and An-dong, where approximately 400 American military and civilian prisoners from several nations had been buried during the winter of 1950.

Subsequently, I was put in touch with Lieutenant Colonel Gilbert H. Eckrich, U.S. Army, assistant secretary of UNCMAC. Eckrich informed me that his commission was particularly interested in obtaining additional information about the location of American and other United Nations prisoners of war in North Korea. My mention of those two villages interested them. In extended discussions at the negotiation site at Panmunjom from 1985 to 1987, the North Koreans had never revealed to the Armistice Commission that Americans had even been held in the Hanjang-ni and An-dong area, much less that hundreds had been buried there.

In an effort to show good faith and to support the negotiations, the United Nations Command had brought to Panmunjom the remains of a small number of Chinese and North Korean soldiers killed in South Korea. The Chinese representatives there accepted the remains of their soldiers; the North Korean representatives, on the other hand, rejected a similar offer, claiming the remains were not really those of North

Korean soldiers. The United Nations documentation was extensive, including photographs of North Korean soldiers being buried with full military honors in South Korea. The North Koreans returned the remains of five Americans on Memorial Day 1990 but have otherwise been very slow to respond.

I took part in more discussions with Col. Donald W. Boose, Jr., U.S. Army, secretary of UNCMAC, who asked for a list of survivors at Hanjang-ni. Using the names and addresses I provided, Colonel Boose and Lieutenant Colonel Eckrich built a file of documents received from survivors of the Hanjang-ni area in North Korea. On May 26, 1987, at the 482d Secretaries Meeting at Panmunjom, Colonel Boose submitted this information to the representatives of the Korean People's Army and the Chinese People's Volunteers. They accepted the documents and said they would pass the information to an "appropriate authority."

Before leaving Seoul in February 1987, I was encouraged by Lieutenant Colonel Eckrich and Tom Ryan of the U.S. Army Corps of Engineers, to prepare my manuscript for publication. I had often been given the same advice by friends in the United States; perhaps I had too hastily rejected it on the grounds that no one was reading anything about the Korean War any more.

Fortunately, when I wrote down my experiences in the fall of 1953, after my return to the United States, my memory of the events had been sharpened by an activity in our North Korean prison that Father Philip Crosbie initiated just before our release. Prison conditions had greatly improved by the fall of 1952, allowing Crosbie to begin keeping a diary. He at once set out to reconstruct the events of our imprisonment since the summer of 1950, using the remaining members of our group as sources. Crosbie held many discussions in the camp from late 1952 to the spring of 1953 regarding our common experiences. Once we had reached a consensus on the details of an event, Crosbie wrote it down. I assisted in this project, not only by supplying the data I remembered but by helping round up ink, paper, and pens—and even pine knots from the nearby forest, which Father Crosbie used as a substitute for candles when writing late at night.

Before our release from North Korea, Father Crosbie rewrote the diary, both to sharpen his memory of its contents and to double his chances of getting it out to the free world. Just as we had feared, one copy was lost and the other discovered and confiscated by North Korean authorities when Father Crosbie was released. Nevertheless, he was able to reconstruct the story and publish it in 1954 and 1955 under the various titles *Pencilling Prisoner, Three Winters Cold,* and *March till They Die.*

I have made a concerted attempt to ensure the accuracy of the material in this book by checking it against several sources. First, I compared my 1953 notes with Crosbie's book and Philip Deane's two books, *I Was a Captive in Korea* and *I Should Have Died.* Second, I made use of the collective memories of many survivors, whom I often see at the annual conventions of former POWs of the Korean War.

I differ with Crosbie's account in *March till They Die* in only two very minor instances. One involves the identity of a North Korean official in an episode at the prison camp in Hanjang-ni in the winter of 1950; I agree with Deane's version of that same event as recorded in *I Was a Captive in Korea.* The other involves a very insignificant date: Crosbie's account puts the U.S. Air Force bombing of the international bridge at Chunggangjin, North Korea, on March 30, 1951; I believe it was one day later. According to Robert Futrell in *The United States Air Force in Korea, 1950-1953,* the bridge at Linchiang, China, just across the Yalu River from Chunggangjin, North Korea, was bombed with disappointing results on March 31, 1951. That Air Force evaluation agrees with the report of some of our prisoners who were in Chunggangjin when the bombs fell: the bridge was damaged but not destroyed. As far as I am aware, from memory and research, there was no other bombing of that bridge during the weeks before or after that event.

I wish to express my gratitude to both Philip Deane and Father Philip Crosbie; their books have provided me with very valuable background material for this account. Crosbie's book was especially helpful because it contained the names of all the people of our group, and also because it recorded some incidents from the Death March that only he would know about.

The spelling of some North Korean village names differs between one writer and another and may confuse the reader. Crosbie's book gives the spelling of three North Korean villages of interest to our story as Jungkanjin, Hajang-nee, and Ando. Deane spells the first two Chung Kang Djin and Ha Djang Nee. In conformity with the United Nations maps that I first saw in Seoul in 1987, I have used the spellings Chunggangjin, Hanjang-ni, and An-dong.

On my return to the United States in May 1953, I was interviewed by Murrel Muller on the *Today* television show and by many newspaper reporters in New York, Georgia, and Texas. A few weeks later I was debriefed for a week by the CIA in Washington, D.C. It was between speaking engagements in various parts of the country that I began writing down my experiences, a project I completed in the fall of 1953 while attending Drew University in Madison, New Jersey.

All the conversations, interrogations, and lectures that are recorded in this book actually took place, though the reader will appreciate that I was not able to remember them word for word and had to reconstruct them as best I could. I also wrestled with the problem of the poor quality of English spoken by some of our North Korean captors and how to make it more intelligible to the average reader. Among those who could speak English at all, language skills varied from excellent to very poor. Some spoke with a cultivated Oxford accent; others could be understood only with great difficulty. Therefore, in the interest of clarity, I have changed all dialogue and speeches by the North Koreans to standard English.

Two books present opposing viewpoints about the conduct of Americans in North Korean prisons. Each writer presents strong arguments supporting his particular point of view. Eugene Kinkead's *In Every War but One* strongly implies that Americans gave a much better account of themselves in captivity in all wars before the Korean conflict. Albert Biderman's *March To Calumny* is largely a refutation of Kinkead's book. Biderman feels that the conduct of Americans in the North Korean prisons was not unique but was indeed similar to the conduct of our soldiers in all our previous wars.

My position inclines toward Biderman's—his book contains some very good research and his conclusion are restrained. However, Kinkead does raise some very disturbing issues about the conduct and survival rate of American POWs in North Korea that I cannot answer: the performance of the POWs of other nations was apparently better than that of the Americans.

It must be remembered that those who were with me in prison were the very first to arrive in Korea from bases in Japan. The youngest had had only minimal combat training; there had been no time for more. Given inadequate training and weapons that did not always function, these men had been thrown into South Korea on a piecemeal basis to engage their small units against a vastly superior North Korean army flushed with victory.

After being taken prisoner, the men suffered incredible hardships: cold, hunger, physical abuse, lack of medicine, fatigue, fear, isolation, and intimidation. They had all seen enough unprovoked beatings and summary executions of their friends to know that they had to take seriously any North Korean threat. They felt cast adrift in a hostile, alien environment. Without resources for coping, in time many of these younger men gave up their chain of command, their friends, their hygiene, their pride, and their sense of belonging. Having no discipline, no maturity, and seemingly no faith in anything, they turned their faces to the wall and died.

It is perhaps difficult for those who have not experienced similar situations to understand how death by voluntary starvation—painless in its latter stages—would ever present an apparently reasonable option, but it did to some. For them the "unreasonable" demands of survival finally became too great.

Many people have raised serious questions about the conduct of our Korean prisoners of war, and the conduct of some did leave much to be desired. I have written about many of those failures in this story. But any general condemnation of those prisoners will come from someone else—not me.

This is a delicate issue, but I must make one observation relative to the difference in the general conduct of American prisoners in North Korea with those in North Vietnam: it would not be fair to compare the behavior of mature, well-motivated, professional pilots from the Army, Navy, Air Force, and Marines in North Vietnam prisons with that of many of the young, immature draftees in North Korea.

In addition to the notes that I wrote down soon after my release, some of my later work assisted me in writing this book. While serving as an instructor at the U.S. Air Force Survival School at Stead Air Force Base, Nevada, from 1962 to 1965, I lectured on various subjects, including "Inner Resources for Survival in a Prisoner of War Camp," "What Communist Interrogations Are Like" and "The Code of Conduct." All Air Force flying personnel were required to attend the school at Stead to receive training to help them survive in five hostile environments: the ocean, the Arctic, the jungle, the desert, and the hands of the enemy. In many different areas where I was stationed during my Air Force career, I also spoke to military personnel at alert facilities, Commanders Call, which is an Air Force information program, and schools and to civilian service and fraternal organizations. I continue to lecture on these subjects at military installations and for church and civic groups.

I owe a great deal of gratitude to Vice-Admiral Charles A. Lockwood, USN, Retired, who was in command of all submarine forces in the Pacific during World War II. It was through his efforts that in 1956 and 1957 I was first exposed to the U.S. Fighting Man's Code, commonly known as the Code of Conduct. Admiral Lockwood arranged for me to appear in California with him and others on many programs dealing with the code—on television and radio, at military installations, at the University of California in Berkeley, and before civic groups in the San Francisco–Oakland area.

The Code of Conduct was formulated by the Advisory Committee of the Secretary of Defense on Prisoners of War, of which Admiral Lockwood was a member. Signed by President Dwight Eisenhower in 1955, the code was intended to serve as a guide to any captured American military personnel. It was put to the test in the Vietnam War with very positive results among American military pilots, who gave it high marks. I support the code, but it would be unrealistic to expect that it would have produced similar results among American POWs in North Korea except perhaps for those who understood the words duty, honor, country, faith, sacrifice.

Beyond relating a historical account, my second objective in writing this story is to introduce brave men and women who pushed their survival instincts to the limit and, with whatever strength was left in them, gave to others—and those others were not always in more desperate need. Much has been written concerning the negative aspects of the entire Korean prisoner-of-war experience; I resolved to present the human face of those who fought so desperately against such overwhelming odds.

My third objective is to describe what it was like to face my own death for so long that I came to terms with it. What thoughts went through my mind while I was awaiting death? And there were many ways to die: by execution in a death cell; by being shot for falling behind on the Death March; by starvation, physical abuse, disease, or freezing to death in the winter of 1950 at Hanjang-ni. How is it possible, though, to arrive at a kind of peace about imminent death, a peace without sadness or resentment or what we normally think of as resignation? With the advent of each new danger I prepared myself to live or to die. I have tried to put into words my strategies for survival in each of those brink-of-death situations and to discuss candidly my doubts, my failures, and my successes.

There is one more point that I would like to make clear: I don't want anyone to feel that these lines, or the ones that follow, are self-serving in any way. When the most terrible part of this whole episode took place, it had failure written all over it. Only when we later became free enough, and sufficiently far removed from these events in time, did we feel any joy at still being alive.

Near the end of our imprisonment a fellow prisoner from England, Commissioner Herbert A. Lord, asked me if I would write something about my experiences when I got out.

"No, Commissioner, I'm afraid not," I replied.

"Why not?"

"Commissioner, there are no words to describe what we have been through."

"That is ridiculous! There are words for every human emotion and every experience. If you haven't found them yet, then it means that either your vocabulary isn't large enough, or you haven't thought about it enough, or you haven't felt deeply enough about it. If you dedicate yourself to the task, you will find the right words!"

I hope that I have found the right words to give honor to those for whom it is long overdue and to show that even in a hostile prison environment one can still achieve a certain serenity. If the overall impact on the reader is one of sadness, then I will have failed. It is my purpose to make this story a celebration of life for those who fought against great odds to survive; to keep faith with their God, with something inside themselves, and with their fellow prisoners; and to be human and caring, sometimes at added risk to themselves. Some did not try to help others. Some died trying. Some tried and lived.

I wish to acknowledge the invaluable assistance of a number of people in the preparation of this book. Freddy Cox, J.T. Cox, and Lem Bray read the first draft of the manuscript and made many helpful suggestions. Editing was done by Carol Skiles, teacher at Weatherford High School, Jim Doss, and Anita Conlee, teacher at Weatherford College. My heartfelt thanks to them all.

CHARACTERS

AMERICAN

Military: Maj. John J. Dunn, 34th Regiment, 24th Infantry Division, U.S. Army—Senior Ranking Officer; Sgt. F.C. Henry Leerkamp, Alphonse Baranski, Cpl. Shorty Estabrook, Lt. Cordus H. Thornton, Dr. Alexander Boysen, Maj. Newton W. Lantron, Charlie, Lt. John Fox, Jesse Sizemore, Sgt. Billy Knowles, and other officers and men of the U.S. Army
Lt. Donald S. Sirman, U.S. Air Force
Capt. Dave Booker, U.S. Marine Corps

Civilian: Father William Booth, Bishop Patrick Byrne, Louis (Danny) Dans, Nell Dyer, Walter Eltringham, Bill Evans, A. Kris Jensen, Helen Rosser, Bertha Smith, Larry Zellers

AUSTRALIAN

Father Philip Crosbie

AUSTRIAN

Dr. Ernst Kisch

BRITISH

Diplomatic: Capt. Vyvyan Holt, minister to South Korea; George Blake, vice-consul; Norman Owen, secretary

Civilian: Bishop A.C. Cooper, Sister Mary Clare, Philip Deane, Father Charles Hunt, Commissioner Herbert A. Lord

FRENCH

Diplomatic: Georges Perruche, consul-general, Seoul; Jean Meadmore, vice-consul; Charles Martel, chancellor

Civilian: Mother Béatrix, Father Joseph Bulteau, Father Joseph Cadars, Maurice Chanteloup, Father Celestine Coyos, Mother Eugénie, Fathers Antoine and Julien Gombert, Simone and Mansang Hoang, Madame Martel, Mother Mechtilde, Mother Thérèse, Father Paul Villemot

GERMAN

Lotte Gliese

IRISH

Father Frank Canavan, Monsignor Thomas Quinlan

KOREAN

The Tiger, Hak Pong Moon, and six other South Korean politicians

RUSSIAN

Mary Daulatsch, Madame Funderat, Ilian Kijikoff, Ivan and Maria Kilin and family, Smirnoff, Ivan Nicolai Tihinoff, Dimitri Verosiff

SWISS

Alfred Matti

TURKISH

Ahmet and Sophia Demirbelek; Salim, Faiza, Sagid, and Sagida Salahudtin, and other members of the family

In Enemy Hands

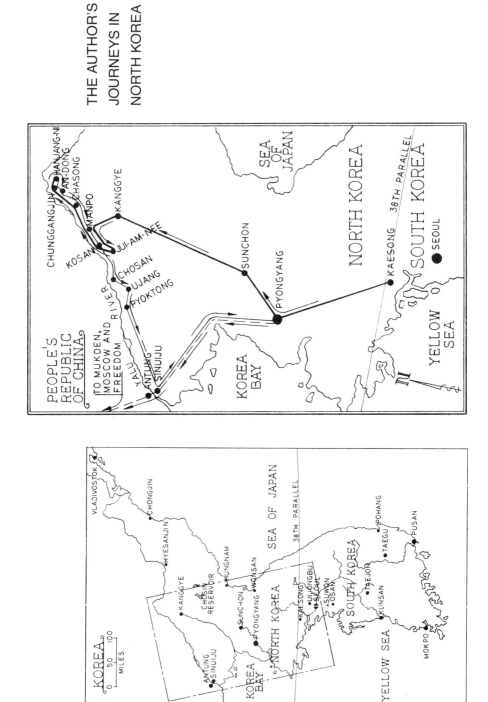

THE AUTHOR'S
JOURNEYS IN
NORTH KOREA

1. FIRST ENCOUNTER

THE North Korean Communist attack began a little after four o'clock in the morning on June 25, 1950, less than two miles from my home in Kaesong. I was awakened by the small arms and artillery fire, but I then did something foolish: I decided that it was simply another border skirmish between North and South Korea. I even turned over in bed and tried to go back to sleep.

In my two years in Kaesong, I had learned that most such outbreaks of fighting along the 38th parallel took place during the early morning hours. And like many people all over the world who live with danger, I got used to it.

On that Sunday morning I had no way of knowing that sometime during the night the North Koreans had slipped across the 38th parallel and relaid the torn-up section of the railway that runs north out of Kaesong. Then, in a brilliant maneuver, they had loaded a train with soldiers and taken it boldly into the train station at Kaesong.[1] I did not realize that I was hearing the beginning of the Korean War, and that soon we would be effectively cut off from the free world. We would not see it again for three years.

We Americans living in Kaesong had had plenty of warning, from both the American Embassy in Seoul and the U.S. Army. In early 1950 one embassy official asked me, "Why don't you people leave Kaesong and move closer to Seoul? You'll have a better chance to escape if the North Koreans attack." Even the mission that sponsored our work had suggested that we close our border station and move farther south.

We had also been warned by events along the border just the year before, when the 38th parallel had erupted with such ferocity that none of us left our homes for three days. Then there were the refugees from North Korea who for a time had flooded Kaesong at the rate of 3,000 per day.

In fact, part of our mission was to help provide temporary shelter to the thousands who were voting with their feet and leaving the North for the South. They were supposed to remain in Kaesong for only three days before being relocated farther south, but every day some remained and more arrived, taxing the already overburdened resources of the city to the breaking point. All these refugees had crossed the border at great risk to themselves; some had lost everything they owned. (They used to tell us, "All it takes for us to pack our bags is to stand on our feet"); and they brought horror stories of conditions north of the border. They had even told us of the massing of thousands of North Korean soldiers less than ten miles from Kaesong.

Yet we had faced only the possibility, not the probability, of open hostilities between North and South Korea. Moreover, Captain Joseph Darrigo, a U.S. Army officer assigned to the Korean Military Advisory Group, agreed with us that if an attack did take place, Americans would not be harmed.

So we were still not overly concerned when, at about seven-thirty that morning, my friend Kris Jensen and I saw the shadowy figures of armed men in strange uniforms moving south through my yard. "They are only South Koreans dressed up in different uniforms. They are having a military maneuver of some kind," said Kris, summing up the matter. And when the young men fired their weapons into the air from time to time without bothering to aim at anything, "This is to make the exercise look and sound more like the real thing," I said to Kris.

Nevertheless, when Dr. Ernst Kisch hurried into my room to observe what was going on, Kris and I, for some reason, jerked him away from the window. I don't know why we did it, but the situation had begun to look suspicious. Then I looked farther down one of the streets and observed that all electric and telephone lines had been cut and were lying on the ground. That was my first real clue that this "maneuver" *was* the real thing.

"The South Koreans would certainly not cut all the electric and telephone lines in the city just to make a military exercise look more authentic," I told Kris. We all agreed. Listening carefully, we could discern the sound of small arms fire moving farther to the south. Had our area already fallen to the North Koreans? We could no longer see anyone from my window. A heavy fog had cut visibility to a few hundred yards and added to our growing feeling of uneasiness. But we were still optimistic: "The South Koreans will launch a counterattack today or tomorrow," Kris said. I agreed with him. We had been led to believe that the South Korean Army was more than a match for the North Koreans. Having achieved the element of surprise, the North Koreans had made some initial gains. When the South Koreans recovered, they would be able to defend their land, we thought.

At approximately ten o'clock, knowing that the wounded would be taken to Ivy Hospital, which was part of our mission station, we walked over to see if we could help. North Korean soldiers were being brought in, and we tried to show our concern by offering them water to drink. They refused; in fact, we were met with such hostility and suspicion that Kris and I decided to leave the ward. Soon Dr. Kisch joined us: "Even the Nazi SS sought out and accepted my medical skills when I was in Buchenwald and Dachau," he said. "These men have been poisoned against us. They will not permit me to help them."

As we stood in the front entry way, an old, dilapidated bus pulled up, loaded with wounded men. Standing in the open door of the bus, wearing a red armband, was a familiar figure. Sa-mu, a young teenage refugee from North Korea, had arrived in Kaesong approximately a year before—looking, he said, for his father and mother. Rev. L.P. Anderson and his wife, missionaries at our station, who were in America on vacation at the time of the attack, had taken him into their home and cared for him as their own son. Before World War II, the Andersons had known Sa-mu's parents—his father was a Christian minister—in what is now North Korea.

Now, the red armband, assuming that he wore it willingly, indicated that Sa-mu was either a Communist agent or a sympathizer. When the bus stopped directly in front of the hospital, he was the first one off. He had started up the steps of the hospital when he looked up and saw me. For an instant he hesitated. Then he turned around and walked back in the direction of the bus. Sa-mu may have been trying to save his own life; I'll not be the judge. But I never told the Andersons about the incident. They are now deceased; if they were not, I would not be writing this, even four decades later.

Moving back into the hospital, I heard someone from down the hallway shouting my Korean name. Dr. Suh, the chief surgeon, came running up to me to explain that without electricity they could not use their x-ray machine to locate shrapnel in the wounded. Kris and I decided that it would be safe for us to go to the city hall where, presumably, the new regime would already have installed itself, and request that electricity be turned on at Ivy Hospital. We felt this to be a reasonable request because their own soldiers stood to benefit. Seeing no civilian vehicles moving in the city, we decided against driving my red jeep, opting to walk instead.

We had gone about three-quarters of a mile when we were confronted by two armed men dressed in civilian clothes but wearing the now familiar red armband. "We are in trouble," Kris whispered.

"Don't act afraid." The two men swung American-made carbines in our direction and demanded to know what we were doing. One of the men pushed his carbine into my stomach: "Who made this gun?"

Presumably, the weapon had been left by some hapless South Korean who had been killed or captured. Being very naive, I answered rather forcefully, "The Americans made that gun, just as the Russians made the guns for your army." Apparently, he did not like my answer.

"You ill-bred American. I could kill you. Do you understand that?" He added some phrases under his breath that I did not understand; I suppose my Korean language instructor never thought I would need to know such words.

"Yes, I understand," I replied at last, trying to sound as unperturbed as possible.

My antagonist very quickly got down to the business of showing me in sign language what he had in mind. He poked the barrel of the carbine into my stomach repeatedly, making certain that I could see his finger on the trigger by turning the weapon sideways. Pulling back the breach to ready it for firing and shoving the barrel harder into my stomach, he waved away the people who were standing directly behind me. I understood why: if I am to be shot, the people behind me will be in danger, I thought. He is clearing the deck for action.

Suddenly, I detected a pungent odor like that of scorching hair, and I noticed a strong chemical taste in my mouth. I learned something that morning: death has an odor and a taste; I was to experience them again. I knew I might be dead before my next breath. During the next few seconds there was little time for anything but prayer.

"Who made this gun?" he demanded once again. This time I was more careful with my answer.

"The Americans made it," I replied in a much less aggressive tone of voice than before. He laughed and then pulled the trigger. There was a sharp snap of the empty chamber, followed by even more loud laughter. The large crowd of people who had gathered around us relieved their apprehension by laughing a little as well.

It suddenly dawned on me that this whole episode had been a show for the people who were watching. All these two performers needed now was a great finish to their flawless act of humiliating the ill-bred Americans. They were pretty good. One of the men kicked me in the shin, spun me around, and gave me a tremendous shove; Kris received the same treatment from the other man, and we moved off in our original direction toward the city hall.

"Don't look back," Kris whispered. It was unnecessary advice.

The officials at city hall were more "correct" but not friendly. On hearing our request, they responded that they were doing all they could to restore power to the entire city. With so many power lines lying in the streets, the task would take a long time, they said. We thanked them politely and took our leave.

Back at Ivy Hospital, Dr. Suh was breathless as he tried to speak. "We ran out of medicine in the hospital so I went to the Anderson house to get more. A Communist official went with me. There was a rifle in the medicine storeroom. The Communist official was very angry and took the rifle. He said that it had belonged to one of their soldiers. He said that things would be very bad for us!" Dr. Suh was trembling as he spoke.

"Don't worry. We have nothing to do with that rifle," I tried to reassure him. For some reason, I did not share Dr. Suh's apprehension. The rifle had, indeed, previously belonged to a North Korean soldier. He had defected the year before, bringing his rifle with him. A U.S. Army officer had given the rifle to Mr. Anderson, who was the director of Ivy Hospital. Anderson had placed the rifle in the medicine store-room for safekeeping. I could not have guessed the problems that rifle would cause me during my imprisonment.

Making one more round of the hospital rooms, we suddenly realized what should have been obvious to us all along: there were no wounded South Korean soldiers. For the first time, I began to be concerned about the kind of people that we were dealing with.

We had just returned to my house when there was a knock at the door. When I opened it, two North Korean officers and two soldiers bowed slightly in greeting and told me that they wanted to search the house. Inside, they informed me that they were looking for weapons, radio transmitters, and electric generators. They opened each drawer and cupboard as they moved about the house, always insisting that we precede them into each room. When it came time to inspect the basement, they asked that Kris and I jump up and down on the stairway before they ventured down.

The inspection team left in about forty-five minutes and, as far as I know, took nothing. "They seem to be people that we can reason with," Kris said. I hoped he was right, but remembering our encounter with the gun-toting actors in red armbands, I was not so sure.

The young wife of one of our workers came to see us that morning as well. She was almost hysterical as she told of the arrival of the *Inmen Gun*, the North Korean People's Army. In part, we understood her great concern. She and her husband were refugees from North Korea, which meant that they were marked for some kind of punishment at the hands of the new regime. Such was to be the lot of hundreds of thousands of North Korean citizens who had tried to escape the repression of their government by coming to South Korea. We tried to comfort her; Kris kept reiterating that the Americans and the United Nations would put the matter right in due time. Finally, she left. Sad to say, I never knew her first name. Following the custom of the time, the Koreans always referred to her as "Mother of Choon Young," her only son.

Not wanting to take any unnecessary risks, we waited inside the house most of the afternoon. At one point I saw several people standing on a small hill just outside my house. They were looking toward the south from which could be heard the sounds of heavy explosions. I joined them, thinking that the South Korean Army might be launching a counterattack and would soon be recapturing Kaesong. That small group of South Koreans, as it turned out, were hoping for the same thing.

From our vantage point we could not only hear explosions but see dark columns of dust and smoke rising in the south toward the Imjin River where, presumably, fighting was still going on. There was talk among the group of trying to move south by night and so escape from North Korean control. Each had his own reasons for wanting to try, but I knew better than to make such an attempt. My six-foot-one height, my 175-pound weight, my blond hair—everything would be against me. I decided that it would be best to wait for what I considered the inevitable counterattack by the South Korean Army.

While we were standing on that hill, we were surprised to see a flight of twelve to fifteen single-engine aircraft pass overhead from north to south. They were flying in a loose formation at about 5,000 feet. I could not identify them, but I felt sure they were not American or South Korean. It had never occurred to me before that the North Koreans had such aircraft or that they could fly over South Korean soil unopposed. My Korean friends were also downcast by this turn of events and left immediately. When I returned to my house, I did not share the depressing information with my two friends. It was just as well that they not know, I thought.

I did a lot of thinking that night because sleep was impossible. Since my arrival in 1948 I had gotten to know many of the U.S. Army personnel assigned in Korea; now I was remembering some of our conversations. Until the early part of 1949 the army had maintained a small garrison, Easy Company, in the center of Kaesong, and I had once asked the first sergeant if he thought the North Koreans might attack the small hill that his company defended. "They wouldn't have any trouble taking it if they wanted to attack. But I don't think they will; they would have to take on the United States." After the U.S. Army units had been withdrawn from the country in 1949, the Korean Military Advisory Group (KMAG) was established on July 1 to train the South Korean army, and only a small detachment—three or four army officers and perhaps two enlisted men—was quartered in Kaesong to question refugees coming from North Korea.

The South Korean Army's 12th Regiment was quartered a few miles south of Kaesong, and in early 1950 I had asked a U.S. Army officer about a weapon I saw there that looked like a very small artillery piece. "That is a fifty-seven millimeter antitank weapon," he said. "But we don't have to worry about tanks. In most of South Korea, they would have to travel down roads built up out of rice paddies and would be sitting ducks for aircraft and bazookas." A tacit assumption behind his remark—or so it seemed to me—was that there would be no need to prepare for a defense against tanks. Apparently no one knew then that "the North Korean People's Army (NKPA), meanwhile, had amassed an invasion force of some 90,000 men, supported by 150 T-34 tanks, a low-silhouette medium tank that had been the standard for the Soviet Army at the end of the Second World War."[2]

It later occurred to me that the attitude of the U.S. Army officer, who may have been merely reflecting his own ideas, was like that of the French Army, which before World War II had built the Maginot Line between France and Germany but had neglected to extend it to the North Sea. Germany bypassed the defenses of that line by attacking France through Belgium.

In January of 1950, Secretary of State Dean Acheson signaled to the world, at least by implication, that South Korea was outside of the U.S. defense perimeter.[3] I'm certain that Russia and North Korea received that information—I know that some of the staff in my school in Kaesong learned about it. My good friend and fellow teacher Cho Dong Yun discussed the matter with me at length. Mr. Cho said at last, "Well, as long as you Americans remain in Kaesong, we Koreans feel that it is safe." Lying awake that first night of the war, I wondered what should have been our greater obligation—to run or to sit tight.

I do not hold the American government responsible for my capture by the North Koreans; my being in harm's way was entirely my own decision, and I had had plenty of warning from the U.S. Embassy. But I do blame the government for sending mixed signals to Russia and her client, North Korea, about our resolve to defend South Korea. Had they believed us committed to defend South Korea, I don't think the North Koreans would have attacked.

We spent the next three days lying low, uncertain what our course should be. At five o'clock on the afternoon of June 26, a rather amiable-looking man in civilian clothes but wearing the red armband knocked at my door. I could not determine whether he was armed.

"Sir, do you have a jeep?" he asked politely.

"Yes, I do. It is in the garage," I answered.

"The People's Government has need of it. I will bring it back tomorrow."

Both my jeep and one belonging to Rev. L.P. Anderson were kept in a garage located in front of Ivy Hospital. I unlocked the door and handed my official visitor the entire set of keys.

"Here is a key to the garage and the keys to my jeep and the other one as well," I said. I wasn't being overly generous. Once my polite young man realized that there was an extra jeep in the garage, he or someone else would be back for it; I thought I might as well save myself the trouble of having to deal with them again. He smiled as though a little embarrassed and asked me to back my jeep out of the garage for him. Immediately, my mind went back to our first visitors from the new regime, who had refused to go down into my basement until Kris and I had jumped up and down on the stairs, assuring them that it was safe. When the jeep had been backed out, he bowed and thanked me. In all of his conversation, he had used the polite high form of the Korean language.

"I'll bring it back tomorrow," he said as he smiled, waved, and drove away. I knew he was lying.

June 27, despite our fear and worry, was uneventful, although that night the North Koreans established a refueling point just outside the house and kept us awake with the clanking of gasoline cans.

About midmorning of June 28 I heard an aircraft circling over the city, then the distinctive sound of an aircraft flying low and firing its machine guns. I ran to the west window just in time to see a Douglas B-26 Invader climbing and banking in my direction, the U.S. Air Force marking in plain view. There was no doubt in my mind about the identity of that aircraft. I had first seen the twin-engine light attack bomber during the closing days of World War II at the U.S. Army Air Force Base at St. Mawgan, England. Then it had been known as the A-26; it was later redesignated B-26. (The original B-26 was the Martin Marauder, a two-engine medium bomber.) A minute or so after the

B-26 had disappeared to the south there was the sound of more strafing. The plane reappeared, circled the city at low altitude, headed south, and vanished. Apparently, it was one of a group of twelve B-26s that had taken off from Ashiya Air Force Base in southern Japan on June 28 at 7:30 A.M. Their mission was to attack rail targets near Munsan, a village on the banks of the Imjin River, a few miles south of Kaesong.[4]

The aircraft had not been gone for more than five minutes when I saw boys spilling out into the road from the middle school and moving off quickly. My Korean friends had advised me not to report to school after the Communist invasion.

"The Communists told us to close all schools immediately after the attack by the airplane," Cho Dong Yun, my fellow teacher, told me a few minutes later; he had dropped by my house on his way home. He explained why the students had been dismissed: "They were afraid of the airplane," he said.

I warned Mr. Cho to leave my house immediately and not to come back; he was probably already in trouble with the Communist authorities for having been so closely associated with me. He said goodbye and he left. I was afraid that I would never see him alive again.

Other Korean friends were more discrete. Having learned their lesson well under the pre–World War II Imperial Japanese regime, they knew that we would understand if they did not come to visit after the Communists came to power. It had been dangerous also in the late 1930s for the Koreans to associate with Americans.

About an hour after the middle school was dismissed, I saw what would prove to be the forward element of a long column of men and vehicles moving north past my house. Three men carrying flags were leading the procession. I immediately assumed that the North Korean forces were retreating and heading back across the 38th parallel. So did Kris; "The United Nations has ordered them to withdraw!" he shouted. Then I saw the marchers turn right into the middle school compound, at that time one of the few places in South Korea that had many tall trees. "They must be hiding their forces because they are afraid of being attacked by aircraft," I remarked to Kris. Our hearts sank as the entire column of men and machines moved into the school compound and disappeared among the trees.

Around noon the next day, June 29, we saw more men and equipment moving toward the north. We assumed from their three flag-bearers out in front that they would be joining the 1,000 or so other soldiers who had earlier taken refuge at the middle school. Just before reaching the bridge over the canal, however, they turned sharply left and then left again, coming up the road that led to our compound. A tank lumbered along about 100 feet behind the fifty or so marching men. When the tank made the second turn onto our road, I shouted, "Let's go to the women's compound!"

There was no discussion. Moving as one person, the three of us jumped to our feet, ran out the back door, and headed south past Ivy Hospital.

"How do we get there without going back out on the main road?" Kris asked as we trotted along.

"I know a back way," I replied.

The house where the three American women missionaries lived was located on the campus of the Myung Duk school for girls and was surrounded by a high concrete wall. We were admitted through the back door; as we walked through the kitchen, we noticed No Sunsang, their driver, standing by the stove and trying to keep out of sight. He was in hiding because at an earlier time he had worked for the South Korean police.

The women were all right; they had been obliged to flee when the sounds of battle came too close and had taken refuge in nearby houses until the immediate danger had passed. Now back in their own house, they were gravely concerned about the future.

As we talked, there was a knock on the back door. It was an old man, perhaps in his seventies, from a country church located about ten miles west of Kaesong. He had somehow managed to walk all the way to bring us some vegetables that he had gathered from the neighborhood.

"Are you all right?" he asked. "We knew that you could not go out and buy food. We were worried about you. Can you use these?" He held up a bag of onions and turnips.

The sight of that old gentleman standing there holding those vegetables and smiling was one that I shall never forget. It was a brave thing to do, even for an old man (a younger person, male or female, would not have gotten through the police barricades). When we inquired about his safety, he dismissed the question immediately.

"They won't bother an old man like me," he said, smiling. We were not so sure.

2. ENTER, THE SECRET POLICE

HOW had we six very different people—three men and three women—come to find ourselves together in this uncertain situation?

Growing up on a farm, I had attended high school in nearby Weatherford, Texas, and Weatherford Junior College, graduating in 1942. Then I went marching off to World War II, where I served as a radio operator on a C-87 transport aircraft operating out of England. Having decided during the war to enter full-time Christian service, I returned home to enroll at North Texas State Teachers' College in Denton, Texas. I graduated in 1947 with a Bachelor of Arts degree and a major in Latin American history, thinking that I might someday become a missionary in that part of the world. But after attending Perkins School of Theology at Southern Methodist University in Dallas for one year, I enrolled in 1948, at twenty-six years of age, in a special missionary teaching program to Japan and Korea sponsored by several religious denominations in the United States. The program was staffed by some seventy young men and women, including Frances, the girl who would later become my wife.

I met Frances in New York that summer while attending a Columbia University training seminar on teaching English as a foreign language. A native of Georgia, she had graduated from the University of Georgia and had already taught school for a few years. We arrived together in Korea in 1948, were assigned to the mission station at Kaesong, and were married in Seoul in November 1949.

By a stroke of sheer luck or Providence, Frances was not with me in our home in Kaesong when the North Koreans attacked. I will be eternally grateful for that. The day before the war began, we had attended a wedding in Seoul; my wife was matron of honor and I was best man. When the time came for us to return home, Frances became ill and was ordered to bed by the doctor. Kris Jensen, in whose home we had stayed in Seoul, volunteered to go with me to Kaesong for the weekend and return to Seoul on Monday. The North Korean attack the next morning changed his plans.

Kris, from New Cumberland, Pennsylvania, was born in Naesborg, Denmark, in 1897 and had made his way to the United States when he was seventeen years old. He knew so little English that he had a difficult time at first. But he knew how to learn and how to work hard; in fact, Kris was one of the few people I have known who spoke English without an accent after having learned it as an adult. In time, he became interested in missionary work and in 1928 married a young woman who had already been serving as a missionary in Korea. They left for Korea the next year where they worked for eleven years. In 1940, when the Japanese administration that ruled Korea at that time became too hostile to all foreigners, Kris, Maud, and their two children were ordered out of the country by the State Department.

Following World War II, Kris returned to Korea in 1946 and devoted himself to the difficult task of trying to rebuild the lives of people who were almost beyond hope. He and Maud made their home in Seoul, yet here he was with me in Kaesong, not quite a prisoner yet but destined to become one—all because he was a nice guy and had volunteered for a job, as he always had.

My other companion, Dr. Ernst Kisch, who lived with Frances and me, was born into luxury in 1893 in Vienna, Austria. He grew up surrounded by the best of Jewish and European culture and learned to play the classics on the piano. He went on to become a medical doctor, but the Holocaust was already brewing, and the world was about to be plunged into war. An early victim of Nazi madness, he spent time in both Buchenwald and Dachau. But for a brief period in 1938-39 Germany allowed Jews to leave if they had money and if they could find a country that would take them.

Dr. Kisch established his home and medical practice in China for nine years, until he was driven out by the Chinese Communists in 1948. He lived in the United States for a short time but remained an Austrian citizen, before volunteering in early 1950 to work in Ivy Hospital in Kaesong, "to be near my beloved China." He brought many trunks full of gifts for his friends in China and stored them in our house. "You wait," he used to say. "One day I will return to China."

The three American women were of differing ages, training, and backgrounds, but concern for those in need and a willingness to share were the reasons they were there.

Nell Dyer was the one American teacher at the Myung Duk school for girls, on whose compound the women lived. In her late forties, tall and erect, she presented a striking presence in any group. Her blonde hair was always a subject of curiosity among the Koreans. Nell had wanted to be a missionary ever since she was a little girl growing up in the home of a Methodist minister in Conway, Arkansas. She first went to Korea in 1927 to teach in a mission school. With the increasing hostility of the Japanese toward Americans living in Korea in the late 1930s, Nell had been forced to leave the country and go to work in the Philippines, where she was trapped by World War II. After being interned by the Japanese for three and a half years, she returned to Korea to teach school in Kaesong. Whether because of her commanding presence or her excellent grasp of the Korean language, Nell was usually singled out by the Koreans to be the spokesperson.

In her early sixties, Bertha Smith of Marshall, Missouri, was ready for retirement in years but not in spirit. Her long, jet black hair was pulled straight across her head and rolled into a bun at the back. Her manner of dress and life-style were very conservative. The one room that she could call her own in their communal living arrangement was devoid of anything except the bare essentials. She spoke Korean better than anyone in our American group. In Kaesong, her mission was to work in building up the local churches that had been devastated by Japanese repression during World War II.

Helen Rosser, in her middle fifties, was a public health nurse who first went to Korea in 1924 from her native Macon, Georgia. With a mild and pleasant personality and her credentials as a registered nurse, Helen had done pioneer work for many years in establishing rural public health centers in Korea.

As we shared our experiences of the past four days, we were interrupted by a knock on the front door. Nell Dyer admitted a very young man dressed in plain khaki shirt and pants. It seemed strange to me that he wore no hat, carried no weapon, and displayed no insignia on his clothes. The fact that he did not even wear the red armband made me suspicious. The authorities must know who he is, I thought.

But our young man was the picture of proper manners. On being asked to sit down, he graciously accepted. Tea and cookies were served, and we talked for perhaps an hour before he broached his main subject.

"Have you been to the city hall to pay your respects to the new officials?" he inquired.

The Korean expression "pay your respects" has much more meaning and strength than does its English equivalent.

"We have been intending to do that," said Nell, "but we know that your officials are so busy." Our young visitor laughed politely as he settled back in his chair, tea cup in hand.

"But don't you think it would be appropriate to go and pay your respects?" he continued.

"Well, yes," Nell said, "I think it would be a good idea."

"Good, but don't you think you might have waited too long already?" he inquired, continuing politely to press the matter.

"Oh, I hope not. What should we do?"

"It might be well to pay your respects as soon as possible."

"When would that be?"

"What about now?" he concluded.

We all stood up and moved toward the front door. The three women turned back momentarily to get their coats, and there was some discussion about taking an overnight bag.

"That won't be necessary. You will be returning before night." The young man paused when he came to the door. "Don't you have a jeep that we could ride in?" he asked, turning to Bertha, indicating that he knew who owned it.

I volunteered to go and get the jeep from the garage.

"It is going to be very crowded. Don't you have an automobile that some of us could ride in? And don't you have your own driver?" our polite young man asked, turning to Helen.

We should have been alerted at this point—our guest knew too much about us for an ordinary public official.

Poor No Sun-sang was routed from his kitchen hiding place to drive the automobile.

The two vehicles moved down the rather steep hill by the side of the girls' school and turned right on the main street of Kaesong. We had driven only about a quarter-mile when our visitor told us to stop in front of a nondescript-looking building.

"Why are we stopping here?" someone asked. "This is not the city hall."

"You will wait here for the officials to be brought to visit you," our young escort announced.

It was a brilliant performance! One young man, unarmed and alone, had succeeded in rounding up six Americans and their two vehicles, plus one Korean driver, without firing a shot, without any unpleasantness, and without their even knowing what he was doing. Not only that, but he and the other Communist officials now had the run of two well-stocked American houses to loot at their own convenience.[1]

Parking our vehicles, we entered a plain building located about 100 yards from the center of the city. Our polite visitor disappeared about this time; we never saw him again. Two North Korean officers escorted us into a large room containing a table and chairs. They were neither as polite nor as friendly as our house visitor had been, but they did invite us to sit down.

"You know what this place is, of course," was their first comment.

"No, we do not," someone answered.

"I don't believe you," one of them sneered.

"Why should we be familiar with this place?" Nell asked. We did not know it, but the building was a prison.

"But you walk or drive by here almost every day. Anyway, you work for the OSI [Office of Special Investigation] and the CIC [Counter-Intelligence Corps], so you would know about this place."

As it became obvious that these two officers had nothing but contempt for us and everything we stood for, we settled down for a night of verbal abuse and vicious charges: spying and working for the American government, exploiting the people of Korea, being members of a capitalistic society, lying. They were not even going through the motions of trying to be pleasant. From time to time we would inquire about our seeing the high-ranking officials at city hall, the alleged reason for our being there in the first place. We were put off with assurances that they would arrive soon.

At nine o'clock that night the siren sounded the city curfew; only security forces were allowed on the street after that.

"It is curfew time. You cannot go home now. You will have to wait until tomorrow morning."

It was a long and miserable night, but the officers seemed to enjoy it—I suppose because they had someone to play with. They rotated in and out of the room, replacing one another every hour or so. An official would leave the room wearing a uniform and return from an adjoining room a few minutes later dressed in civilian clothes. Thus attired, he would walk out the front door, only to return about an hour later with some terrified South Korean in tow. Disappearing for a few minutes into the adjoining room, he would emerge again in full uniform. Several officers carried on this practice throughout the night. One of them changed from uniform to civilian clothes and back again at least three or four times.

Sometime after midnight, one of the officers brought out and introduced a young high school student, still in his school uniform, whom I recognized immediately. Although he was enrolled at the Commercial School, not the middle school where I taught, he attended a modern literature class that I conducted in my house each Tuesday night. "This young student will now be your guard for a while. We will be away for a short time," the officer announced. I was shocked to learn that the student was not a prisoner but was actually going to serve as our guard. It must have shown on my face. The officer looked at me and smiled.

"Oh, yes, he is a member of your modern literature class," he added as he walked out of the room. The student glanced at us only once or twice as he took his seat by the side of our table. We were left alone with him for about an hour, during which time we talked quietly among ourselves. He kept his head bowed and never looked at us or said a word. It would be interesting, and perhaps tragic, to know the real story behind his being there.

When the officer in charge returned, he dismissed our student guard and then tossed a box of American-made matches on the table near where I was seated. Those matches looked familiar. The officer noticed my interest.

"Oh, yes, we took these from your house," he said, laughing. The urgent business that had taken him away for an hour was now obvious. They had been plundering our houses.

Only then did we really understand what had happened to us that day. We had unknowingly been players in a battle of wits in which we were totally outclassed. They repeatedly told us that they had known all along who their real enemies were. The fact that we did not accept the label made no difference to them.

We soon came to realize that they were not interested in our concept of truth. Insisting that they be addressed as "honorable teachers" in the Korean language, they showed no interest in engaging in serious dialogue. It was the first time that I had met anyone so possessed with "invincible ignorance." That would turn out to be a common disease among the Communists of North Korea.

About halfway through the night several officers walked in and ordered the three men to stand in the middle of the room. Dr. Kisch, Kris, and I were then treated to the humiliation of being thoroughly searched and of having our trigger fingers examined minutely—presumably to determine whether we had fired a gun recently. They also wanted to know where we kept our pistols and seemed angry when we told them that we had no weapons.

The interrogators were merely sparring with us that night, as I'm certain they had been told to do. Our situation would soon change for the worse. Communist teaching was that the war against capitalism was to be fought everywhere on every level. Writing on the history of battles, John Keegan makes the observation that battle "is essentially a moral conflict. It requires, if it is to take place, a mutual and sustained act of will by two contending parties, and if it is to result in a decision, the moral collapse of one of them."[2] An interrogation in a controlled environment conducted by a determined interrogator surely qualifies to be called a battle, according to Keegan's definition of that word. And resisting interrogation requires a moral decision to fight, however unevenly, with moral weapons.

It was nearly eight o'clock the next morning when the long night of interrogation ended. We were again searched, this time more thoroughly. They took money, fountain pens, and my wedding ring, permitting me to keep only a small picture of Frances when I explained who she was. We were then placed in a large cell containing about thirty men and women. The concrete cell was about twenty by thirty feet, and there was no light in the room except for what filtered through a small window at the top of the wall. When I first entered the room, I could not see anything. Several of the Korean prisoners took us by the hand and guided us to a place to sit down on the concrete floor. As my eyes became accustomed to the darkness, I began to see the forms of people sitting on the floor all around us. In one corner, I noted what appeared to be a large container, which I later learned was the toilet. It became full during our stay there and overflowed on the floor, making a small stream that ran across the center of the cell. People moved together to keep from getting wet.

During the next twenty-four hours we were occasionally taken out for interrogation. These experiences were repeat performances of the first night. They seemed to prefer the night for conducting their interrogations. We were allowed no food or water during these twenty-four hours, but given our state of apprehension, that was not as great a hardship as one might think.

By the next morning our toilet was in very bad condition. Suddenly the door swung open behind us revealing an officer whom we had not seen before.

"What's that smell?" he demanded.

"Honorable teacher, it is very difficult to talk to you about this, but the toilet is full and running over," replied some brave soul from the darkness.

"That's ridiculous! Empty it immediately and clean the room!" the officer ordered. Two young Korean men jumped up and hastily carried out the command. A mop was provided to finish up the cleaning. On inspecting the floor afterward, the same officer ordered, "Do it again.

The floor is not clean yet!" To his credit, and for whatever reason, the officer stood by until the job was finished to his satisfaction.

Soon after the room had been cleaned up, we foreigners were taken to a patio that separated the front offices of the prison station from the cells. Here we were provided water for washing and drinking. For a few minutes, we stood on the patio observing South Korean prisoners being brought from other cells for brief interrogations. Some were kicked; others were struck about the face from time to time. One prisoner's glasses did not prevent him from receiving the same treatment; the interrogator asked him to remove his glasses and hand them over, then proceeded to slap the man a few times before giving back the glasses. The treatment was administered several times until the suspect's face became quite red.

Soon we were taken into one of the offices and given a bowl of rice to eat. After breakfast, an officer walked up to us and made a very startling announcement.

"We are sending you to Pyongyang, Seoul." I jumped at what the official had said.

"Pyongyang, Seoul! That means that they are sending us to Pyongyang, and then on to Seoul!" I shouted, thinking that we were being freed. Nell Dyer, the missionary from Arkansas, was quick to put me straight.

"*Seoul* in Korean means capital. He is telling us that they are sending us to Pyongyang, the North Korean capital."

It is not a long trip as the crow flies from Kaesong to Pyongyang—less than seventy miles, according to my Air Force friends—but it took three hours to cover it. It seems longer when you are traveling in the back of an old weapons carrier truck overloaded with people, with a guard's submachine gun constantly poking you in the ribs. Actually, there were two guards, but one of them decided to attach himself to me. Seating himself at my right, the sling of his weapon over his neck and one end of the weapon braced on the floor, he wedged the business end into my right rib cage, never showing any mercy.

Our journey took place in the afternoon of July 1, 1950. We had not gone more than a mile when we passed the burned-out bodies of several trucks by the side of the road. The trucks were riddled with large-caliber bullet holes, and from their location just west of my house, I assumed that earlier in the week they had been the target of the attack by the B-26 aircraft with U.S. Air Force markings. Delaying the trip were frequent stops to check on the possible presence of American aircraft in the area, the bad road conditions, and one bathroom stop—during which the women were herded off to one side of the road and the men to the other. (Even that little consideration was far better than the barrel provided for thirty men and women in the Kaesong dungeon.)

There were about twenty-five men and women in that small truck. In our American group there were three men and three women. The rest were Koreans of different ages and manner of dress. We could only conclude that we were considered to be very dangerous people.

We arrived at the headquarters of the National Internal Security (secret police) in Pyongyang near sundown, yet the place was still humming with activity. Secret police, whether in North Korea or elsewhere, frequently do their most important work at night. We entered the compound through a guarded gate and stopped in a small courtyard. The entire compound was surrounded by a wall about ten feet high, topped with barbed wire. We were almost surrounded by long, low buildings of a dull gray color that gave the whole setting an ominous look. Climbing out of the truck, Kris whispered to me, "It doesn't look very friendly, does it?"

On being marched into a large building and warned not to talk, we noted very quickly that the other prisoners who came with us were taken away, leaving only the western group. We were moved into a large room and instructed to be seated at one of many tables. Our two guards immediately took a seat and placed their submachine guns on one of the tables. As we waited, we were treated to a strange sight: the two guards would take the cartridge drums from their weapons, remove all the bullets, count them one by one, put them back—and then repeat the procedure.

Some women brought rice to the two guards, who moved a couple of tables away to eat it. No food was brought to us, but that didn't matter; we were so traumatized by fear and uncertainty that we could not have eaten anything.

Several North Korean officers standing in one corner of the large room did not seem to be interested in us at the moment. Suddenly, they all snapped to attention with the arrival of a short, heavily built officer. We could see that he was very much in charge of the situation. With a wave of his hand and a grunt, he put the others at ease and then turned in our direction. A younger officer came forward and addressed us: "This is our commandant." We Americans attempted to stand on our feet to show respect but were dismissed by a similar wave and a grunt.

An older officer walked into the room about this time and went straight to the commandant. He began speaking to the senior officer by apologizing for something, the nature of which we did not understand. As he talked, the commandant began to beat the air, moving his right hand up and down from the elbow, and presently became verbally abusive. In obvious anger, the commandant dismissed the officer and departed with him.

I then asked Kris why we had been brought here.

"We represent everything they hate," Kris said.

"Is there nothing we can do?" I asked.

Dr. Kisch answered that question for us. "Larry, they already know what they are going to do with us, no matter what we say or do. We can do nothing, Larry. Nothing! Nothing!"

That note of finality made me shudder inside, coming as it did from a survivor of Buchenwald and Dachau. If any man alive had the insight, based upon personal experience, to summarize our situation, it was he. By that remark, Dr. Kisch introduced me to the fatalistic philosophy, which I was to adopt, that my answers during interrogations would have no bearing on whether I was to live or die. That belief was strangely comforting to me for a time—but only for a time.

Still not satisfied, I continued to speculate that the United States would act on our behalf in some way. Dr. Kisch had a ready answer for that also.

"What can America do? If they ask for us, will these barbarians listen? And if America threatens to punish them, these people will kill us. They don't care about us. They don't care about anyone!" Sadly, I had to conclude that the man with the experience knew what he was talking about. We would have to face alone whatever these people had in store for us.

Kris thought perhaps he could reason with the commandant. "Jensen," Dr. Kisch said, "do you think you can reason with the commandant of the secret police? How do you think he got to be commandant—by being reasonable? Jensen, you are mad!" Dr. Kisch always spoke his mind.

At that point we were approached by two officers. "Why are you working against the people of this country? You come here telling everyone that you love the Korean people and want to help them. But you lie! You are secretly working for the American Office of Special Investigation. Your airplanes come and kill our people—they bomb our schools and hospitals. Do you think that is good?" None of us said anything.

When the commandant returned, Kris obtained permission to

speak with him. Dr. Kisch was right; it was a wasted effort. "We are not your enemies," Kris said as he approached the commandant.

The commandant was ready. "Then why are you supporting that American puppet president Syngman Rhee in South Korea, and his clique of Wall Street lackeys? Why are you telling the people lies about a God who does not exist? Why are you working against us? Why are your airplanes bombing us?" The commandant was fully capable of answering his own questions. "You are doing all these terrible things because you are reactionaries, just like all the other religious people of the world." Beating the air with his hand to stress his point, the commandant turned his back on Kris to signal that the conversation had ended.

Head down, Kris returned to the rest of us seated at the table. "His mind was made up before we started," he said somberly. We were to meet the closed mind on many occasions in North Korea. But that must be expected in a country where truth, to quote Communist ideology, is a servant of the state.

The officers seemed to be in no hurry to make their next move. Most of the night still lay ahead for them, and they apparently wanted to save some of the fun until the early morning hours. One of them came over to our table holding some papers and began to question us. "Why do you work for the Counter-Intelligence Corps?"

Nell Dyer corrected him. "We do not work for the Counter-Intelligence Corps. Anyway, the job of the CIC as I understand it, is to catch spies, not to send them out." The interrogator showed no reaction.

"Which one of you speaks the best Korean?" All eyes turned to Bertha Smith, that strong little woman from Marshall, Missouri.

"Auntie" (a term of respect), the interrogator said addressing Bertha, "why did you come to Korea?" Whenever Bertha spoke in either English or Korean, she wanted to be grammatically correct. She hesitated too long forming her answer.

"And why did you come?" he asked, turning to Helen Rosser, the public health nurse from Macon, Georgia.

"I came to Korea to try to help the Korean people," Helen answered. The interrogator looked back at Bertha, who was waiting to speak.

"I came because I wanted to help the Korean people, and I felt that I had something to share with them."

"Well spoken, Auntie. You speak very good Korean, but you speak it so slowly," he said.

"Yes, I know," Bertha replied. "I speak English that way also."

"And you," he said, looking directly at me. "What do you do?"

"I teach English in a middle school in Kaesong."

"But you are an American soldier, aren't you?" he commented.

"I was a soldier in World War II, but not now."

He pressed the attack. "Then how is it that you can be a teacher in a middle school when you don't speak Korean very well?" I knew then that my limited ability to speak Korean would be a problem for me. The North Koreans could, and did, use that issue to try to prove that I was really an American agent and not, in fact, who I said I was. "I teach conversational English in the middle school. I don't need to know Korean very well for that," I said.

"But you are still a soldier in the American army," he remarked as he walked away.

My companions looked at me, but no one said anything.

3. DEATH CELL IN PYONGYANG

AN officer walked me down a long hallway and turned into an empty office that I at once thought must belong to the commandant. It had better furniture and more of it than any other room I was ever to see in North Korea. On the walls were five large pictures: Marx, Engels, Lenin, Stalin, and the Communist leader of North Korea, Kim Il Sung. Those pictures and what they stood for dominated not only this room but everything in North Korea. The next item that caught my eye was a very expensive-looking shortwave radio on a shelf just behind the impressive desk at the end of the room. How I wished that I could be left alone with that radio for a few minutes to find out from the Voice of America what was going on in South Korea.

The commandant walked into the office about that time. His first question was, "Don't you have a passport?"

"No, I don't. I have one in my home in Kaesong." I was not about to tell him what I already knew concerning the thoroughness of his secret police. They had already plundered my house and had taken whatever they wanted.

"Are you an American?" he asked.

"Yes," I answered.

"What do you do?"

"I teach English in a middle school."

"But you are an American soldier," he charged.

"Not anymore. I was a soldier in World War II." I was reluctant to tell him more than he asked for.

"We know that you flew in airplanes, and you know about radio." He must have seen my look of surprise.

"We have our ways of knowing these things," he said with a slight smile.

Then the commandant stood up and walked past me to the door. He returned to his desk carrying a military rifle in both hands. A young officer followed who would now act as interpreter. Standing to his full height and with shoulders erect, the commandant directed a charge against me that made my blood turn cold.

"We found this weapon in your house in a closet where you tried to hide it. You used it to kill our brave soldiers when they liberated Kaesong," he said, looking me straight in the eye.

I didn't trust myself to answer right away. I recognized the rifle he was holding as the standard weapon carried by most foot soldiers in the North Korean army—exactly the same kind of weapon, as far as I could determine, that had been taken by a Communist official from the Anderson house in Kaesong on the first day of the war.

This must be the same rifle, I thought, that Dr. Suh had tried to warn me about. I continued to speculate to myself: doesn't the commandant know or doesn't he care that the rifle didn't come from my house?

My heart was pounding in my head, and my palms were sweating. Somehow I managed to stare back at him and stammer, "You didn't find that weapon in my house."

The commandant changed the subject.

"We were attacked on June 24 by the bloodthirsty Syngman Rhee's puppet regime in South Korea and his Wall Street lackeys who support America. The puppet forces were immediately overwhelmed. They were well armed by the reactionary government of America. The puppet forces were so strong that they would have conquered us if we had not been ideologically prepared through Marxism-Leninism. But even though they had more weapons and men, we were stronger. We have a right to defend ourselves, so on June 25 we counterattacked and drove back the imperialist armies. We won because we have a clear conscience. Our victory was brought about by our desire for peace. Did you know that we have liberated Seoul?"

"No, I didn't," I answered. I did not take issue with his absurd declaration that South Korea had attacked first. On Saturday, June 24, Kris and I had driven a jeep from Seoul to Kaesong. On our route of travel, which had taken us very near the 38th parallel for many miles, we did not see or hear any military activity. Arriving at my house in Kaesong, we were met by Dr. Kisch, who kept a wary eye out for signs of military activity; he told us that the border had been quiet during my two-day trip to Seoul.

In light of the actual comparative strength of South Korean and North Korean forces, what the commandant said was untrue. The South Koreans had been told by the Americans that their forces could repel any North Korean incursion; in the patriotic fervor caused by the attack from the North, some South Koreans believed that their forces were capable of successfully invading North Korea and reuniting the country under one government.[1] According to General Douglas Mac-Arthur, a deliberate decision by the American government not to supply sufficient arms to South Korea had been based on a fear that Syngman Rhee, if strong enough militarily, would attack North Korea.[2]

The reverse, in fact, appears to have been the case: the weakness of the South Korean army invited the attack. Regardless of what Syngman Rhee may or may not have had in mind, the North Koreans beat him to the punch. There is now ample evidence that the South Korean army was not prepared to fight even a defensive war, a fact that was certainly taken into consideration by the North Korean Communists before they attacked. MacArthur wrote about this matter, "It was a vital and a fatal error not to prepare South Korea to meet an attack from the north. The potential of such an attack was inherent in the fact that the North Korean force had tanks, heavy artillery, and fighter aircraft with which South Korea was not equipped."[3]

The commandant looked sternly at me and spoke with measured words. "We know you are a Wall Street agent, a spy, an ideological saboteur, a soldier. You fired on our soldiers when they entered Kaesong. All over the world such people are shot. All of this makes you an enemy of the state. Do you know what this means?" I was soon to find out.

"I am only a teacher. I haven't done any of those things you accuse me of."

The commandant had heard enough. Growing visibly impatient with me and my answers to his questions, he suddenly rose to his feet and with a wave of his hand indicated to the soldier standing in the room that I was to be taken away.

The armed guard took me out of the commandant's office and ushered me into another room. A short time later an officer came and took the other four Americans, Dr. Kisch, and me down a long hallway. A steel door opened as we approached it. Walking past yet another steel door, we stood in an area of death cells. The three American women were led off and disappeared as the second steel door slammed shut behind us. We three men were taken in another direction into a small room and ordered to strip completely. Two stone-faced guards removed our ties, belts, and shoestrings before returning our clothes to us.

After being placed in the cell, Kris, Dr. Kisch, and I were instructed not to talk and to go to sleep at once. We would be required to arise at six and retire at ten o'clock. During the day, we would be given three meals and allowed to use the toilet in the corner three times. Otherwise, we were to sit cross-legged and remain perfectly still in the middle of the room, facing the back wall. Except for the three small meals and bathroom calls, we had to sit still for sixteen hours each day without any back support. A powerful electric light burned continually overhead. A clock tolled two o'clock from somewhere down one of the long hallways. There was no desire to sleep. Too much had happened.

The guard came at six o'clock to awaken those who were asleep. I wasn't. This was much too early a beginning for what was to be the worst day of my life. My first job was to carry to the latrine the old wooden bucket that served as our toilet. While I was there, the guard motioned for me to come look out the window. He pointed to a corner area where sandbags were piled high, lining the inside of the wall that surrounded the complex. "Bad men are killed there," he said, putting his index finger to the back of his head and making an explosive sound, mocking execution. So that's how they do it, I thought. When you are an expert merchant of death, there is no need to waste extra bullets using a firing squad. If I were ever taken there, I'd know why. But I'd probably be blindfolded and wouldn't know where I was.

How do you prepare yourself to die? They didn't teach that in school—at least, not in the one I attended. I would have given anything to know.

We assign different priorities to our lives on the basis of what we think is important. In that death cell that morning, my two priorities were to live with some kind of honor and to avoid torture if possible. I would learn to cope with death, but I couldn't come to terms with the possibility of torture.

On returning to the cell, I was given a mop to clean the wooden floor. Pushed through a small door was breakfast—a bowl with vegetable soup and another of rice. Using three small spoons, we were obliged to lie on our stomachs around the two bowls and share the food. There wasn't much, but we were under so much stress that our appetites had disappeared. It was to be some time before eating became a priority issue.

With breakfast out of the way, we were instructed to assume our cross-legged positions on the floor. This manner of sitting that is so easy for Orientals, who begin the practice as children, can tire adult Americans and Europeans in a few minutes. Once we were in place on the floor, I noted the sound of heavy hobnailed boots in the concrete corridor behind us. The steady footsteps passed by our cell, turned right at the end of the cell-block for about twenty paces, and after three more right turns were in front of our cell again. The owner of those boots never varied his pace unless he discovered someone in one of the cells breaking the rules: doing physical exercise, whispering to a fellow cellmate, looking around or sitting with the head down (I never learned whether the heads-up rule was aimed at preventing sleeping or praying or both). Whenever the guard observed someone breaking the rules, he would either scream at the offender or report the violation to another guard. Punishment was immediate, administered by slapping the prisoner about the face with the hand or by applying a heavy leather belt to the back.

From somewhere outside the cellblock came the sounds of gunfire, one or two shots at a time in perhaps five distinct groups. I did not immediately connect those sounds with what was apparently occurring. Then I suddenly realized the truth: those "bad men" that the guard had told me about in the latrine were being executed. For some time I was too stunned by this startling revelation to react in any way. In our very constrained environment we were not allowed to communicate with each other. I turned my head very slowly to see whether Kris and Dr. Kisch had heard the gunfire. In the periphery of my vision I was able to see that Kris was looking at me. His face was grave. Dr. Kisch sat very still with head bowed. They must both have been aware of the tragic situation.

We heard groups of shots throughout that day and each day during our incarceration in the death cell. It was common practice for men to be hauled out of their cells at any time of the day or night. Unless you have heard the hobnailed boots stop at your cell door and the guard call out your name to lead you away, you can't imagine the terror that accompanies such a call. Some were taken out for interrogation and were later brought back. Others never returned. I never got used to it, but my feelings did become numbed.

Later that morning I was taken from the cell to a small room where an officer was waiting behind a table.

"Did you sleep well?" he asked.

"Yes," I replied, knowing it was a lie.

"We want you to write your life history for us," the interrogator said, wearing a smile for the first time. "We want to know everything about you." He handed me a piece of paper and left the room.

After writing for about two hours, I decided to stop. I knew they would have difficulty reading my writing and would have to study it for some time. When the interrogator returned, he picked up what I had written and had me taken back to my cell, a welcome relief. Terrible though the cell was, it was far better than being interrogated.

Lying on the floor with our heads together during the noon meal, we were able to share a few whispered words. Dr. Kisch spoke of his morning's research.

"There are two guards out there in the darkness of the hallway. One wears the heavy boots, and we can hear him wherever he is. But there is another who wears no shoes at all. Watch out for him. You never know where he is."

I began to think about what Dr. Kisch had just said. Only that morning a shout had come from the darkness when Kris had made a slight movement to straighten his back. This occurred when the hobnailed boots were in the opposite corridor. I decided to learn more about the system.

After lunch, I assumed my position at left center of the cell. I turned my head very slowly and held it there as motionless as I could. Very soon, I saw the dim outline of a small man darting past our cell making no noise whatsoever. I soon saw him pass our cell again from the opposite direction. Meanwhile, the hobnailed boots continued to clomp around the square cellblock like a metronome. Later that afternoon, the little guard with no shoes left for an hour or more. I considered our situation; there were, indeed, two guards watching us. The invisible guard might not be there at all times, but we had to assume that he was. A slight movement of the body to try to ease the pain of sitting cross-legged on the floor could earn us a reprimand or worse. It was a dismal prospect.

That afternoon, sirens wailed to signal an air raid. It was not much of an air raid compared with those that followed, but it was enough to thoroughly upset the internal order of the prison system. Even the guard with the hobnailed boots disappeared for a time. When the siren sounded, guards and officials ran helter-skelter for about thirty seconds. After that, quiet descended on the whole place except for the booms and blasts of the bombs and guns. For some reason, I was not worried about my safety. I had the feeling that those bombs were for someone else.

When the "all clear" sounded after about an hour, the guards and officials returned, so angry that they shouted insults at us. Some grabbed the iron bars and rattled them. For once I was happy that my cell was constructed so well.

Near suppertime, one of the officials came to our cell and announced, "Your American bombers destroyed two hospitals and a school today. But they paid the penalty. They were all shot down. Your supper will be late because of the action of these murderers." Supper did arrive about an hour late. The cook had a few harsh words to say about the air raid, but the food was only slightly worse than usual.

"Sit down, Rarry," said the seated officer at my next interrogation with a wry smile (they never could pronounce my name correctly). "You die now, Rarry. We have been chosen to be your executioners." He nodded in the direction of another officer standing at his side. "Don't blame me. The choice was not mine to make. Your capitalistic world is about to die with you." I could feel the blood drain from my face.

In my cell I had tried to think about every possibility, everything that the Communists might do to me. I had imagined that they might just take me out and summarily shoot me in the back of the head without warning. I had even given thought to the possibility of some kind of trial in which I would naturally be found guilty. I had not considered that two smiling, friendly young men, very much in control of their emotions, might calmly inform me that I was to die at their hands.

"But I haven't had a trial!" I finally exclaimed.

"History has already judged you, not us. We are only the instruments who have been chosen to carry out your execution. We can carry it out at any time. When we do, you will have no reason to complain."

Somehow it would have seemed less sinister if they had been angry with me.

"But what have I done?"

"You are an advance agent of Wall Street and a soldier who fired on our brave soldiers in Kaesong. Where is your uniform, Rarry?"

"I don't have a uniform because I am not a soldier." Even as I spoke I wondered how much choice I really had in what was going to happen to me. Were they serious, or were they playing a role?

"You know," he went on, "it is a very bad thing for a soldier to be captured when not in uniform. Things are very bad for you."

"But I came to Korea to help people, not kill them." I could tell that reasoning with him was useless.

"That was only a disguise. Since your arrival in Korea, you have taught a vicious ideology of deception concerning a God who does not exist. You have spied on our military fortifications from your house in Kaesong and reported by radio to the Office of Special Investigation, and with this gun," he said, holding up the rifle first shown to me by the commandant, "you killed some of our brave soldiers when they liberated Kaesong. We know all about your skill in radio. We know all about you. We know everything. We make it our business to know everything."

There was always that rifle! I remembered when Anderson had proudly displayed it to me in the fall of 1949. It would make a wonderful souvenir, said Anderson—who was now safely in America on vacation—coming as it did from a defecting North Korean soldier and having been given him by a U.S. Army officer. I considered telling my interrogators the truth about that rifle, that it had come from the Anderson house, not mine. Something told me not to. Later I verified that in North Korea mere knowledge of something could make you guilty. The best policy was not to know anything. You lived longer that way.

I didn't know what to say to my two interrogators. Several times I tried to formulate some reply to their preposterous charges. Nothing I could think of seemed adequate, and I was afraid that anything I might say would only make matters worse. I have no idea how long their harangue lasted. The extreme fatigue from lack of sleep and the stress caused by the uncertainty of my fate were beginning to take their toll. The interrogation continued until the early morning hours, but I could never develop a strategy to counter their line of attack. They always had the advantage and most of the time were skillful enough to use it. I was too tired to do any more than answer their questions.

Perhaps Dr. Kisch was right. His experience as a concentration camp survivor had prepared him for what was to come. He had told me on our arrival at Pyongyang that the North Koreans had already decided our fate. To believe Dr. Kisch would be to believe that my life was predetermined and out of my hands. I decided that I would prefer it that way. The alternative, believing that avoiding execution depended upon how I conducted myself during interrogations, was more than I could bear.

Normally, I am not a believer in fatalism—that whatever will be, will be—but there are times when it becomes very comforting. To imagine having my life depend on something I might say during interrogation was too much—I couldn't handle that pressure! It was far better to agree with Dr. Kisch, to admit my lack of control over my life, and to say my prayers.

Kris and Dr. Kisch were not in the cell when I returned that night. I lay down on the hard wooden floor to sleep. When Dr. Kisch arrived, he was very agitated. "Larry! I was interrogated tonight by someone who spoke German. Almost all of the questions were about you. They are after you for some reason."

"What did he ask you?"

"Well, he tried to tell me a lot, but when I didn't agree I just kept quiet. He said that the North Koreans counterattacked against South Korea on the 25th of June. When he said that, I knew enough to keep my mouth shut. But Larry, be careful. They wanted to know all about you."

Kris returned about that time, agitated and nervous. He didn't want to talk at first as he joined us on the floor and tried to sleep, so I didn't ply him with questions or mention what had happened to me. Then I noticed that Kris was crying. "Jensen, what did they do to you?" Dr. Kisch demanded. Kris faced me for the first time. I could see that he was deeply troubled.

"Larry, I did a very foolish thing," Kris whispered. "You remember those empty cartridge shells that I picked up outside your house after the battle for Kaesong, the ones you told me to throw away? Well, I was afraid to go outside again—there were so many soldiers around—so I hid them in the coal bin of your basement. They are after you, Larry. They asked me all kinds of questions about you. They know that you were in the service, and they know that you were in airplanes and that it had something to do with radio. They showed me a gun they said was taken from your house, and they said that you used it to kill their soldiers during the battle. Larry, that must have been the gun they took from the Anderson house!"

I was simply too stunned to say anything. I instantly knew that I would have no possible defense if the Communists searched my house and found those empty cartridge shells that Kris had hidden in my basement. The rifle in Anderson's house, which was now in the hands of the commandant, was a North Korean weapon. Those incriminating shells would almost certainly fit that rifle.

Kris continued to cry, and I knew that he was crying because of what he had done to me. During three years of prison together, this was the first of only two times I saw him so carried away. In both cases, his tears were shed for someone else. For a long time I said nothing.

After what seemed an eternity I had to conclude that the Communists were, indeed, after me. I knew that once they found those empty cartridge shells in my basement, that my fate would be sealed. That was the one time in my three years in North Korea that I never expected to see my wife again. Then I thought about my wife and family. Even though they were thousands of miles away, they were also vulnerable. They were more innocent than I was, but they would have to suffer after I was gone. I considered how insignificant I really was when measured against the few people who would be directly affected by my death. I tried to count the number of those who might grieve for me and came up with twelve, at most—not very many, I thought. After that, prayer, grief, and thought became intertwined and indistinguishable. Time became irrelevant, and nothing beyond the inside of the mind had any real meaning.

I suspect that the mind creates its own private world under such circumstances. What is actually occurring is much too strong to be taken full strength. There were times during my three years in prison when hope manifested itself out of the flimsiest evidence, but in that death cell that night, there was absolutely no evidence on which to base what we generally regard as hope.

Somehow during that night, what little was left of it, I made my peace with God and with death. My conviction was that everything would be all right, no matter what happened. It was my first victory in that prison.

During that night, I became aware that I was faced with a strange irony. When you feel you must die and are prepared for it, the act of living can become a burden. I could face my own execution now if I had to. Would I feel the same way tomorrow morning? If not, why not get it over with now?

In another ironic twist, you become ambivalent about time. If I am to die tomorrow morning, then the night will be too short. Yet if I am to die, I don't need that much time to pray. Prayer becomes very efficient in a death cell. Too little time to live, too much time to pray.

In fact, I concluded that death might become a welcome friend under conditions of extreme torture. I didn't worry any more about dying, but I did worry about what I might have to endure before my death. My execution: would it be painful? I was in the hands of people who had the mind-set to make it painful if they chose.

Would my death have any meaning to anyone? Perhaps that was the last selfish thought of a person going to his own execution.

How would I conduct myself during those final moments? Would I cry out? Would I plead for mercy? I hoped not!

On returning to a little sanity, I asked myself why it would matter how I acted, being in the hands of professionals who had seen it all before. But would it make a difference to me? Yes, I supposed it would, but not for long.

Torture, pain, and the feeling of futility in the face of my own execution were issues that I never resolved. I simply had to learn to live with them. I had packed my bags and was ready to go. For the first time since coming into that death cell, I felt some comfort. I was still worried. I knew that they could hurt me. Yet the evidence against me was so overwhelming, I thought, that I might not be tortured at all—just taken out and shot. If you can relate to that possible turn of events as good news, then you will better understand my mental state in that death cell.

Those who hate you are there to trouble you every day. It is their business to create pain. It is yours to find another horizon and to live by faith. Their weapons are both external and internal. Yours, by definition, are internal only—not subject to being lost, used up, taken away by the guards, or worn out. The only thing you can count on in such a struggle is what you have inside yourself.

It was morning again, and the same guards were there to make us do the same things we did the day before. After breakfast, we took our positions cross-legged on the floor, looking toward the rear wall. The guard with the heavy boots made his rounds as usual. In all the time I was·in that cell, I never saw him face to face.

I was certain the interrogators hoped they could increase the pressure again today. If so, they were wrong. Nothing could surpass the harrowing events of the day before—not only their demonic techniques for making my life miserable but also the bombshell dropped by Kris the night before. They already had a rifle that they said I had used to fire on their soldiers in the battle of Kaesong. By now they must have also found the empty cartridge shells in my basement.

But it was time to go to another interrogation. By this time I felt certain that continuing interrogations would have no bearing on whether I lived or died; I could take them because my fate was already sealed. I sat down at a table in a different room, one containing three chairs, a table, and an old makeshift desk. Feeling strangely detached from my surroundings, I thought it really didn't make any difference what went on during that interrogation. "Please write the story of your life," the new interrogator instructed me.

"But I did that yesterday."

"Yes, but you wrote so little. What are you trying to hide? You are not writing enough."

I thought about that for a moment. If I don't write enough, they accuse me of trying to hide something. Yet the more I write, the more likely I am to get into trouble. Also, something I write today may conflict with something I wrote yesterday. I lose either way.

I was in the hands of people who were not content merely to control the body; they wanted the mind and heart as well. They had the training to make us pay dearly for thoughts and attitudes that were not "correct." These people felt that they were doing us a favor when they caused us all forms of deprivation: loss of freedom, controlled starvation, controlled fatigue, controlled fear, controlled confusion, confinement. The purpose was to assist us in learning the "truth," according to their definition of it.

We were required to call them *Sun-sang-nim*, "honored teachers." Their job as teachers was to motivate learning, and they had many skills available to them to accomplish that purpose. Such radical reeducation might involve some rather harsh discipline, they readily admitted. "But Rarry, we want you to learn the truth freely. We could force you to agree with us, but we want you to see the truth from your heart. This way you can have a clear conscience."[4]

"But I don't agree with you," I said.

"We understand that. You are poisoned by capitalistic thinking. But we want you to see the truth on your own so that you will have a clear conscience. When you do, you will thank us for our efforts on your behalf."

This time my two self-styled executioner-interrogators were waiting for me when I entered the room. "Rarry, in spite of all the bad things you have done, you can still have a happy future. Do you want that? Here is how you can do it. Confess all you have done! Tell us who your contacts are in South Korea. Whom did you report to with your secret radio messages? What are their names? What information did you give them? Tell us all this! Confess your bad thoughts and you can have a happy future. We would like for you to join us in our struggle against imperialism. We like you. We need you. You believe me, don't you?" I didn't say anything.

"But Rarry, we must first talk about your bad thoughts. You don't understand; we will have to teach you. Is it possible that you are a college graduate, and yet you do not know about Marxism-Leninism? What did they teach you in America?" Again, I let them do the talking. We were seated around a table in an informal fashion. They offered me some tea, which I accepted.

"But Rarry, we will not kill a good person. Right now, you are not a good person. You are a bad person. We can kill you. We can kill you now. So examine your thoughts and heart, Rarry. Wouldn't you rather join the peace-loving peoples of the world than remain with the Wall Street pigs and their running-dog lackeys? We will have to teach you."

I could hardly believe what I was hearing. In contrast to their threats of the day before, they were now almost kind by comparison. But I knew more was coming.

"Rarry, you are nothing as you are now. Look at you—an ideological saboteur, a spy, a soldier without a uniform who killed our brave soldiers in Kaesong, a reactionary, an advance agent of Wall

Street under sentence of death. But we want you to have a happy future." They went on for some time, but they were coming to the end with another riddle.

"Rarry, you cannot help yourself without our help. And we cannot help you until you help yourself. Sleep on it, Rarry. Sleep on it."

I tried. The body was ready for sleep, but the mind would not turn off. It isn't possible to sleep under such circumstances until the body grows so tired that it finally forces the mind into submission.

By offering hope, they had succeeded in doing to me what they could no longer do by threatening my execution. I had quickly made my peace with death, but I would have to take more time to come to terms with hope, however unwarranted it might be.

They knew what they were doing. If death is faced long enough, the human psyche makes an accommodation with it. To further harass me, the interrogators held out the possibility that I might save my life without compromising my country or my beliefs. It was a very seductive ploy. I knew that the pricetag exacted for my newly found hope would be high indeed, but I wanted to know about it anyway. Part of their game was to make you lie awake at night and deprive yourself of much-needed sleep.

After a long time of not being able to sleep, my mind also became so fatigued that it did not function properly. Philip Deane, a war correspondent for the *London Observer* who was captured in South Korea and later joined me as a prisoner, experienced some of the same kinds of treatment that I did, and some of his reactions paralleled my own: "I spent a great deal of time in dissociation."5

I occasionally retreated into my life as a child on a small farm near Weatherford, Texas. We had problems then, but they were problems that we could handle. In that death cell, sleep and semiconsciousness would often blend, as though the mind simply would not let go and give real sleep a chance to take over. But even in that never-never mental state, I escaped for a few minutes from that terrible place.

Perhaps your conscience becomes more active when you believe your death is near. Lying there trying to sort out the many ideas that were struggling to find a place in my mind, I was suddenly shaken by something I had forgotten: those student essays I had left in the study of my house! I had assigned them to my students in the middle school as part of their homework. I had already graded them and would have returned them at the next class session. The subject of those essays was "Why I Believe In Democracy." In that death cell I became aware for the first time that those essays could create problems; some of them were very critical of Communism. And the Communists had a different definition of democracy from those of the students.

To make matters worse, the author of each essay had spelled out his name on his homework in both the Korean and English alphabets. Just what would be done to those students whose essays had espoused strong anti-Communist sentiment suddenly became a concern to me. During my imprisonment, I had seen that the Communists did not take such matters lightly. I realized that I should have destroyed those essays. The issue bothered me so much that I composed a letter in my mind to my students: "I'm sorry, boys, I let you down. I hope that my failure to destroy those essays has not caused you problems, but I'm afraid it has." The mental letter remained unfinished. There was no way I could undo, or even know, the damage I may have done to the lives of so many people.

We had another problem. We were being eaten alive by fleas. The wooden floor in our cell had been constructed on top of a concrete base with wide gaps between the boards, as much as a quarter-inch. Fleas were jumping through these wide gaps; we could feel them bounce off our hands if we put them down anywhere on the floor. Perhaps the fleas were part of the punishment plan.

That morning I developed a way to while away the hours; I killed fleas and spelled out words on the floor of the cell with their dead bodies. An observant guard walking by my cell looked in and demanded to know what I was writing. When he entered the cell and saw what was happening, he screamed and went running for higher authority. The flea issue was more than he could handle. An officer who could read English arrived and surveyed the situation. On reading my message, "Fleas are bad," he shook his head and walked out, not saying a word to anyone. I continued my new hobby as before, but I doubt very much if I made even a dent in the flea population.

At the noon meal I asked Kris and Dr. Kisch if they had seen or heard anything about the three American women, who had been taken away to an area behind our own cell. We concluded that their situation must have been every bit as bad as our own, and we wondered about the mentality of a country that would hold such women as enemies of the state.

One morning I made the startling discovery that Dr. Kisch and Kris were becoming very thin and haggard. On looking at my arms, I saw that I was wasting away also. I assumed that my mind was being similarly affected. Every day that I spent in this place, I concluded, was one more day that I lost something important to me. Would I continue to be diminished until there was nothing of value that belonged to me? If I should survive, would I really be able to live with the part of me that remained?

I wrestled with this problem for some time before I finally came to a conclusion: I controlled what was most important in this death cell— my relationship to God, and my thoughts. These were things that no one had given me and, as long as I had a mind, no one could take away. At last, a part of me that they could not control! They might suspect that it existed, but they could not get at it, at least not directly. They could destroy my mind, but if they did, then nothing else would matter to me anyway.

That danger was real. But there were other kinds of dangers. I soon realized that I might be tempted to purchase my life by compromising my country and beliefs. I then achieved another breakthrough, one based at least in part upon an earlier discovery. Death was not the worst thing that could happen to me.

After much soul-searching, I developed a strategy for survival. I would strengthen and take refuge in that which they could not control and keep my integrity. I would also remain prepared for my execution at any time.

This plan for dealing with the issues of life and death did serve me well in that death cell. But my interrogators later uncovered a few chinks in that armor.

4. DEADLY DIALOGUE

THERE were many interrogators working on me, each with a different tactic. I have no idea where they got their training—certainly not from the Japanese. They appeared to use techniques against me that were very similar to those of the Chinese Communists, techniques intended to achieve the genuine reeducation of a prisoner's political views: hence their frequent advice to me to purge my old capitalistic thoughts and "have a clear conscience." To the North Koreans, a clear conscience meant correct political thinking.

My views about the intense psychological pressures that I endured in prison are similar to those of journalist Philip Deane. When asked after his release from North Korea whether he had been physically tortured, Deane gave a searching response: "Not in the strict sense of the word. The theory—and I learned the theory after I came out of prison—is that they act on the mind of the prisoner by exploiting fears he already has or implanting other fears. They confront the prisoner with these fears day and night, till he breaks."[1]

With the exception of the controlled sinister climate that caused me at times to fear living more than dying—the sensory deprivation, the interrogations, the chronic fatigue that was just as bad on waking up in the morning as at night—I was not subjected to what we usually consider torture. I don't know why. If they had used torture on me, they would have won whatever they wanted; I have no doubt about that.[2]

My next interrogator, one I had never seen before, apparently worked alone.

"Rarry, where is your pistol? We didn't find one when we arrested you."

"I don't have one."

"You teach ideology in your house in Kaesong."

"I sometimes discuss religion in my house." I was being careful in my answers.

"Then you admit that you teach ideology in your house?" he pressed on.

"I teach a class in modern literature once each week in my house. Some of that literature discusses Christianity. I suppose from your point of view I do teach ideology, but attendance is strictly voluntary."

"You are hiding something. You admit that you teach ideology and yet you do not have a pistol."

"I don't need a pistol. Everyone is permitted to come to my house if he wishes. They are not required to attend." He appeared to be agitated by my answers.

"Do you believe in what you teach?" he demanded.

"Yes, very much."

"If you really believed in what you taught, you would have a pistol, and everyone would be required to listen."

"Does everyone in your country believe in your ideology?" I asked, thinking I might divert him from the subject.

"No, some do not, but they are poisoned by capitalistic thoughts. In any case, they do not matter. But they will at least know our ideology. We require them to know it. You do not require it of your people. You are not sincere."

My interrogator seemed to be a very excitable person and a chain smoker. His questions indicated to me that he had his own agenda. I had never seen him before, and I was never to see him again.

"How can you say that I am not sincere? Do you mean that I am lying?"

"Not necessarily. But if you really thought that your ideology was very important, you would have a pistol, and you would make people listen. Perhaps not all of them would believe you, but at least they would know about your teaching. You are not sincere!"

"Our system believes in tolerance," I replied, thinking that I was on safe ground.

"Tolerance! Ah! It is not tolerance at all. It is lack of conviction!" I could see the problem. In the eyes of the interrogators, either I did not carry a personal weapon, which they could not understand, or else I did carry one and they could not find it, which made them angry with me. There was a pause, and I thought about the general drift of our conversation. I had displayed one of our best ideological weapons, tolerance, and the interrogator regarded it as a sign of weakness.

My next interrogators, a set of three, attacked from still another direction, asking, "How much money did your parents earn per year?" My parents were rather poor farmers, so I had already surmised what the reaction would be to my answer.

"You lie!" they shouted. I soon realized the nature of the problem. It was a question of doctrine. If my parents were poor, then how was I able to attend college? According to their little book, the children of parents who made less than a certain income were not able to go on to higher education. They were obviously faced with a conflict between their ideology and my testimony, and it had to be resolved.

I didn't know what else to do, so I remained silent as my interrogators shouted at me. I realized my plight early in that interrogation. Fact and fantasy alike must be bent to fit the prearranged plan. On certain issues, at least, it really didn't matter what I told them. It was obvious that these particular interrogators were more bureaucratic than the others. They would simply fill in the blanks, in as much detail as they chose, based upon the requirements of their plan. There had to be a way out of this dilemma for them, and there was.

"We will write in our report that your father was a wealthy landowner," one of them said at last, after much consultation with the other two. (My father had a good laugh when I told him about this on my return to America.)

I was beginning to feel like the unwilling participant in an ancient Greek tragedy, where the issues are already decided and the players merely going through the motions, playing out their appointed roles with as much grace, courage, and nobility as possible. With their roles already prescribed, the main characters win or lose, not by whether or not they live (they always die) but by how faithfully they play out their roles to the predictable end. Not a very noble way to make my exit, I thought.

They changed the subject again about that time. "When the peace-loving peoples of the world liberate the earth from capitalism, there will finally be peace." They could become positively misty-eyed when they talked like that. "You are a reactionary who is delaying that wonderful time when all of this takes place. Don't you feel ashamed of your actions?"

"I want you to know," I said, thinking I might make a point, "that I do not consider you to be my enemy." They were ready with an answer. "You may not consider us to be your enemy, but we know that you are ours." I wondered how my sociology teacher in college would have responded to that statement.

Then they returned to a matter that I had been dreading in a way but one that I wanted to know about: that tantalizing offer of hope. "Have you been thinking about what we asked you?"

"What did you ask me?" I reacted cautiously.

"We told you that you could have a happy future, remember?"

"Yes, I remember."

"Well, what about it? Do you want a happy future or not?" I knew that I was in a tight spot, no matter what I answered. It was dangerous to play along with them. From their point of view, there was no polite or acceptable way to turn them down without making them angry; after all, they were the teachers.

"I'm sorry," I replied at last. The three of them became very angry.

"Who do you think you are? Do you think that you are in a position to make bargains with us? You who are about to die?" One of them spat on the floor in apparent disgust as the other two raved on simultaneously.

"We have tried to save your life, but we can see that you don't appreciate it!" They appeared to be offended by my apparent ingratitude.

"My life isn't worth very much to me now anyway."

"Oh, you are complaining about your treatment! Please pay attention: unless you show us in some way that you are trying to change your thoughts and your conduct, you are not worthy of the kind of treatment you are now getting. You should try to be more grateful."

"What is it that I am not doing right?" I asked.

"You must change your attitude and submit to self-criticism. Your thinking is bad. You are poisoned with reactionary thinking."

When at last there was quiet, they all expected me to continue the conversation. I realized that anything I said or asked would be viewed as weakness, so I remained silent.

"Is that all you have to say?"

"Yes," I replied.

"If you continue to do as you are now doing, you will die. You will die soon."

Apparently, they felt that they had made their point and ushered me out of the room to be returned to my cell. When I walked by an adjoining room, my interrogator from the day before poked his head out the door and shouted after me. "You can have a happy future. Many nice things." His voice trailed off in singsong. I did not even look back. I preferred the death cell and the fleas. It was difficult to decide whether these men were more frightening when they appeared friendly or when they were openly hostile.

My mind was very confused that night. I wondered why each set of interrogators seemed to pursue a different approach, yet all were aimed at breaking me down. Confusion reigned between their methods, but it could not be termed random confusion; it all had a purpose.

But I was becoming more and more enticed by the prospect of hope that the interrogators seemed to be offering me. Was there really a way out for me after all? Could I escape execution without betraying my country or compromising my beliefs? The peace of mind I had previously enjoyed was predicated upon Dr. Kisch's belief that our fate had already been decided before we were ever placed in the death cell, that nothing we said or did during our interrogations would make any difference concerning whether we lived or died.

Yet the interrogators at that time were certainly leading me to believe that I could save my life by something I might say. This belief would place a very high premium on how I conducted myself during those interrogations. Little by little, I was beginning to doubt what Dr. Kisch had said. To that same degree, I was becoming more troubled about my conduct during interrogations. Also, to that same degree, I was growing increasingly vulnerable to all the other stresses in that prison.

After a very miserable night in my cell, I was brought into a room to face three new interrogators. "We have been looking over your life history. Very interesting," one of them said with a smile. They always told me that no matter what I wrote.

"We noticed that you did not tell us who your fourth grade teacher was. What was her name?" I paused for a moment, thinking he might be joking. The speaker and the other interrogators sat very still, looking intently at me without saying a word. They were not joking.

"I'm sorry, I don't remember who my fourth grade teacher was," I replied, not even trying to hide my exasperation.

"Rarry, I thought you would know by now how important it is for you to cooperate with us. You seem to remember many other things. Why do you not remember this teacher?"

"I'm sorry, if I knew I would tell you."

"You are showing initiative, Rarry, and that is a very bad thing for anyone in your position to do!"

That word, "initiative" had a habit of creeping into their vocabulary quite often. I didn't know the Korean word for initiative. Inasmuch as English was used in all interrogations, I thought at first that the confusion might have resulted from a mistranslation of a Korean word into English. But the same English word would show up at odd times during the entire three years. Even on the Death March that was to follow, the one catch phrase that the North Koreans shouted up and down the line of marching men and women was, "Don't show initiative!"

It was impossible to convince the three interrogators that I was unable to follow their instructions. "I am sorry that I still cannot remember the name of my fourth grade teacher." They were very unhappy with my answer. Immediately they launched into a tirade against me and everything I stood for. They made it very clear that I would have to answer for not cooperating. Their punishment was to interrogate me longer and more often. Finally, as they were returning me to my cell, they called after me, "If you didn't show initiative, things would be better for you!"

A recurrent theme in the interrogations concerned the relationship between war and religion. This is ironic when you consider that the Communist world in the 1950s did not believe that religion should even be allowed to exist in their society. But the interrogators used the issue of religion against me to try to achieve their own goals. After I could not supply the three interrogators with the name of my fourth grade teacher, they changed the line of attack for a time. "Rarry, we have been wondering about you. Are you a religious person?"

"Well . . . yes," I replied, knowing they were up to something.

"Good. You have told us that you are a missionary teacher working in a middle school. According to your religion, is war bad?"

"Yes, it is," I answered without hesitation.

"Good. Then you will sign this paper condemning America's barbaric bombing and aggression in Korea," they said. They placed a single piece of paper in front of me and indicated where I was to sign. Although I knew better than to look at it for more than an instant, I could see that it was written in English.

"I can't sign this," I replied.

"Why not? You said that you were a missionary and that your religion taught that war was bad. If that is true, then why can't you sign this paper? People all over the world are signing it. Enough signatures will end this terrible war."[3]

"I still can't sign it," I said in resignation.

"Rarry, we know why you won't sign this paper that would end all the bloodshed in Korea. You are not a missionary! You are not a teacher! You are a soldier! We understand now. And since you are a soldier, you are also a spy." They sat back waiting for me to respond. It was a trap, but it was one that I could not have avoided.[4]

Around this time, I accidentally discovered a technique of replying to my interrogators that proved to be invaluable to me. When the interrogators used abstract words such as peace, freedom, justice, democracy, and truth, they gave them different meanings. For example, when they spoke of freedom, they referred to the restricted way their citizens were required to live. Peace to them reflected a world in which Communism had finally triumphed. Truth was whatever helped the Communist cause. To employ my word-clarifying technique, I would pause for a second or two after each question and do my mental exercise before giving an answer. When a prisoner is physically and mentally exhausted from hours of interrogation, he must be very careful not to accept the interrogator's definition of reality. If they could get me to do that, they would have me where they wanted me. They took issue with my delaying tactics, but I told them that I had always been slow of speech.

At the next interrogation, I was asked if I could now remember the name of my fourth grade teacher.

"Yes," I responded, "her name was Mrs. Smith." I had made up a name, as they knew I would.

"Good, now you are cooperating with us and showing a proper attitude. You are not showing initiative. We will leave you alone for a while."

With a sleepless night ahead, I had a lot of time to think in that death cell. I remembered something my father had told me when I was a boy. "L.A.," he said (I go by the initials L.A. to my parents), "there may come a day when someone will offer you something that you want more than anything in the world. It looks like it might be worth any price that you could pay. But they don't want money for what they are selling. They want you to do something that is a little bad. It doesn't look like it's real bad. In your mind's eye it seems like a good trade. But you have to remember, it's still bad."

At the time my father gave me that advice, I thought I understood. But now it occurred to me that what he had said was far more complicated than I had suspected.

Their goal was clear to me: they were asking me to lie in order to receive a reward. I didn't regret playing with the truth when I couldn't remember my fourth grade teacher's name; in that sense, I had played their game. But I knew that in the future, when both the rewards and penalties had escalated, I would have to set my limit.

The same three people were waiting for me at my next interrogation. "Rarry, who started the war?" I had been worried that they would eventually ask me that question. Their lectures still claimed that South Korea began the war by attacking across the 38th parallel on June 24, 1950, and that they (the North Koreans) had counterattacked on June 25. As an eyewitness, I knew that view was false.

"I think North Korea started the war," I said, not knowing what they would do.

"You are lying, Rarry," one of them said in a calm voice. "South Korea started the war on June 24 and we counterattacked on June 25. You are showing initiative again, Rarry. You still do not understand. We will have to teach you." When I did not respond, the three of them launched into another long-winded harangue against me and every value known in the free world. At long last they had me returned to my cell.

With the passing of time in that death cell, another consideration besides that of mere survival began to surface. I decided not to carry any more excess baggage with me to my execution than absolutely necessary. I chose not to hate my captors. Much later, without the stimulation of impending execution, that old emotion would return on occasion, and dealing with it was difficult. But in that death cell, giving up hate was not difficult to do because it was too much of a burden.

Their little games continued every day that I spent in the death cell. I was never left alone for very long. Several times a day a "thought control" guard would test what was going on inside my mind. Throwing open the door of the cell, he would suddenly appear without warning. Jumping directly in front of me and pointing his finger in my face, he would scream, "What are you thinking about?" I'd usually respond that I was thinking about home and loved ones.

"*Napan sangok*—bad thoughts! You should be thinking about your many crimes against the people!" I was never punished for my "bad thoughts" except by screaming lectures, but I always dreaded the verbal examination.

The stress was beginning to make me feel numb. I no longer reacted when I heard the now familiar gunshots from outside the cell. Those shots could be heard several times each day, usually occurring in groups of two to five, beginning at sunrise. The Communists didn't employ what we think of as a firing squad; one pistol shot delivered to the back of the head at close range was sufficient. I wondered how those who had been executed had faced their deaths. It occurred to me that many of those hapless victims were probably no more guilty than I.

I was taken into a familiar room with the same cast of characters as the time before. I now called them the Three Musketeers. "Who started the war, Rarry?" they wanted to know. I gave them the same reply as before.

"What did we tell you last night?" they demanded.

"You said that South Korea started the war."

"We told you nothing of the kind. We told you that America started the war. You are showing initiative again, Rarry. We will have to teach you." Another three-hour lecture deprived me of much-needed sleep.

The Three Musketeers, operating together as a team, took a different approach from that of the other interrogators. It occurred to me that they might have been from the propaganda office. In that capacity they would have wanted to put words into my mouth—perhaps to break me down so that I would agree to make propaganda radio broadcasts for them. Later, in fact, they did ask me to make such broadcasts.

If the Three Musketeers were, indeed, from the propaganda office, they might also have wanted to know more about the convictions of their enemy in matters of ideology; the Communists were always very concerned about what people believed. Except for the fact that I lacked their obvious Communistic convictions, they probably considered me a fellow missionary—each of us engaged in our separate tasks of spreading the Word.

The next session went the same way. "Who started the war, Rarry?" they asked. My answer was the same.

"What did we tell you last night?" they asked.

"You said that it was America, but I still think North Korea."

"We did not say that. We told you last night that England started the war." Another long lecture followed. This bizarre episode was repeated through several interrogations. Other countries were implicated: France, Germany, Canada. It had become a very exhausting game, one that I knew I couldn't win. Finally, they played their trump card.

"Rarry, why is it so hard for you to learn? All you must do is ask us. Ask us anything at any time. We will tell you. You won't have to spend all this time with us when you could be back in your cell. You will never get anywhere by showing initiative. Just ask and we will tell you what we want you to know." That was all. Then I was taken back to my cell to contemplate what had happened.

That particular episode was complete, but I still had to decode the meaning. I was free to tell them what I thought, except that I was harassed for hours for speaking my mind. I was wrong even if I repeated to them what they had told me during the previous interrogation. Even that was showing initiative! Then it struck me: that was exactly what I was doing wrong—I was showing initiative by assuming that I knew the correct answer, based upon what they had previously told me. What they wanted, in effect, was for me to ask them at the beginning of each interrogation session what I was supposed to believe at that moment.

They were following Communist doctrine to the letter: truth was a servant of the state. Truth, then, was whatever they wanted it to be. To play their game was to accept their most recent definition of truth.

They came for me one day after I had been in the death cell for about a week, for what I thought would be my last time. Seeing the back door of the cell open very slowly, I looked up to behold the face of the youngest guard that I had ever seen. He spoke to me almost in a whisper. "Come with me." There was a pleasant expression on his face. He escorted me politely down the corridor in the direction of the guard office. Conflicting thoughts rushed through my mind. This is it, I thought. This is exactly the way they would do it: send their youngest and most polite guard to escort me to the place of my execution.

When I entered the guard room, I found another equally young man sitting in a chair behind a desk. He quickly arose, looked at me for a moment as he walked past me, and then asked the first guard to follow him into the hallway. They talked together in whispers for a few seconds before reentering the room. There was an empty expression on their faces—also entirely consistent with what I deemed to be their ultimate plan for me.

Again, there were all kinds of conflicting thoughts going on in my mind, a part of me insisting that these would be my last few minutes alive, another part taking issue with that train of thought entirely. Suddenly, the second guard left the room and disappeared down the hallway. The remaining guard ordered me to sit down in a chair beside a desk. A deathly silence followed, allowing my perplexed mind to work overtime in conflicting speculation. Yes, this is it, I thought. "Well, Larry, are you ready? As ready as I ever will be," I thought. I wondered why they had picked the two youngest men to be participants in all this. Will one of them be required by his officers to pull the trigger and thus prove his loyalty to the system? Yes, they are capable of that, I concluded.

I caught myself searching the inside of the small guard office to see whether I could locate bullet holes in the walls or furniture. There were none that I could see. "They won't kill me in this office," I thought, "but in that special place just outside the latrine," the execution area next to the high wall that the guard had pointed out the first morning of my imprisonment. But even as I had reached this state of mental preparation (or confusion), part of my mind rejected the idea that I was about to die.

The wait for the first guard to return was a long one. At any moment I expected to see him reappear in the doorway accompanied by at least one officer. That never happened. When the guard did return, he was alone. Following a hurried conference in whispers, one of the two guards politely ordered me to stand. The same courteous guard returned me to my cell, leaving me to ponder what might have just taken place. I finally concluded that I had been taken out of my cell for an interrogation that for some reason never came off. It had been a very emotionally draining experience.

I relate this story, in part, to demonstrate that the mind may work against you under stress. The actions and behavior of the two guards, though a little unusual, did not really warrant the conclusion that I had drawn—that I was on my way to my execution. Perhaps once the mind has been thoroughly traumatized, it sometimes misinterprets the information it receives. For whatever reason, the prisoner must be prepared to fight enemies both from within and without.

My next memory is of our being taken to a large room beyond the two great locked doors that separated our cellblock and interrogation rooms from the rest of the prison compound. My sense of elation at being removed from the death cells was overwhelming. There was beauty to be seen everywhere, even in the drab walls of the prison. The first people we saw were the three American women, who had also been brought from their prison cell. We all looked terrible, but at the moment, that did not matter. I tried to say something to Nell but was cut short by our escort officer. Then the six of us were taken to a large room whose furnishings appeared to be church pews. Our escort officer told us to be seated and then departed, leaving us in the care of a silent, unfriendly guard who sat at a small desk toward the front of the room. Thereafter, though I was still taken out quite often for interrogations by the Three Musketeers, I was always returned to the same room with the others, where we remained for a night or two.

Our joy at being removed from the death cells was tempered somewhat by the slow realization that one of our members (who will remain anonymous) was showing overt signs of emotional stress. Had we been able to talk freely, we would have discovered the problem earlier. Fortunately the condition disappeared, when we were removed from the prison compound and into more normal surroundings.

An officer walked into our room one day and announced that we were to follow him. Entering a large office, we saw someone with Western features standing by a desk. Looking more closely, I could see that he wore the uniform of the Salvation Army; then I recognized him as Salvation Army Commissioner Herbert A. Lord, an Englishman and head of all his organization's work in Seoul. Extending his hand to us, he smiled and said cheerfully, "Hello. Are you all right?"

Wild thoughts raced through my head, and I asked, "Are you here to take us out?" It was a foolish question to ask, but because he was English, I could not believe that he would be a prisoner. Lord was indeed a prisoner, however, along with some other Europeans and Americans who had just been brought in from Seoul.

"They are taking you and all of us out of Pyongyang. They are evacuating the city because of the bombing," he said. That was great news—at least to those of us who had been in the death cells. The others, who had just arrived from Seoul, were very discouraged that they had been arrested and brought to Pyongyang.

There was even greater news. Looking at Kris and me, Commissioner Lord whispered, "Your wives were evacuated by ship from Inchon on June 26. I know that for a fact, as I saw them off." I was overjoyed to learn with certainty that Frances had been able to escape.

An officer who had been seated at a nearby table came up to us carrying some papers. Yes, the paperwork had to be completed before we were turned over to someone else. With that out of the way, we were marched into a second room, where the other Americans and Europeans were waiting. They had been rounded up in Seoul and other cities in South Korea and had now been brought to Pyongyang just as we had.

It may sound selfish, but I felt reassured by the presence in Pyongyang of twenty or so non-Koreans who were obviously in the same boat as we six westerners from Kaesong. I felt it unlikely that the North Koreans would put on trial such a large group of people. After our harrowing experience in the death cells, it did not immediately occur to me that the entire group could be exposed to other equally grave dangers.

We were loaded into three trucks and driven toward the northeast. I must have been wearing a perpetual smile. No matter what the future danger, I was excited and happy to be moving away from that death cell.

5. THE SCHOOLHOUSE

AS our truck moved along the road that took us out of the city of Pyongyang, we were treated to the latest war news. The date was sometime in the second week of July 1950. Commissioner Lord informed us that the British minister, Capt. Vyvyan Holt, and his staff of two from Seoul were on one of the other trucks. We all considered this to be a good sign. With the shield of diplomatic immunity protecting the British diplomats, surely we Americans would not be treated too badly. We tried to reassure ourselves that even the Nazis and the Imperialist Japanese had observed the universally accepted practice of diplomatic immunity.

Some in the group suggested that we were being assembled in one place in order to be returned to freedom in some sort of prisoner exchange arranged through the International Red Cross. Both Nell Dyer and Commissioner Lord, as prisoners of the Japanese in World War II, had been helped by the International Red Cross. We naturally assumed that the North Koreans could do no less than the Japanese. At least, they might permit the International Red Cross to visit us and assure our families that we were alive and well. In fact, the International Red Cross did try many times to arrange for the exchange of prisoner lists as a humanitarian effort. They were always rebuffed, "for why should the anxiety of any prisoner's family constitute even remotely a 'problem' for a North Korean Communist official?"[1]

The truck stopped, and we were ordered to unload. We were parked next to what appeared to be a long schoolhouse with a smaller building in front. At first, we were apprehensive when ordered to arrange ourselves according to nationalities. When the American men and Dr. Kisch were instructed to enter the first room in the building, I found myself walking with two men whom I had never seen. One was short and powerfully built; the other man was taller and older and had a heavy black beard.

The shorter one spoke first. "Well, here I am. I never thought I would wind up in North Korea." This was Louis (Danny) Dans, an

American from Chicago and now a businessman in Seoul. The first thing that I noticed about Danny was his very athletic physique, apparent even through his shirt. When I later asked him about this, he told me that he had been an acrobat at one time.

I turned and looked at the powerful face of the other man. It was not difficult to believe that he had been a coalminer for most of his life. At the time of his arrest by the North Koreans, he was employed as a mining engineer by the Economic Cooperation Administration (ECA) of the U.S. government. His very important job in South Korea was to increase badly needed coal production. His first words to me (slightly edited) were "I'm Walter Eltringham, and if Uncle Sam doesn't kick the daylights out of this outfit within a week or ten days, I'll eat my hat!"

Walter, of Wilkes-Barre, Pennsylvania, had a powerful voice and spoke with authority, looking his hearers dead in the eye during every conversation; he must have been good at what he did in South Korea. In spite of his rough exterior, Walter turned out to be one of our most caring, compassionate persons and in time would demonstrate that quality in a very dramatic way.

The American women were placed by themselves in the next room. When the French consul-general, Georges Perruche, head of the French legation in Seoul, and his staff arrived a few days later, they were located in the third room. Finally, Captain Holt and his staff from the British legation in Seoul were given the last two rooms. Other prisoners from many nations would join us during the remainder of July and August.

Not being allowed to talk between rooms, we managed to communicate in the fairly modern coed bathroom, which was located in a separate building. That bathroom provided the only place where information could be exchanged. Either the guards didn't know about it or didn't care.

We Americans from Kaesong were grateful to hear even news that was, by that time, two or three weeks old. Having been cut off from all outside information on June 25, we had known absolutely nothing about the American involvement or the United Nations resolution to send troops to fight on the side of South Korea. American bombing of Pyongyang was taking place almost daily at this time as we could see by looking out our windows from our vantage point just out of town. Four-engined American B-29 Superfortresses, the type of aircraft that destroyed Tokyo and many other major Japanese cities in World War II, would arrive about noon at moderately high altitude, but they were not high enough to make contrails.

Each morning after we woke at six o'clock, our first duty was to remove the whole row of southward-facing windows by lifting them out of their tracks. We did this in order to be able to see what was going on and for safety reasons. Removing the windows offered us some protection from flying glass in case of a nearby bomb blast. None ever fell very close to us.

The arrival of those B-29s was at first announced only by a swishing sound caused by the flight of the bombs through the air. After a few days an air raid siren would sound a minute or two before the first bombs actually exploded on the ground. Antiaircraft fire at that time was extremely light. In our six weeks' stay in that schoolhouse, while witnessing a bombing almost every day, we never saw a single American aircraft shot down.

So punctual were these bombers that as noontime approached, we in the room would grow nervous. "Walt, what time is it?" Danny once shouted over to Walter, who was one of the few who still had a watch.

"At the sound of the bomb, the time will be exactly twelve o'clock noon," Walter announced.

There were also raids by U.S. Navy dive bombers. They would arrive over the city at medium altitude and begin their dive in groups of approximately nine. In some instances we could actually see the bombs they released at the bottom of the dive. Some of these raids must have been made against bridges because we could see columns of water shoot up from time to time. Antiaircraft fire could be seen bursting around the aircraft near the bottom of their dives.

The most graphic displays of all were made by F-51 Mustangs as they arrived over the city at extremely low altitude to begin their strafing and rocket attacks on the rail yard. Approximately twelve of these aircraft appeared suddenly at six o'clock one morning and attacked a target located nearby. Walter was the first to see them. "Here come the Ponies!" he shouted. The F-51s circled after each attack and flew directly over our schoolhouse. In some instances, those planes were so low that we could see the pilots. We wanted desperately to signal them in some way but were frustrated by the fact that the guards lying outside in air raid trenches were watching us. The only signaling we could do, therefore, was from the inside of the room and below the level of the window ledge. In spite of our efforts I doubt if we were ever seen by any of the pilots.

After an air raid one day, someone asked whether the four-engine aircraft we had just seen were B-29s or B-50s; at their altitude I could not tell the difference. It was not until after my release that I learned that no B-50s were used in Korea; all my references to B-29s reflect that later knowledge. Someone suggested that the aircraft had been B-36s. I knew that was not true. While attending Southern Methodist University in Dallas, Texas, in 1948, I had often seen that six-engine monster fly over the campus. The B-36 Peacemaker, a relatively new and very heavy bomber, was built at the Convair plant in Fort Worth some thirty miles from my home. Just as I started to remark that we had not seen the B-36 over Pyongyang, Kris slapped me on the shoulder: "Don't say anything. Your situation is far too delicate here as it is. From now on you don't know anything about airplanes. Do you understand? You'll be better off that way." Remembering my problems in the death cell, I followed his advice for the remainder of our stay.

We tried to give names to the various guards on duty at our schoolhouse, but it proved to be very difficult because the guards were shifted around so often. One day we were attempting to get around the ban against talking between rooms by whispering out of the open window to Nell Dyer and Helen Rosser. An alert guard soon put a stop to our illegal communication. "The man with the gun is in charge here," Danny remarked. The title caught on. From then on any guard with no name was referred to as the "man with the gun."

Following our arrival at the schoolhouse, we were joined from time to time by other prisoners. Late one night we were awakened by the sound of someone entering our darkened room. It was Bishop Patrick Byrne, apostolic delegate to South Korea, and his secretary, Father William Booth. It was apparent that Bishop Byrne was very weak. He had difficulty walking on his own, and he could speak only in whispers.

"Water, water," whispered the bishop. "I have not had any water since yesterday." The cooks had gone for the night, and the guards did not want to be bothered, so we assumed that water would not be brought until morning.

"What's going on here?" boomed the familiar voice of Commissioner Lord out of the darkness. Hearing the commotion, he asked permission to assist in his capacity as official interpreter of the group. Lord had a way—a persistent yet polite way—of dealing with Koreans; he finally persuaded one of the guards to go for water. Bishop Byrne had to be propped up against the wall and be supported as he drank bowl after bowl of water. By the next morning he was much improved, but it was several days before his voice returned completely. Deprived of the immunity granted them by international law, both Bishop Byrne and the British and French diplomats would have to submit to even worse indignities before the end of the year.

Walter Eltringham, the American coalmining engineer, had arrived in the schoolhouse bearing the marks of a very severe beating. When he was first arrested in Seoul, he had been taken to the police station, made to kneel, and beaten with the broad side of a steel bayonet. There were more than thirty long, bloody marks on his back when he arrived at the schoolhouse. However, his injuries were treated from time to time by a North Korean medic, and he recovered from that ordeal.

I was so happy to be out of the death cell that except for the starvation diet, the wait of six weeks in the schoolhouse was no problem for me. The interrogators were now overwhelmed with work. With so many prisoners to investigate, they were not able to devote as much time to each one. For the first time, there were more prisoners than interrogators—much better odds for the prisoner! The interrogators had to work such long hours that on more than one occasion I was taken for questioning only to discover that the officer sitting in the chair was asleep from sheer exhaustion. The guard would have to go over and shake him gently to wake him up.

The interrogations themselves were more and more turning into anti-American lectures with particular emphasis on the American bombing, leaving less time devoted to my individual "crimes." The bombing seemed to keep the interrogators off guard. During one session, the officer turned to me in midsentence and exclaimed, "We cannot fight the entire world. We are fighting the United Nations!"

It may sound ironic, but I think the American bombing of Pyongyang may have saved my life; it got me out of the death cell and into the schoolhouse. After the Communists evacuated the city, they changed their agenda with me. When I was first arrested, my number one problem was the North Korean military rifle that a Communist official had found in the house of my next door neighbor in Kaesong. I never did learn whether they knew the real source of that rifle or whether they were using it to intimidate me; it certainly caused me a great deal of grief and, I believe, very nearly got me executed. Fortunately, they never did find the empty cartridge shells that Kris had hidden in the coal bin of my basement. Not being aware that this most damaging piece of evidence would never be found, however, I spent many sleepless nights in unnecessary worry.

Even in the death cell, besides the hard-liners who seemed to want me executed, there were others who wanted to use me for propaganda purposes. And after we were moved to the schoolhouse, the Three Musketeers were still trying to get me to make anti-American radio broadcasts for them. I always refused.

Most of my interrogations at the schoolhouse were not very memorable, but one especially comes to mind. Early one evening a guard came running across the schoolyard from the little building used for interrogations. He burst into the American room and demanded to know where "Sellas-su" was (*Sellas-su* was how my name sounded when pronounced from the Korean alphabet). We went running back to the little building and found the interrogator, one of the Three Musketeers, standing by a radio receiver. He looked very tired; most interrogators were now operating around the clock.

"Listen, Rarry," he said, sounding a little weary. "Listen to what some of your American Army friends, who are our prisoners, are saying about America's aggression here in Korea."

Sure enough, there for all to hear was an American-sounding voice on the radio. The speaker identified himself, his rank, his serial number, and his U.S. Army military unit. He then went on to roundly condemn the American presence in Korea. It made me sick to hear such words. I felt both ashamed and sorry for the man whose voice I heard, but I did not condemn him—nor do I today. It is impossible to know what he went through before submitting and making that radio broadcast. There is a limit to what most people, including this writer, are able to endure.

After the radio broadcast, the interrogator looked at me wearily. "Rarry, would you speak on the radio?"

"No," I replied at once. He didn't push the matter; I think he knew what my answer would be. He mentioned that North Korea was now fighting the United Nations, and then drawing a deep breath, he spoke for about thirty minutes of his commitment to Communism.

The man who sat before me had undergone a transformation since he had been my interrogator in the death cell; he was no longer arrogant, and he was no longer playing the role of my teacher. He looked tired and dejected. The young man who had been so filled with words and ideas could now barely talk about anything. He was ideologically bankrupt, the first defeated North Korean Communist I had ever met. With world revolution as Communism's goal, as was the case in 1950, a Communist country that was about to be bested in battle no longer had a message to communicate. MacArthur later said that in the fall of 1950 North Korea was defeated.[2] My interrogator was witnessing the twilight of the gods, or so he thought; he couldn't have known that the entry of the Chinese into the conflict would change the whole equation.

My most pleasant memory of our stay in the schoolhouse is that of listening to the various discussions going on in the room. Bishop Byrne, that humble, quiet, friendly man, told of the world that he had known in both Japan and Korea before World War II. Kris, action-oriented person that he was, shared some stories of his life and work. Walter, the mining engineer, kept us spellbound with tales of his life in dangerous mines in the United States. Danny Dans shared his experiences as an entertainer. Father Booth told many humorous tales about his work in Korea. Bill Evans, a new arrival and an adventurer in areas that none of us had even dreamed about, shared his life in Korea as a businessman and goldminer. We never ran out of things to talk about, and the time passed quickly.

Many other prisoners arrived during the next few weeks. In fact, any non-Korean in a part of South Korea that fell to the Communists was arrested by the North Koreans, and those who escaped being shot—some did not—were brought to North Korea to join our group. We had British, French, German, Austrian, Russian, Turkish, Swiss, American, Australian, and Irish subjects in our group, which soon numbered just under fifty. There were even a few South Koreans and two or three whose nationalities we were not certain of. I was happy to see the arrival of each new group. My reasoning, not entirely valid in light of later developments, was still that North Korea would not kill or put on trial such a large group of foreigners.

News from the outside world brought by these new arrivals was disseminated to all the rooms by means of our "bathroom communications." From time to time, Monsignor Thomas Quinlan, an Irish Catholic bishop, would share some item of information by walking down the hallway past the American room, singing a little song as he did so. The news he wanted to share was in the song; Monsignor had made it up just for the purpose of fooling the guard. He was always smiling from ear to ear as he performed this little ritual, and I am certain that he enjoyed the whole thing as much as we did. The guards never caught on.

Two very good sources of information were British correspondent Philip Deane and Maurice Chanteloup of the French Press Agency, who informed us that the first American troops sent to fight in South Korea had done so poorly they had been called "tourists from Japan." Philip Deane was born into a military family; his father and uncle had become national heroes fighting the German occupation of their native Greece during World War II. After serving in the British Royal Navy during that war, Deane went on to become a correspondent for the *London Observer*. With the outbreak of the Korean War, he went to South

Korea as a war correspondent. When he was wounded in the fighting and captured by the North Koreans, he was treated like everyone else—he had to prove that he was not a spy.[3]

Deane arrived at the schoolhouse in late July and was taken to the British room. We in the American room first became aware of him when we heard someone walking down the hallway toward the bathroom singing "Over There," emphasizing the part that the Yanks were coming. Wearing a big smile and flashing the famous Churchill victory sign with his fingers, he then whispered that the Black Watch was on its way. By mentioning one of Britain's elite fighting units, he communicated to us that England was also sending troops to fight in Korea.

Deane had sustained several minor wounds in the battle during which he had been captured and was often brought to the American room for treatment. Dr. Kisch, who had been placed in the American room, looked over his wounds very carefully, talking and asking questions concerning the military situation in South Korea, while a North Korean guard looked on. Although the guard did not understand English, he could guess what was being discussed when he heard the names of cities in South Korea, and he ordered them to stop talking about the war. But Dr. Kisch was ready for that; he continued the same conversation with Deane, while pretending to examine him, by using letter abbreviations: "S" for Seoul, "PY" for Pyongyang, "TG" for Taegu. Dean immediately picked up on the deception and continued to tell us about the war while pointing to various shrapnel wounds on his body.

By being careful not to overdo it, Deane was able to visit the doctor many times and share much information with us. The guards never caught on to that deception either, and the practice of using code letters for names of cities was immediately adopted by the rest of us in our conversations with one another.

The American room was always the first to be visited by high-ranking North Korean visitors, an honor that we did not welcome. They would enter our room and vent all their anger on their captive audience. During the course of these one-sided conversations, we were never physically abused, but we were frightened from time to time. Some visitors, however, merely wanted to peek in and see what we looked like. One was heard to exclaim as though in amazement, "Why, they don't look so bad, except for their big noses!"

On September 5, 1950, we were told that the entire group would be moved to an unnamed place where we would be safe from the bombing by the "bloodthirsty Americans." We were then taken by trucks back through Pyongyang to the railway station. We could see areas of bomb damage as our trucks made their way through the city, and as we neared the rail terminal the devastation increased markedly. With the exception of a few people in uniform, the streets were deserted.

When we first saw our long train, we expressed hope that we would not be crowded on our trip, but we were in for a surprise. All the seats had been removed, and two tiers of wooden decking had been installed to increase the carrying capacity, leaving only a narrow corridor on one side. The two layers of decking and the floor provided three surfaces to lie on, like bunk beds. I decided on the middle level because it had access to the windows, but on crawling into the small space, I discovered that I could not sit up because of the deck above me. Nor was I able to stretch out my legs completely without blocking the hallway. The North Koreans would not permit that, so I had to manage the entire trip in a cramped position.

Still, my situation was far better than it had been in the death cell, I reassured myself. I paid special attention to the weapons carried by the guards and the officers but saw no sign of the rifle that had caused me so much grief, the one that I had been accused of using to kill North Korean soldiers in Kaesong. If we were taken far away from here, I thought, we would be among strangers who would know nothing of who we were or what "crimes" we were each supposed to have committed. It also occurred to me that since the North Koreans had evacuated Pyongyang, they probably had other things to do than keep accurate records on their prisoners. As the train departed that night for an unknown destination, I was even optimistic enough to believe that I might never see that cursed rifle or hear about it again. For once, I was correct!

6. NIGHT TRAIN TO MANPO

WAITING in the train at Pyongyang, we discussed where we might be taken. I heard Monsignor Quinlan, from somewhere out of sight, talking to someone. Catching bits and pieces of what he said, I was able to understand that over 500 American military prisoners of war were boarding the train. Soon this information was being whispered about in the various languages of the group. We could not understand what it all meant.

I tried to look out a window from my crowded position to see what was going on. Long lines of haggard-looking young American soldiers were marching past my window to board the coaches in front of ours.

I couldn't believe what I was seeing. These ragged, dirty, hollow-eyed men did not look like any American soldiers that I had ever seen! I had worn that same uniform until five years before, but I could hardly recognize it on the men walking along that railway platform in front of me.

The North Koreans had provided no special consideration for the wounded. Some of the more badly injured prisoners were half-carried by companions; others limped along as best they could. Communist guards walked along side and behind POWs but made no attempt to assist in any way. We were all so stunned that we watched in silence.

Even after the train had been loaded, it did not move for a long time. We later learned that the North Koreans were waiting for darkness to fall in order to escape possible attack by American aircraft. Once under way, I discovered that being by a window had its drawbacks; cold night air rushed through the broken glass. A young Catholic priest from Australia was located next to me on the decking. When Father Philip Crosbie saw that I was growing cold, he took off a light yellow zippered jacket and handed it to me.

"Here, put this on," he said.

"I can't take this," I protested.

"Wear it for awhile. We'll share it," he replied. I noted that he still had a watch.

"I'll wear it for thirty minutes and then give it back."

"All right, and then I will wear it for thirty minutes," he replied. The agreement stuck, and so did the friendship. All my life I had heard talk of someone who would give you the shirt off his back. I had found such a person.

Father Crosbie looked much younger than his thirty-five years when I first met him on that train. Before that, I had only seen him among others in the schoolhouse at Pyongyang as they walked by our room on their way to the bathroom. The life he had chosen was a hard one, and his manner of living did not make it any easier. He studied for the priesthood in St. Columban's Seminary in Melbourne and then for four years in St. Columban's in Ireland, graduating in 1940. World War II broke out not long after his arrival in Korea as a missionary, but he was repatriated to his native Australia, through the good offices of the International Red Cross, until the war was over.

Now after only ten years he found himself a prisoner again. The North Koreans had arrested Father Crosbie when they captured his mission station in the South Korean city of Hongchon on June 29, 1950. He was held in a crowded local jail for a time, then taken to Seoul and finally to Pyongyang, like all of the other foreigners who were not shot. But this time he would not be repatriated. Never shirking hard work of any kind, this dedicated man of God would set a high standard for all of us in compassion and self-sacrifice during the difficult three years ahead.

Many of the older missionaries had been well acquainted with train travel in pre–World War II Korea, when North and South were one country. Our primary concern, as we moved out of the station, was whether we would be taken south or north. There was considerable disappointment when our train failed to turn southward. We had hoped that we might be returning to South Korea for a prisoner exchange.

Our train moved only at night and never very fast during our six-day trip. There were frequent delays as we were shunted off to sidings, giving priority to other traffic. As a consequence, we covered very little distance during each night. With the coming of daylight, the train pulled to a stop in an open area, and we were immediately removed and marched into the nearby hills. We spent the first day lying under pine trees on the hillside overlooking our train half a mile away. The locomotive had been driven about 500 yards ahead, where it disappeared into a tunnel under a mountain. With our train parked on the main track, there would be no other train traffic that day.

Our conditions during those days spent in the mountains awaiting the arrival of darkness were not too bad. We could not go anywhere, but there was freedom to talk and to move about within the group. There were still large rice balls and good potato soup left over from the night before.

Shortly after we arrived at our hillside location for the day, we looked back at the train and saw the figures of American soldiers moving in our direction. It was not a pretty sight. They moved as though in slow motion, probably because of their bad treatment. We soon found out that they were members of Task Force Smith and other units of the 24th Infantry Division of the U.S. Army and had been stationed in Japan before the Korean War broke out. The senior ranking officer was Major John J. Dunn of Rome, New York, a member of the 34th Regiment. Task Force Smith, the very first group of American soldiers rushed to Korea to try to stem the tide of North Korean aggression, had been defeated by a vastly superior North Korean army trained and equipped by the Russians to win an offensive war.[1]

Later we learned that the POWs numbered 726 when they left Pyongyang in the fall of 1950. Another thirty prisoners joined them later in the year. When we last saw them on October 10, 1951—more than twelve months later—their numbers had dwindled to 292 (a number easy for me to remember because my address in Kaesong before the war was 292 Man Wul Dong).

The American soldiers were marched in our general direction for a few minutes and finally settled on a slope near us. We were not permitted to talk to them. But a short time later we noted four men carrying one of their group on a blanket. At first we thought that it was perhaps one of their wounded, but when two of the men began to dig in the ground, we knew otherwise. Sgt. Hank Leerkamp received permission to walk over to our group, accompanied by a guard, and request the services of a Catholic priest for a funeral service. "His name is Kelley, and I'm sure he is Catholic," the sergeant commented.

Monsignor Quinlan was selected to conduct the funeral, but a snag developed when another guard countermanded the order. Then a North Korean colonel wearing the red braid of the regular army was called into the discussion (we had been placed under Regular Army control for our trip on the train). The colonel agreed to permit the Monsignor to conduct the funeral.

Later that morning, the same colonel swaggered over to our group and engaged us in conversation for a time. His gait was like that of all the high-ranking North Korean officers we saw; such an affected walk was probably a part of their training. The custom did have a practical application, which may have been the real reason for it: by his manner of walking, a person of high rank could easily be identified, even from a distance. The colonel was, in fact, a very polished, well-educated, and thoroughly professional soldier. Though tough, he would at least listen to reason. Unfortunately, we were not to see his equal again.

Following quite a long discussion in Russian with Minister Vyvyan Holt and Vice-Consul George Blake of the British Legation in Seoul, the colonel called the entire civilian group together for a long lecture, making certain that we Americans were standing in the very front.

"America is the most barbaric country in the world," he began. He proceeded with a litany of crimes and abuses that the Americans were supposed to have committed. Then came the climactic ending: "The American soldier is the worst and most cowardly in the world. In fact, one soldier of our army is the equal of ten American soldiers." He paused for a moment; then, with a smirk, he threw back his shoulders and concluded, "I think I might be able to handle eight myself."

Late that afternoon I heard the sound of aircraft. Presently, three F-51s came into view, flying so close to the ground that we could see the pilots. Two continued to circle while one disappeared to the rear of our train. Soon we heard machine gun fire as the single aircraft came into view. The machine guns operated for only a second, and it was clear that not all of them were firing; possibly the pilot had already expended most of his ammunition on other targets. The F-51 carried six 50-caliber machine guns. When all were working, they made a much different sound; you could not distinguish each individual round being fired.

Dust kicked up around the train as some of the bullets struck the ground. Suddenly, we caught sight of the lone figure of an American soldier jumping off the train and running in our direction. He was followed by a guard and other American soldiers. Some of the wounded and their medics had been left on the train that morning. None were hit in the attack, however.

The aircraft made only one pass over the train, and then it left with the other two. Had all the machine guns on that aircraft been working, and had the other two aircraft joined in the attack, I shudder to think what might have happened to those left on the train. On returning to our coach that night, we noted bullet holes in the cars and wondered how they had escaped being injured or killed.

Our short train trip that night took us to the town of Sunchon. I first heard the name when Kris made a remark to Father Booth as we slowed down to stop: "Say, this is Sunchon. I remember this town had quite a few Christians before the war."

"Yes, I remember it well," Father Booth answered. "We had some strong churches here."

As our train drew up to the station at daybreak on September 7, 1950, we noted many women and children standing outside. We had no idea why they were there. But as we stepped down from the train, we could see some of them bowing in our direction, and many made the sign of the cross when the priests and nuns came into view.

7 Sep 1950
Sunchon

When I saw what was taking place, I whispered to Kris, "Isn't it dangerous for them to do this?"

"Yes, I suppose it is, but they seem willing to take the risk."

We civilian prisoners were then marched down a wide street in the direction of a schoolhouse. Looking back, I could see some of the American military prisoners huddled together in open boxcars. They had ridden through the night buffeted by the cold wind.

Walking along, we were joined by many of the women, who inquired about our health. An almost carnivallike atmosphere prevailed as children ran back and forth through our group. Everyone seemed to be having a good time. When we reached the schoolhouse, we were placed in three rooms and instructed to wait there for breakfast to be served. It was obviously the intent of the authorities that the two groups not talk to each. The Korean women had been ordered into adjoining rooms where food had been brought. The plan was simple: the women were to serve up the food into bowls, and the children were to bring it to us.

The segregation worked for a time, as long as there were officials around and sufficient guards on hand to enforce it. But soon some of the guards were called away to other duties guarding the American soldiers, and the remaining guards were not able to keep the local citizens and the prisoners separated. By that time the high-ranking people had departed, and the guards who were left probably didn't want to be bothered.

Soon the Korean women were coming to our rooms and engaging us in conversation. Many of the older missionaries actually knew some of these women from nine years before, when all of Korea was one country and travel was easy. Sunchon had been a center for the Christian work of many different groups before the Communist takeover in 1945. Listening to the conversation, I heard the names of priests, ministers, and other well-known people in various churches. In light of our circumstances, it was truly a strange spectacle.

After a time I left the group and walked out of the schoolhouse to see where the American soldiers were located. The guard on duty just outside the door seemed to have no objection to my standing there and looking around as long as I did not go any farther. Sensing what I was looking for, he pointed to a nearby cornfield where, on closer examination, I could see American soldiers seated or lying on the ground. Considering the warm daytime temperature, I concluded that at least they were not suffering undue hardship at the moment.

Soon Kris came out of the building and joined me. "Have the American soldiers had anything to eat?" Kris asked the guard. The guard indicated that they had. Not knowing whether he could be trusted, we went back into the schoolhouse and asked some of the Korean women. They did not know, but the children, who could come and go as they pleased, confirmed that what the guard had said was true.

Having enjoyed three large meals and the friendliness of the people, we were reluctant to leave the schoolhouse for the train when night came; this was the greatest outpouring of kindness from North Korean civilians that we were ever to receive. Knowing how the Communists felt about such things, we knew that the actions of our hosts might later cost them dearly. As we were marched back to our train, we said goodbye to the villagers, but they had one more courageous surprise for us. The train had left the station about half a mile behind when suddenly we began to hear the shrill voices of children: "*Me-gook man-sai. Me-gook man-sai.*" Not certain that I had really understood what they were shouting, I turned to Nell. "Does that mean what I think it does?"

"It means, 'America, ten thousand years,'" she said—roughly equivalent to shouting "Long live America" in our society. Quickly looking out the window, I saw long lines of children standing near the railroad track, waving their hands and continuing to shout as we moved past. There was not an adult anywhere in sight, but there were too many children and they were too young for this demonstration to have taken place without the complicity of the parents. The Communist authorities would be aware of that as well.

The plan for the train to move only by night almost backfired on at least one occasion near the end of our trip. Like their Japanese counterparts in World War II, the North Koreans did not notify the International Red Cross of their intention to move enemy prisoners, nor did they mark our train with a large red cross. Our situation in that train was like that of Manny Lawton in 1945 when he was one of 1,606 American prisoners loaded into three Japanese ships bound for Japan from the Philippines. The Japanese did not properly mark these prison ships to preclude attacks by American aircraft and submarines; as a result, fewer than 400 American prisoners arrived in Japan.[2]

It was not at all unusual for the train to make sudden stops to permit other trains to move though or for other reasons that we could not determine. I remember one such instance when the train came to a sudden halt in the middle of the night at a grade crossing. We had waited for a time in almost total darkness when suddenly I was able to see the outline of a long line of trucks waiting to cross the track that our train was blocking. Everything was bathed in an eerie red light, bright enough that we could see houses and discern individual vehicles waiting on the road.

Although I could not see the source of the light, it had to be an infrared flare dropped by an American aircraft in search of North Korean targets. It seemed logical to me that those targets would probably involve transportation because no trains or trucks moved in the daytime. Such a system involving the use of infrared flares in coordination with specially designed and equipped night-fighting aircraft had been developed in the closing days of World War II. I remembered seeing red flares being dropped over Pyongyang at night during the latter part of our stay in the schoolhouse.

The gravity of our situation stunned me. How ironic, I thought, to come this far and then be killed by our own side. We were on a train stopped at a grade crossing, holding up dozens of trucks, while somewhere overhead crews on American aircraft were looking for just such a tempting target. It was to be the first and only time while a prisoner of the North Koreans that I was ever really afraid of American aircraft. I said nothing to anyone; I didn't even move.

After what seemed like an eternity, the light of the flare began to dim and finally went out. If they dropped another one immediately, it would mean that they had seen the train. Minutes passed. We sat in darkness and silence. Presently, the train began to move slowly forward, and I breathed a prayer in thanksgiving. We were on our way to Manpo.

7. AUTUMN ON THE YALU

ON September 11, 1950, when I departed the train at Manpo, the first person I saw was Commissioner Lord. He was running up and down the platform trying to relay to the prisoners the many directives of the North Korean colonel. I looked off in another direction for a moment, and when I looked back, the commissioner was not there. Moving forward, I finally saw him lying on his back on the concrete platform with Helen Rosser holding his head in her hands.

"What's the matter, Commissioner?" I asked.

"I just felt a strange tick in my heart and felt suddenly weak," he answered.

"Larry, run and get Dr. Kisch," Helen called out to me.

Immediately, we were surrounded by other prisoners crowding around to see if they could help. I went running for Dr. Kisch. Having no stethoscope, the doctor put his ear to Lord's chest to listen. Everyone stopped talking. After a few minutes, Dr. Kisch said quietly, "There is no way we can know what happened, but I don't think you had a heart attack. But be careful, Commissioner, be careful!"

I looked up and saw the North Korean colonel standing just behind Dr. Kisch. He had not said a word until now: "Be careful, old man [a term of respect]. Don't let anything happen to you. I couldn't have done all this without you." Commissioner Lord started to get to his feet, but the colonel told him to wait a bit longer. After about thirty minutes, Lord got up and told the colonel that he was ready to move.

Our new living quarters were part of a compound that had been an old quarantine station during the Japanese occupation of Korea; it was composed of two long buildings approximately fifty feet apart. A high wooden fence connected one end of the two buildings, forming a "U" shape with a courtyard in the center. On the opposite end was a large administrative building, which was used to accommodate the guards, seven South Korean politicians, the six diplomats, and the two journalists.

Here we were required to do our own cooking for the first time.

Our daily ration included plenty of rice, vegetables, cooking oil, and dried fish. Occasionally, there would be meat and sugar. We were well fed here, and that good fortune came at just the right time. We had experienced near-starvation at the schoolhouse in Pyongyang, but here most of us regained some of our health and vitality for the very hard times that lay ahead.

We received more medical supplies and attention at Manpo than we were ever to receive again. A Korean doctor from Manpo came twice a week to visit us and look after our medical needs. He even managed to have some medicine delivered to us on one occasion. With these supplies, Dr. Kisch held a clinic each afternoon for the prisoners. His two trained assistants were Mother Eugénie, a French nun, and Helen Rosser, a public health nurse.

Water for cooking and washing had to be drawn from a well located about 100 yards away from our complex. A work roster was drawn up each day detailing all duties in the camp and who would do them.

Walter Eltringham, the American mining engineer, volunteered to take charge of the water detail. It was the general intent of the group that the duties would be shared, but Walter must have felt otherwise. He continued to carry all the water by himself every day until we stopped him.

One morning Father Crosbie and I were drawing water at the well when we were approached by a young Korean boy in a school uniform. For a while he stood and watched us as we drew up the well bucket and emptied it into our container. We were preparing to return to our compound when the young boy moved forward, bowed low, and announced that he was a Christian of the Presbyterian faith. He then handed me a piece of paper and quickly departed. Not wanting to advertise what had happened to anyone who might have been watching, I put the paper in my pocket and returned to our kitchen.

Once inside, I looked at the piece of paper and found that it contained Korean writing. There were others in the camp who could read Korean quite well, but I went immediately to Commissioner Lord, who read the contents. The paper proved to be a handwritten copy of the daily U.S. Army communiqué read over Radio Taegu, located in South Korea. It reported the landing of the U.S. Marines and Army at Inchon under the direction of General Douglas MacArthur. The piece of paper was dated September 15, 1950, at 0800 hours—not more than two hours old.

Apparently, someone had decided to risk delivering that very important message to us. We knew that the danger would be far greater for our benefactor than for us. Nevertheless, the next day as I went for water, the same boy was standing by the well with another piece of paper. That communiqué from MacArthur's headquarters concerned the favorable progress of the landing at Inchon.

I began to worry about the procedure of the schoolboy in openly handing me such messages and tried to think of a better way. The next morning the messenger was there again, and I motioned for him to come near and pretend to assist me as I pulled the bucket from the well. Once our two hands were down inside the well and out of sight of anyone standing nearby, I told him to give me the piece of paper. That proved to be a good method of accepting delivery of the notes. Subsequent messages detailed the fall of Seoul to the advancing American forces and the collapse of North Korean resistance to the south, once they had become aware that they were trapped by the Inchon landing.

These reports continued to be delivered each morning, and everything would probably have been all right except for one thing: too many of our people became party to the secret, and the authorities found out. One of our group, in a moment of incredibly bad judgment, had boasted to a guard that we had a better source of information concerning the progress of the war than he did and went on to reveal that we received a secret radio message each morning at the public well.

Fortunately, the guilty person was overheard by someone else in our own group. Informed that our secret had been compromised, we decided not to show up at the well the next morning at nine o'clock, the appointed hour for our rendezvous with the messenger boy. Once the guard had been tipped off, we knew that it was very dangerous to try to continue our operation. Our problem concerned the little boy: he would very probably be walking into a trap. By looking through a hole in the back wall, we were able to observe the well without being seen. Our plan was simple: delay the water detail until the boy with the message grew tired of waiting and went home. He showed up just before nine o'clock, as usual, and waited for about two hours before disappearing.

Deciding it was now safe, I went to the well to draw water. Three men of military age were standing next to some buildings about 100 yards distant. I had never seen young men in the village before. The well bucket was drawing near the top when I noticed someone approaching me; it was our little messenger boy! Apparently, he had not gone home at all but had been waiting out of sight. He gave a little bow and was smiling as always. Remembering the three strange men standing nearby, I was frozen in my tracks, and I don't know what I did or said for the next few moments. I do remember trying to act nonchalant and uninterested, turning my back to the boy, hoping he would get the idea and leave. But I had underestimated the tenacity of my messenger; he stood right behind me waiting to make his delivery.

I had filled up my water container and was preparing to leave when suddenly I heard the sound of an air raid siren and the clatter of antiaircraft fire, followed a few seconds later by the roar of jet aircraft high overhead. People were running for cover in all directions. Using the air raid as an excuse to get away from the messenger, I ran toward an old dilapidated building and threw myself on the earthen floor inside. It was no use; the boy was right behind me. Looking through the cracks in the walls of the old house, I could not see the strange men, but I knew they had not gone far. The faithful little boy handed me his message. I took the piece of paper and shouted to him in my stilted, choppy Korean, "Thank you for all you have done. You have worked very hard. Coming here is now dangerous. Please go home and do not return. Now!" The little boy jumped up and ran through the open door at high speed. I breathed a sigh of relief as he disappeared around the corner of a building, but I was sure he had been identified.

I decided that the confusion created by the antiaircraft guns would provide a good cover for me to make my break for the kitchen. Realizing that the strange men were secret police, I was aware that they would probably want to talk to me, and I did not want them to find the radio message on my person. I knew better than to try to hide the message somewhere in the old building; their finding it there would only incriminate me more than ever. With about 100 yards' head start, I thought I could reach our kitchen and burn the message in the fire if necessary before the police caught up with me.

Arriving at the kitchen, I looked back and was surprised to see that I was not being followed. Commissioner Lord took the message from me, swiftly inserted it into a crack in one of the beds, and left the room immediately, whispering to me, "Later, Larry, later. Don't be seen with me for a while." Lord knew his business well. During World War II, as a prisoner of the Japanese in Singapore, he had worked in secret radio communications. The penalty for such activity in a Japanese prison was execution. After the war, King George VI had awarded him the Order of the British Empire for his very courageous work.

Several times during that day, people asked Commissioner Lord about the contents of the radio message. He had no comment to make. Later, he verbally revealed the contents to me and a few others, but he did not tell everyone. His practice had been to make a written copy of the message in English and pass it around for all to see. We had learned the hard way not to talk openly in our group about sensitive information.

It was a sorry ending for our best and most reliable source of news, and a terrible blow to all of us. Our loss would be difficult to explain to anyone who has always lived in the free world with access to an almost infinite quantity of news and information. At a later stage in our prison experience, when we were on starvation rations again, we would discuss the relative value of a bowl of rice and an up-to-date American weekly news magazine.[1]

One day a smiling young North Korean Army officer, who had just arrived that morning, addressed the assembled prisoners. "You are most fortunate to be in the care of people who are concerned about your welfare. Even in the middle of a war against the imperialist Americans, we are able to look after your needs," he assured us. With Commissioner Lord serving as translator, he went on. "I am here because our government believes that you should be well cared for and happy. You will be here only until the inhumane bombing by the Americans stops. We are now going to have a 'be-happy' program." There should have been some sighs and groans from our group about that time, but we gave the personable young man a fair hearing. "I will now lead you in some happy singing. First of all, we will sing the famous song praising our glorious Korean People's Army." The officer paused and raised his hand as though to lead us in singing.

"Honored Teacher, I regret to tell you that we do not know that song," Commissioner Lord interjected.

"What! How can anyone not know that song?" He was right in a way. No Korean over four or five years of age could not have known the famous song praising the great Korean People's Army. One could hear it sung many times a day, both by the guards and by the school-children who marched by our compound. We prisoners must have been the only people in all of North Korea who did not know it.

The young officer's enthusiasm was not to be dampened.

"Well, what about the song praising the glorious success of our railroad system?" he asked. We all knew that the Japanese had built the railway system all over Korea before World War II.

"I regret to say that we do not know that song either," Lord announced, pretending to be sad. The officer looked dumbfounded for a moment but quickly recovered.

"I will permit you to sing any song you wish from your own

culture. I will permit this, even though some of your songs may be decadent."

It was quite a concession, but I think the young man really wanted us to sing and be happy. He urged us on and told us repeatedly that we were expected to have a good time. Discussing this incident later, we all concluded that we were being secretly photographed for propaganda purposes, probably from the administrative building. It would have been useful to the Communist cause to have such photographs to "prove" to the world that we were being well treated.

Our master of ceremonies never lost his temper, but some of our guards did. They became visibly angry and shouted for us to sing. We shouted back that we could not sing when we were far from home and unhappy. The guards only became more angry and swung their automatic weapons in our direction.

Finally Kris called out, "Honored Teachers, you and your comrades have taught us many things, for which we are very grateful. Now it is time for us to teach you about how we feel." So saying, he walked toward the front of the group, in the direction of the leader and two guards. Suddenly, as though on cue, the two guards grabbed Kris by both arms, turned him roughly around, and marched him back toward and through the group, knocking some of us out of the way. The rest of us were released and told to go back to our rooms. The "be-happy" interlude had been brought to a close.

At eleven-thirty that night, Kris returned to the darkened room and lay down on his straw mattress. I wondered if he had been hurt in any way but was afraid to ask. It wasn't long before I had my answer: Kris began chuckling to himself.

Our obligation to sing and be happy was never brought up again at that location. We would have to wait until our first Christmas to face that issue again—and at that time we would have a choice.

Although the days were still warm, the nights were turning cold at that latitude in early fall. Every morning we would get up early and move into the enclosed courtyard to await the sunrise. The floors closest to the kitchen were heated very well, thanks to the fact that we were cooking for seventy-four people at that time. The extra heat was appreciated by the French nuns who were sleeping in the first room. In a Korean house, the heat that cooks the food also warms the floors. The first room is too hot for most Americans, the second just right, and the third too cold.

We were allowed, during our sojourn at Manpo, to take advantage of our proximity to the Yalu River. Almost every day we were marched to the river under guard to while away the hours bathing, washing clothes, or simply lying in the sunshine.

During our return from the river, Commissioner Lord would often catch a glimpse of a bulletin board located outside our camp where official information about the war was posted for the benefit of the local people. While we were still meeting our messenger at the well, it was especially interesting to compare the news from these two very different sources. Our secret radio messages would always report events two or three days ahead of the bulletin board; we got the news of the Inchon landing on the day that it occurred. The North Korean version was that the "attempted landing" at Inchon by American forces had failed. A few days later, the information on the bulletin board conceded that North Korean troops were consolidating their forces and shortening their supply lines in "strategic withdrawals." We recalled hearing nonsense like this from both the Germans and Japanese in the closing days of World War II.

At our camp in Manpo we became acquainted with the diplomats from England and France, the British and French journalists, the South Korean politicians, the Turkish and Russian families, and many others who had been taken prisoner. They represented many cultures and temperaments but all were interesting.

I had several conversations with George Blake, who, I knew, was British vice-consul in Seoul before his capture by the North Koreans, but I did not know the nature of his job. I discovered after my release that he had been station chief in charge of intelligence operations for the British government in South Korea. Blake was always very interesting to talk with. He told us of escaping from his native Holland under the noses of the Nazis during World War II. Arriving in England, he had joined the British forces in the common struggle against Hitler. After the war, he had gone into the British diplomatic service and had risen quickly in rank. Blake was a likable person, possessing what might be called a boyish charm. He was a good conversationalist who was also a good listener, was widely read, and was not snobbish in any way.

After our release from North Korea, Blake secretly renounced his political loyalty to the West and defected to the Soviet Union. When he returned to England in 1953, he landed an extremely sensitive position with MI6 (British equivalent of the CIA), which enabled him to learn the names of Western agents operating in the Communist countries of Eastern Europe. It has been estimated that he "betrayed more than forty British agents to torture and many to their death."[2] His other major accomplishment for the Russians involved his work in heading up the secret communications tunnel in Berlin that allowed the British and Americans to tap in on high-level telephone conversations in East Germany. Blake had blown the entire project to the Russians at the very beginning, while pretending to work for the British.[3]

These disclosures came as a great shock to those of us who thought we knew him—but I wonder if anyone really knew him. The British Foreign Office and MI6 were also fooled: "British complacency [was] sorely shaken by the revelation that the diplomat George Blake, captured in July 1950 when he was serving as vice-consul in Seoul, had been successfully 'turned' during the three years that followed. He operated undetected for years as an important Soviet agent."[4]

Many people have asked me if I had any indication when I was with George Blake that he might one day defect to the Communist side. My answer is, absolutely not. Yes, I was fooled by Blake, but apparently I wasn't the only one. Journalist Philip Deane, who spent much more time with Blake than I did, didn't suspect him either. Deane even made the statement after his release from prison in North Korea that he did not think Blake was a Communist, a comment that almost landed him in hot water with some members of his own Greek government.[5]

Herbert Lord was also shocked to learn of Blake's arrest on espionage charges in England in 1961; it was only after Blake had been tried and found guilty that the commissioner "was prepared to accept the conclusion of the attorney general that Blake had become a convert to Communism in Korea in 1951, but he was emphatic that he would never have believed it when he was with Blake."[6]

The interrogator who may have converted Blake was a Russian whom we called "Blondie."[7] He questioned me several times in 1951 and was by far the most skilled of the interrogators I met in North Korea. We now know a lot more about "Blondie," thanks to some research work by E.H. Cookridge: "Although I have been unable to discover his real name, I found out that he was known as Gregory Kuzmitch, or 'Kuzma,' for short. He was an official of the Political Education Department (*Prosveshtcheny Otdfel*) of the M.G.B., the Ministry of State Security, which controlled all espionage activities abroad."[8]

There are a few things about Blake that I especially remember. He would come out of his room alone at the old quarantine station only when he wanted to talk with someone other than his roommates. In our conversations he would ask specific questions about life in America and seemed to enjoy learning about the history of the American Southwest. He occasionally showed some antagonism for the U.S.

government and its involvement in the Korean War but never toward our American group. He seemed to feel that we were being held prisoner only because America had sent troops to fight for what he considered the very corrupt regime of Syngman Rhee in South Korea.

One thing that bothered me about Blake was his unwillingness to share his knowledge about life and events in England. I was very interested in England and had been all my life, but he told me very little. He was always friendly, but when he wanted to leave, he would simply walk away, and at other times he didn't want to be bothered.

Blake knew how to put us in our place if he wanted to. The British and French diplomats often met in the patio and conducted their discussions in French, even though the French diplomats spoke excellent English. While this was going on, most of us stood around wondering what was being said. After one such conference, I asked Blake what had occurred. He could have told me to mind my own business, but instead he answered with a question that was also a put-down: "Larry, don't you know French?" I told him that I did not but that I could struggle along in Spanish. He did not consider my remark worthy of comment.

Apparently Blake successfully fooled people on both sides who thought they had known him. After he broke out of Wormwood Scrubs Prison in England in 1966 and defected to Russia, with the help of Sean Bourke, he turned on the man who had helped him escape: "Gone was the ever-ready smile, the patient and understanding disposition, the willingness to listen and sympathize. Blake was now sullen, intolerant, arrogant and pompous. . . . In Moscow, George Blake had suddenly, dramatically, reverted to type."[9]

Many people have observed that the best method of operation for a secret agent, and especially one who elects to become a double agent, is to live a double life. In that, too, Blake evidently succeeded. Even his wife later claimed that "she had never really been married to him because he had turned out to be someone quite unknown to her."[10]

We were relatively well looked after at Manpo. Thanks to the abundance of very nourishing food, the relatively freer regime of the army (as opposed to the prison system that we had known before), the adequate accommodations, the medical attention, the lack of interrogations, and the provisions for bathing, our stay was not too bad. Except for our final few months of imprisonment, our experience at Manpo was as free from hunger, fear, pain, and harassment as we were ever to know again during our captivity.

Then we received the disturbing news on October 7 that we were to be moved. We were very depressed to hear this because we had hoped to await the arrival of the American forces in our current location. We were told to pack everything and prepare to move. Walking in the direction of the international bridge that spans the Yalu River, we grew concerned that we might be taken into Manchuria. It is strange when one considers that on the night of our departure from Pyongyang, we were hoping that we would be taken either South for a prisoner exchange or, if that did not materialize, into Manchuria. But that was before the Americans had begun their advance into North Korea.

During our stay in Manpo, we had received information from time to time concerning the American military prisoners we had met on the train. We were always told that they were being treated well and that their rations were on a par with our own. We did not know whether to believe such reports. On several occasions we were told that the POWs had been given flour with which to bake bread, that a proper oven was being constructed, and that we would be sent some of the bread. It arrived on the day that we walked out of our compound on our way to an unknown destination. The cooks must have had to work under very primitive conditions, but they turned out a good piece of bread.

Originally, we were told that we would move to our next location by riverboat. After waiting by the banks of the Yalu River for two days, we became convinced that we would have to walk. We were encouraged to see that some boats had been provided for the sick and wounded American military prisoners. We watched them glide by, pulled along by the swiftly flowing river, and wondered when our time to move would come.

At the end of each of the two days that we waited by the riverside, we had to walk back to our old quarantine station for another night. Few of us had much personal gear, but we were required to take with us all our big cast-iron cooking pots and other kitchen accessories.

In spite of all the promises that had been given, we did not travel to Kosan by riverboat after all but eventually made the trip of about twenty miles on two trucks that were greatly overloaded with people and cooking gear. We were located in a school building in the village and told that we would be required to prepare our own cooking facilities. Such a prospect worried us until an old Russian gentleman named Ivan Nicolai Tihinoff, a fellow prisoner, volunteered to help us. We did not think much of his offer at first because he was sixty-eight years old. But then the other Russians told us that he knew what he was doing.

By way of explanation, the Russians in our group were not Communists—far from it. They were actually refugees or descendants of refugees from the Russian Revolution of 1917 and 1918. Not wanting to be a part of the Communist political system emerging in Russia at that time, they had moved to Siberia, where they were safe for a few years. But with the political influence of the Soviet government in Moscow moving steadily eastward across Siberia, many of these Russian people became refugees once more. Their flight took them into China where, again, their safety was only temporary. When the Chinese Communist forces began their final offensive against the Nationalist government in 1949, the only place left on the continent of Asia for these now stateless people to go was South Korea. Then the North Korean Communists attacked their last refuge in June 1950. These Russian refugees from the Communist revolutions were promptly rounded up and treated as enemies. After thirty years of running, they had reached the end of the line.

It was easy for us to understand when our first efforts to approach the older members of the Russian community were met with hostility and suspicion. Their world had not been kind to them. During the early part of our imprisonment, we were obliged to spend quite a bit of time reassuring them that we were not trying to take advantage of them. There were some confrontations at first, but in the end we were able to work together. One had to admire their determination, faith, and courage. These must have been the qualities in their character that had helped keep them alive in a hostile world throughout the thirty years of their roaming over the face of Asia.

The first test of our ability to work together as a group was provided by the building of our kitchen. With the able assistance of Tihinoff, the old Russian gentleman, we pitched in to the task of installing our cooking pots. We discovered that plenty of mud, rock and a little know-how was all that was needed for the job. Even the other Russians, who would not normally have allowed themselves to be ordered around by Tihinoff, were content to carry out his every wish. I thought the whole project would take us days to complete, but it was finished in one afternoon. The Russians could work so fast that it was no wonder they snorted through their noses when we Americans and Europeans volunteered to help. They were not very patient with our inexperience, but they did teach us. In time, I think we were able to work as well, though not as fast, as they did.

Up to that point, Herbert Lord had served as both our official interpreter and leader. But the Korean major in charge at Kosan, decided to replace Commissioner Lord with Hak Pong Moon, one of seven South Korean politicians who had been captured and sent by the North Koreans to join our group at the schoolhouse in Pyongyang. Although he was also a prisoner, Moon was not trusted by most of us; even the other South Koreans were openly suspicious of everything he did. As a politician, however, he knew how to make the most of his newly appointed position. He would sit behind a makeshift desk in the guard shack for most of the day, and in the late afternoon he would wander through the group spreading good cheer. "Don't worry, Mr. Rarry! Every ting going be all right!" he used to say in a voice that boomed out from a very large body.

Shortly after our arrival at Kosan, there was a memorable confrontation between a guard and Commissioner Lord. We were standing inside the schoolhouse one morning when a guard came in and ordered us to fall out to do some work. Because of the attitude of the guards, we felt that our rescue was near and did not want to comply. Lord, in his very military manner, walked up to the guard and announced that we were not going to carry out his order. At that, the guard leveled his submachine gun at Lord's chest and repeated the order. The commissioner instantly threw back his shoulders and stuck out his chest, as though to provide a better target. What immediately followed was totally unprecedented in our prison experience. I think that it was Danny who made the first move; nothing was planned, but within two or three seconds there was a general movement among the prisoners in the guard's direction. I felt myself being drawn along with the others; I did not even think about what I was doing.

The guard did not know how to respond. Apparently, his orders and training did not cover this sort of prisoner behavior, and he went running out of the room. Soon he returned with the major and several other guards.

The Major called it a riot. That sounded like strong language to us, and we wondered what he would do to punish us. In fact, we were not punished at all for our rather serious breach of discipline. "You have caused a riot," he said. "Why do you disobey the authority of those who are appointed to protect you?" This issue of "protection" was one that we had heard many times. The official North Korean position was that we were being "protected" from the American bombing and from the civilian population—although with one possible exception, which was a staged propaganda show, we would have been perfectly safe in the hands of the North Korean civilians in every instance that I witnessed. The reaction of the civilians to us depended upon the presence or absence of the Communist officials: in the presence of officials the people appeared hostile, but on a one-to-one basis and out of sight of authority, they were friendly. At any rate, the major took no action other than to rebuke us for our lack of appreciation for all that they had done for us. Then he turned to leave the room and ordered the guard to follow him and take up his position outside.

Early one morning we were ordered to assemble outside in the schoolyard. When we were all in place, the major made his appearance and gave a very strange speech; later, we were to call it "The Major's Swan Song." He said, "You will be going home soon, and when you do, please tell your people what we have tried to do in this country to improve the living standard of the people. We have tried to look after you, but our job has been complicated by the bad American bombers." Then he mentioned specific areas where the Communist regime was supposed to have made great improvements in the country. The major really got our attention with his last remark: "When you do get home, we hope you will have happy memories of North Korea, and what we have tried to do here."

The lecture was quite brief by Communist standards, only about twenty minutes. When he had finished, the major turned and went back into the room that served as his office. We were electrified and questioned Commissioner Lord about the contents of the speech. "I'm as lost as you are," he said. "In fact, I think my English translation made more sense than the major's speech." The questions kept coming about possible hidden meanings in the speech, but Lord kept reiterating that he had translated everything; whatever else he might say would be mere speculation. Finally, he walked away to avoid further questions.

Then we were suddenly ordered to move again! Having just barely made our present accommodations livable, we were in no mood to start over again in some other place. We could not understand why we had to leave—and on foot. Within a week we would know why.

Soon after beginning our march we left the main road that parallels the Yalu River and turned south through the deep forests that cover most of that part of Korea. We followed roads and trails too narrow for automobiles. After a couple of hours, we were told to move off the trail to allow the American military prisoners to pass.

Whenever we saw the POWs, we always had mixed feelings. We were grateful that so many were still alive, but some were too weak to keep up with the group and dropped out to rest. Then there were always the wounded, who never seemed to get well, though at that time (late October 1950) their wounds were at least three months old.

On October 21, our one-day move took us to the old mining town

21 Oct 1950

of Jui-am-nee. Arriving at our new camp near nightfall, we were surprised to learn that we had traveled only twelve miles from Kosan. We had been delayed not only by the mountainous terrain but also by the many rest stops along the way, in deference to the sick and the aged.

Given the deteriorating condition of some of the wounded POWs and the general debility of our elderly, with every day of captivity meaning that more lives might be lost, there was an attempt at this time to make contact with the nearest United Nations forces.

The origin of the idea is not clear, nor how far the planning had progressed, but a disturbing piece of news forced a decision. We were told that we were moving back to Kosan, which would take us farther from the front lines and possible rescue. We were all greatly disappointed, so it is understandable that once this news had been received, those planning to contact the United Nations forces were given an even greater urgency.

In the absence of their officers, who in this very uncertain situation had left us, the North Korean guards didn't know how to organize our march back to Kosan. We set out late one day but had to return to Jui-am-nee because of rain and the approach of night. When we set out again the next day, this time better organized, we were not surprised to discover that some of our group could not be located. All the diplomats, the two journalists, the Korean politicians, Danny, and Mr. Moon were missing. We assumed that they had left in an attempt to reach the United Nations forces. They had taken with them two guards who believed their Communist cause was lost.

Our guards were now becoming friendlier. They asked us what kind of treatment they would receive if the Americans came and liberated us. None of us had counted on the appearance of the Chinese into the equation. Although we were very near the Yalu River in Jui-am-nee, we were not aware at that time that the Chinese had entered the war on the side of North Korea. Our little mining camp must have been off the beaten path because we saw no Chinese soldiers until we returned to Kosan.

The group moving south to contact the United Nations forces encountered increasing numbers of Chinese soldiers, however, and the escorting North Korean guards became more and more nervous. Even more dangerous than the Chinese were the remnants of the badly beaten North Korean army, who were retreating in small groups across these very same mountain trails and at times were openly hostile to the group of prisoners. Finally, the guard in charge of the would-be rescue party decided that it was too hazardous to continue south and turned the group around. The attempt to make contact with the United Nations forces had failed.[11]

Preparing to leave Jui-am-nee the next morning after our abortive attempt in the rain the night before, I spotted Walter Eltringham coming out of a hut carrying something wrapped in brown paper. "Walt, what have you got there?" I inquired. Walt didn't say a word as he unwrapped the object. It was a small mirror which he flashed to the sky. We all understood that the mirror was to be used to try to signal American aircraft. I don't think Walter ever got a chance to use it for that purpose.

The trip back in the direction of Kosan was agonizingly slow, and we were obliged to spend the night in a small village a mile or so short of our destination. When we entered Kosan the next afternoon, we beheld a totally deserted town that only a week before had been home to several hundred people! Every outside door in every house had been removed, presumably taken by the occupants. "That is an old Korean practice," Commissioner Lord remarked. "It discourages squatters." The traditional Korean sliding doors cannot be locked, and can be removed with ease in about three seconds. It was then that some of us remembered seeing a small group of Korean families the day before with five or six crude wooden sleds pulled by oxen. These sleds were stacked with blankets, bundles, and cooking pots, and on the very top of each load was a door.

We walked up and down the empty streets for more than an hour as though in shock, never seeing a single Korean. Having grown thirsty, we were equally surprised to learn that none of the wells in the village had a bucket, though in some we could see the bucket or attached rope lying at the bottom. "Another attempt to discourage squatters," Commissioner Lord remarked.

Late that afternoon, we saw our first Chinese soldiers as they moved quickly through the village, following the road to the southwest. Noting that they were armed with rifles and automatic weapons, we thought it prudent to keep out of their way. Then we realized why the village was deserted: the North Koreans were afraid of the Chinese. At first we thought that the villagers might have taken to the hills for fear of American bombing. However, that would not explain their removing doors and throwing buckets into their wells. Lord was right; they had made such efforts to discourage squatters. Korea had for centuries been a pawn between its larger neighbors, China and Japan; once again, it was being invaded by a traditional enemy.

We now had to face the probability that China was entering the war on the side of North Korea. Just before dark, horse-drawn light artillery pieces began to make their appearance, followed by oxcarts of all sizes and shapes. Behind these came Chinese coolies with their characteristic trotting gait, which is carefully synchronized with the flexing of the shoulder stick loaded front and back. Some of these men can carry as much as 200 pounds for a full day. We saw no heavy artillery, no tanks, and very few trucks. "None of this will bother the U.S. Army very much," someone remarked, summing up what we all wanted to believe.

Walking down the street, we came across a young American soldier. His name was Alphonse Baranski, and he was a medic who had volunteered to remain behind to look after a dozen or so wounded. Baranski told us that the main body of the POW group had left for Manpo that day and that the North Koreans had promised to send oxcarts to transport the wounded in his care. If Baranski had any fear about the future, he never showed it.

"I'm getting ready to feed my men," he said in a matter-of-fact manner. Some of us inquired if there was anything we could do to help.

"No, I found some millet, and there is plenty of wood around. At first we couldn't find a well bucket, but now we have everything we need." Hearing that Baranski had found a bucket, all of us went to the well to quench our thirst. As we talked, the flow of Chinese soldiers continued on the road, not more than 100 feet away.

We had entered Kosan that afternoon with two guards. After an hour or so, they were not leading us any more but merely following. They disappeared shortly after we met Baranski, and Kris later discovered them hiding in a nearby storage building where he had gone looking for firewood. They told Kris that they were afraid of the Chinese. Even after all that we had been through, we considered our situation in Kosan that night absolutely bizarre by any standard.

Gradually it became clear to us why we had lived in a kind of limbo for the past week—not quite prisoners but certainly not free. The North Koreans holding us were in a quandary: should they cast their lot with us or not? We surmised that all the officers and many of the guards had adopted a wait-and-see approach in the matter, waiting to see whether the United Nations forces would make their appearance. The North Koreans in charge of us would have been in deep trouble if they had prematurely come to us asking for protection from the U.S. Army. In Communist thinking that would have been traitorous; they would have been vulnerable to any radical elements of the Communist government who appeared on the scene and would have been dealt with accordingly. A radio broadcast by Kim Il Sung to North Korean citizens and the army on October 14, 1950 had specified: "Traitors and agitators were to be shot on the spot, regardless of rank, and a new 'Supervising Army' of politically reliable veterans was to be formed." [12] The situation was fraught with uncertainty and danger for all of us, North Koreans and prisoners alike.

The guards decided that most of us should not remain at Kosan but should return to the farmhouse in the village where we had spent the previous night. It was agreed that Kris would remain in Kosan to look after the ill and the elderly civilian prisoners. When I reached the farmhouse, I was too tired to know which craving cried out the stronger within me, sleep or food. I lay back on a bundle of straw to contemplate what to do and was overcome by sleep.

The next morning, we walked back into Kosan to discover that Kris and the other civilians and the wounded POWs in the care of Baranski had already gone. There was more delay, and several of us went through the deserted village looking for any kind of clothing. I found a small piece of cloth and wrapped it around my head for warmth. This was my only hat for several months.

We did not get under way until midmorning, with Mr. Moon setting the pace. "Go slowly, please," Mr. Moon told us repeatedly. This was an order that we were happy to follow. We did not want to create any additional distance between us and possible rescue by United Nations forces. Apparently the pace was so absurdly slow that it angered the South Korean politicians, who were walking just in front of us. They occasionally communicated their displeasure to Mr. Moon.

The one or two guards with us never intervened in any way. When the diplomats, who were marching in front of the South Korean politicians, were ordered by Mr. Moon to increase their speed, we civilians in the rear decided that we would set our own pace regardless of what Mr. Moon said. Our guard, who wanted to be our friend in case the U.S. army liberated us, willingly slowed down or speeded up according to our pace.

We met many Chinese soldiers that day on our march in the direction of Manpo. Seeing them pouring into North Korea, we tried to remain optimistic about our chances of early rescue, but we had to face facts. Everything we saw was disconcerting. As we met one group of Chinese soldiers, a man lifted up his submachine gun with one hand and patted it with the other, making some threatening comment to us in Chinese as he marched past.

"What did he say, Monsignor?" I asked.

"He said, 'I could kill you with this,'" Monsignor Quinlan replied. All the Chinese soldiers stared at us, but very few showed such signs of hostility.

At one afternoon rest stop we had grown so hungry that we made a dash for a nearby turnip field.

"Look out, Dogpatch. Here come the turnip termites!" shouted George Blake as he ran through the field pulling up bunches of turnips with both hands. Blake's outburst came right out of the American comic strip *Li'l Abner*. I was surprised that someone of his background would have known about those "funny paper" characters from Dogpatch, USA. We gulped down the unwashed turnips, sand and all, ignoring for the moment that they had been fertilized with human wastes.

Most of the day passed in the indecisive battle between slow and fast pace. We spent the night in a Presbyterian church that was located near the main road. The next day we resumed our march at a normal pace, arriving at our destination just after noon. We were shocked at what we saw. It had been our expectation to find those who had gone ahead by oxcart living in our old quarantine station just west of Manpo. Instead, our group was directed off the road toward an old hut with the roof missing. The sick and the elderly civilians who had gone ahead had spent the night there; we knew at once that we could expect no better.

When Kris came walking out to greet us, I asked him where the American military prisoners were staying, and he pointed upriver to the east toward a large cluster of people about half a mile away. It was clear to me that they were living totally out in the open without even a burned-out building to protect them.

Later that day I spotted Mr. Moon seated on a log with his back against a building. I had never before seen him so dejected.

"What's the matter, Mr. Moon?" I asked the big man.

"Rarry, we-e-e m-u-s-t all-l-l die-e-e," he boomed out as though on a Shakespearan stage. Mr. Moon was a man with great swings in temperament, so I didn't pursue the conversation. I thought that he was merely going through another one of his difficult moods. But this time, Mr. Moon was right; he had just met The Tiger.

We built a fire and maintained it all night, but even so, we were very cold. The fire offered little protection against the wind that blew across the Yalu River about 100 feet to the north. The women, children, and elderly slept inside the old burned-out building, which offered a little protection. I learned something that night that was to come in handy later on: with the temperature so cold, one is better off to stay awake and continue moving around from time to time. Dr. Kisch had already warned us that the greatest danger in our present circumstances was pneumonia. The next day I found that I could catch a little sleep by leaning against the south wall of our old hut when the sun was shining.

We were informed that we were to be turned over to the prison system that had tried so hard to take us away from the army when we were in the old quarantine station. Remembering life at Pyongyang, we knew that our treatment would now become much more harsh.

George Blake escaped during that night of October 30. We were not surprised to learn that someone from our group had tried to escape, but we all felt that such an attempt was doomed to failure. When we saw him being returned the next morning, we were not surprised either. He hadn't gotten very far; in fact, he had made it over only one hill when he walked right into the headquarters of the prison system and was picked up by a guard. By coincidence, Blake had stumbled into a meeting of Korean officers, including the man we were later to know as The Tiger. But Blake told us, "I met the major who will take control of us today, and he seemed all right." We were encouraged by what he said.

That day we took our leave of the major who had given us the swan song at Kosan a week or so before. We had not seen much of him after that, and his control over us seemed somewhat tenuous. We always found him to be a man of reason and intelligence, however, and we were sorry to see him go—and to hear him confirm that we would be turned over to the prison system very soon.

The day went very slowly, especially since we were in such uncertainty about our future. Guards stood around in the background but did not seem to take any interest in what was happening within our group. Finally, we saw some movement among the American military prisoners: the POWs were on their feet, standing at attention, apparently listening to a group of Korean officers. After a few minutes we saw them sit down, and the Korean officers headed in our direction. A tall thin major with a quick step led the way, and it was obvious even from a distance that he was the ranking man. He offered no greeting but got right down to business by having all of us line up. With Commissioner Lord once more serving as translator, he made a speech.

"We are going on a long march. I am in command, and I have the authority to make you obey. From now on, you will be under military orders." There was a pause. "You see," he said, pointing to his military epaulette, "I have the authority. Everyone must march. No one must be left behind. You must discard at once anything that can be used as a weapon. After all, you are my enemy, and I must consider that you might try to do me harm." Having said this in a strong, clear voice, he proceeded down the line of assembled prisoners, pausing to inspect each one. Father Paul Villemot, an eighty-two-year-old French priest, stood at the very head of the line, leaning heavily on a wooden cane. The major marched up to him and tapped the cane with his swagger stick. "Throw that away. That is a weapon."

The major moved swiftly on down the line of prisoners, looking at what each one was carrying. When he came to me, he tapped the rolled-up straw sleeping mat slung across my shoulder. "That can be used as a weapon. Throw it away."

With one task out of the way, the major returned to the front of the group and once more addressed us. Apparently trying to justify what he had just said and done, he continued as before. "You are my enemy, and I must protect myself from you." By this time, several members of the group were trying either directly or through Commissioner Lord to reason with the major. The consensus was that many of the prisoners would not be able to make a long march. I remember Father Villemot speaking up in French with Monsignor Quinlan translating: "If I have to march, I will die." Similar sentiments were voiced by others.

"Then let them march till they die. That is a military order," the major concluded. So saying, he gave the order to move out.

By this point the major had earned his new name: by common consent, he was referred to as The Tiger. Soon the long march ahead of us would also have a name—the Death March. The man to lead it was in a hurry, and we could never move fast enough to satisfy him.

To the east, we could see the American POWs also lining up and preparing to march. Our group was brought to a halt while things were being sorted out between the POWs and one of the North Korean officers. Putting the few minutes to good use, The Tiger made his first propaganda speech.

"Suppose you were the engineer on a train and the locomotive broke down. What would you do? Would you kneel down and pray that it would run? Or would you get an expert who knew about such things to repair it? In this country we know what we would do. We don't need you religious people anymore. You are parasites. There are things in this world that need repairing; we know what to do about that too." Indeed, they did.[13]

We were in the process of crossing another threshold. For some four months we had been introduced to a world that rejected everything we held dear. It was a world in which education, the wisdom of the ages, cultural heritage, Jesus Christ, Mohammed, Buddha, Socrates, and Aristotle were set aside as irrelevant. But there was an even more bizarre world in the offing. With The Tiger as our guide, we were now moving into an existence in which the most ordinary, decent human emotions would evaporate in the face of the gun; raw power would replace conscience, and the man with the gun would become all things to all men.

8. THE DEATH MARCH BEGINS

OUR journey took us by the old quarantine station about three miles west of Manpo where we had been quartered before. It had been extensively refurbished, and we noted something by the gate that we had rarely seen in North Korea: a large, expensive car. Suddenly, two men with European faces ducked out of sight when they saw us, but they were not fast enough; French Consul-General George Perruche recognized one of them as a former staff member from the Russian embassy in Peking (Beijing), where Perruche had formerly been stationed.

Up ahead, the guards were making sport of the weaker POWs. They took turns kicking the stragglers in the rear, laughing and jumping up and down as they did so. They were not yet using their rifle butts to beat the prisoners over the head; that would come later when this first game was no longer considered fun. But at the moment, any hapless POW who lagged behind the main group was considered fair game by the guards.

General William F. Dean wrote in his book *General Dean's Story* that as a prisoner he caught a brief glimpse of a group of prisoners marching through Manpo on October 31, 1950; he saw them for only a second in the center of the city but was certain that they were American.[1] Cpl. Shorty Estabrook, 19th Infantry Regiment, confirmed this event with General Dean after the war. It is ironic that the only American prisoners Dean ever saw during his three years in prison were from his old 24th Infantry Division, the unit that he had commanded before his own capture in South Korea (Dean was awarded the Congressional Medal of Honor for heroism).[2]

With night falling, it was a terrible time to begin a march. Nell Dyer remarked to me, "This is the time that you should end your travels, not begin them." The somber occasion was made worse by the growing cold that came with the approach of darkness. We knew that we were in for hard times, and we were right. As Philip Deane wrote concerning this part of our experience, "These, perhaps, were our worst moments."[3]

I agree with Deane's assessment of our situation at that time, with two reservations. First, perhaps it was more painful to see men shot who could not keep up on the Death March than it was to see a greater number die of cold, starvation, physical abuse, and disease during the coming winter, our first as prisoners. But on the Death March we had a glue that held us together, the cruelty of one common enemy—the guards—and, perhaps as a consequence, we helped one another. Second, during that first winter there was far more cruelty from cold, starvation, and disease, and, yes, in some instances, even from ourselves.

Nevertheless, we were already so hungry and chilled to the bone that even the walking didn't help much to warm us up. There was no escape from the cold wind that blew lightly from the north; the temperature must have been just above freezing at the time. Most of us were wearing the same clothes that we had worn into captivity—all summer-weight outfits. We discussed as we walked along that the North Koreans would have a difficult time finding a place for us to sleep out of the cold. Our group was such a ragtag collection of military prisoners, diplomats, journalists, very old missionaries, women, young children, that only a madman would even dream of conducting a march under such conditions. About this time the word had been passed back to us: the man in charge would be known as the Tiger.

We marched through Manpo and headed east as darkness fell. By that time there was no doubt in our minds about what was happening to us. The war would indeed continue, now that the Chinese had entered the conflict, and we were unlucky enough to be caught in the middle. The few North Koreans who were truly hard-core soldiers were still fighting, but without the Chinese they would not have lasted very long.

There was some light snow and sleet, but none built up on the ground. By that time there were some who required the help of others to keep going. Nell Dyer and I took turns assisting Sister Mary Clare, an Anglican nun. For others, the lack of footwear was proving to be a problem; their shoes had been either worn out or stolen. In Korea, you leave your shoes outside when you enter a house. Many of the people in our group who had small feet had awakened at some earlier time in their imprisonment to find their shoes missing. My feet were larger than most, and as a result I never lost my shoes.

We covered about six miles before being ordered off the road by The Tiger to spend the night in an open field. It was to be a miserable night, made even worse by the realization that things would probably not get much better for us in the near future. For warmth, people huddled together on the cold, wet ground, praying for the morning to come. Again, I did not try to sleep that night, though moving around to try to stay warm was not permitted. In a way, we were fortunate to have marched until midnight, because it made our time in the cold open field seem less than an eternity.

The next morning we did not have to wake up—we just stood up. I doubt if anyone had slept, certainly not very much. It was time for breakfast, but I wasn't hungry; you can be so cold for so long that you don't think about food. After a meal of boiled corn, we were off again with The Tiger setting a fast pace. Immediately, the group began to spread out; the weaker ones couldn't keep up. The word was passed back and delivered by Philip Deane that we were not to show "initiative." That word had a familiar ring; I had heard it before in the death cell. With time I had learned what it meant in the earlier context, but what The Tiger had in mind on the Death March, I could only guess.

At the Tiger's order, everyone was assigned to a group with one person in charge; that responsible person was to ensure that no one be allowed to drop out. The Tiger was putting the group leaders on notice that he would hold them personally responsible.

We had traveled for only a short distance when several American military prisoners fell out of march and were left by the side of the road. The Tiger was so angry that he called the march to a halt. He ordered the ranking officer, Maj. John J. Dunn, and all officers who were group leaders and had permitted men to drop out to report to him. When five officers stepped forward, The Tiger lined them up by the side of the road.

"I will shoot these five men for disobeying my orders," he announced.

"Commissioner, try to save us," the men pleaded. When Commissioner Lord tried to reason with The Tiger, he was ordered not to speak: "Shut up, or I will shoot you too. You are only the translator."

We were later told that when the officers saw some of their men dropping out of the march, they had asked the guards what to do, but even the guards were not really clear concerning The Tiger's policy about the sick and wounded. The guards replied that such men should be left by the side of the road where, presumably, they would be picked up later by oxcart; that had been the procedure followed until the time of The Tiger.

Commissioner Lord tried to explain to The Tiger that the guards had given permission to leave the men by the road. "Where are those guards? Show them to me!" ordered The Tiger. It was obviously an impossible demand under the circumstances.

"Honorable Leader," Commissioner Lord continued, "it is unjust to punish these men for doing what they thought was permitted."

"Then I will shoot the man whose group lost the most men. Who is that leader?"

Lt. Cordus H. Thornton of Longview, Texas, stepped forward. He stood tall and erect, as he did throughout his entire ordeal. "Save me if you can, sir," he whispered to Commissioner Lord. At that point The Tiger was in no mood to listen to anyone; he ordered Lord not to speak under the threat of being shot.

"Death is the penalty for disobedience in wartime," he informed Lieutenant Thornton. "Isn't that true in the American army as well?"

"In the American army, sir, I would have a trial."

The Tiger turned around and for the first time surveyed the curious onlookers who had gathered on the public road. In that group were a number of North Korean soldiers who were moving in our same direction, away from the front lines. They were a seedy-looking lot. Having been beaten in the war at this point, they were probably in retreat to some staging area where they would be regrouped. Their uniforms were tattered. Most had no hats. Only one or two carried weapons, and all appeared haggard and exhausted.

These men would be Lieutenant Thornton's jury. "What is to be done to a man who disobeys the lawful order of an officer in the Korean People's Army?" asked The Tiger.

"Shoot him!" they all shouted.

"There, you have had your trial," The Tiger announced.

"In Texas, sir, we would call that a lynching," Lieutenant Thornton responded.

"What did he say?" The Tiger demanded. Commissioner Lord had not translated the last remark. On hearing the translation, The Tiger made no comment but proceeded swiftly about his business of preparing for an execution. He asked Thornton if he wished to be blindfolded. Hearing an affirmative answer, The Tiger handed a small towel to a guard. Another towel was used to tie the victim's hands behind his back. The Tiger's moves were fast and efficient. He threw off the large padded coat he was wearing, revealing his rank.

I was seated by the right side of the road, looking to my left to observe the actions of The Tiger. Directly behind me Nell Dyer was wiping tears from her eyes, and Sagida Salahudtin, a young Turkish girl, was crying softly. Father Crosbie, seated on my left, had met The Tiger before—in a jail in Chunchon, South Korea, a few days after the

Communist invasion. At that meeting, The Tiger told Father Crosbie that they shot only bad people and then asked if he had ever seen a man shot. When Father Crosbie replied in the negative, The Tiger indicated that he had seen a man shot, dropping his hand and touching the pistol at his side as he spoke.

Now, Father Crosbie lowered his head into his hands and whispered, "Larry, I can't watch this." Following his first meeting with The Tiger, he had considered how he would respond if he became aware that a man's life was going to be taken: "A few months later I was to have the opportunity of seeing a man shot—and shot by the same hand and that same pistol. When the time came I would forgo my opportunity, forced by horror and revulsion to avert my eyes."[4]

"You see," The Tiger said, pointing to the epaulettes on his shoulder, "I have the authority to do this." He moved smartly to face the victim and ordered him to turn around. Pausing for a moment, The Tiger pushed up the back of Thornton's fur hat. But like Father Crosbie, I had seen too much already; my eyes snapped shut just before The Tiger fired his pistol into the back of Thornton's head.

When I opened my eyes, I saw that the brave young man lay still without even a tremor. The Tiger knew his business well. Quickly putting away his pistol, The Tiger called for Commissioner Lord to come to his side and translate for him. "You have just witnessed the execution of a bad man. This move will help us to work together better in peace and harmony."

In that one brief speech, The Tiger managed to outrage both the living and the dead.

The Tiger waited for a few minutes for the impact of his words to sink in before ordering, "Bury him!" It was an order given to no one in particular, and for a few horrifying moments it seemed that no one moved or spoke a word. Out of nowhere a tall blond sergeant appeared, moved down the steep slope to a level place about fifteen feet below the road, and began to dig away the stones with his bare hands. When someone threw a shovel down, Sgt. Henry Leerkamp began to dig a grave with it. The Tiger stood on the knoll by the side of the road, watching but not saying a word. The digging was very difficult in the hard and stony ground, and finally the sergeant looked up and asked, "Won't some of you come down and help me?"

The calm appeal for aid by this one brave man in the midst of horror spurred the others into action. Immediately, several people moved forward to assist. They finished the shallow grave, laid the body of the victim in it, and piled large stones on top.

Following the execution The Tiger ordered that all dog tags be turned over to his guards as they moved through the group. He must have been well aware that identification of bodies would be made more difficult without dog tags. The removal of the dog tags didn't shock me; I don't know why. Perhaps at that point I was prepared to believe that The Tiger was capable of anything.

After my return from captivity, some people asked me why a man like Thornton would cooperate so willingly with his executioner, since it would appear that the condemned one would have nothing to lose by refusing to do what he was told. The answer is simple. The executioner has at his disposal the only reward that really matters in such a situation: he can make your execution swift and painless . . . or he can make it otherwise. In the face of such a choice, I think the average person would cooperate to the limit with the executioner. It was fitting, in light of all that followed—when cold, hunger, pain, fear, and often death became our most common experience, that Thornton would become our greatest hero. Others would die, often after enduring much suffering, but he had shown us how to die bravely and with honor.

The Tiger gave the order to move out. This time the guards were not playing their innocent little game of kicking the stragglers in the rear as they had done the day before; they were using their rifle butts as clubs to drive the GIs along like cattle. We were all now convinced that the man in charge would go to any length to move us forward at a pace that agreed with his timetable.

But no pace was fast enough for The Tiger. He moved up and down the group of marching humanity, covering much more distance than we did, shouting at the top of his voice. Guards ran up and down the road, urging us to move faster: *"Bali, bali, bali!"* Even Commissioner Lord was ordered to move up and down the line to speed us along. Marching up close to us, the commissioner would first speak in a low voice—"This doesn't mean a thing"—then, throwing back his shoulders, he would shout out, *"Bali! Bali! Bali!"*

The various groups stretched out on the road with the GIs in front, setting the pace. As a result of this arrangement, The Tiger spent most of his time with them. It was easy to see that the guards took their cue from their leader; they screamed at us and became more nervous when The Tiger was near.

At our first rest stop that morning, we all sat down on the ground by the side of the road. There was little conversation. Looking up, I saw a guard who was either a corporal or a sergeant walking slowly in our direction, looking back over his shoulder occasionally. This senior guard ordered away two other guards who were standing near us.

After they had walked beyond hearing distance, he knelt down and addressed us in a quiet voice. "We do not like to see what happened this morning. Our commander is a very determined man. He will do whatever is necessary to complete this march. Please do as he says." The ranking guard then got up and walked toward the front of the group. Within a few minutes our two former guards had rejoined us and taken up their positions. We realized that the guard had tried to warn us. It was probably dangerous for him to say what he did. His carefully disguised remarks would have to suffice as the only apology we would ever receive for the execution of Lieutenant Thornton.

As we resumed the march, one of the French nuns, Mother Thérèse, showed signs of failing strength and found it difficult to keep pace. We constructed a makeshift litter and carried her for perhaps two hours until our next rest stop. The four of us sat there by the side of the road and agreed that we simply could not go on; we sadly admitted that Mother Thérèse would have to walk. Yet when the signal was given to resume the march, as one man we walked over to the litter, picked it up, and proceeded on our way as before. We had gone perhaps a quarter-mile when Father Frank Canavan turned around and shouted at the other three of us, "We agreed, didn't we, that we couldn't continue? What are we going to do?" All four of us stopped and gently lowered the litter to the ground. Mother Thérèse struggled to her feet and, with the assistance of another nun, began walking and managed to keep pace with the march.

I spoke with Father Crosbie about this incident a couple of days later when we both observed Mother Thérèse still marching along with the rest of us.

"Bing," I said, using Father Crosbie's nickname, "how does she do it?"

"At this stage it isn't physical strength anymore. She ran out of that a long time ago."

"But she is so weak. And look at her—she doesn't even weigh eighty pounds," I commented.

"When you are as weak as she is, you put one foot in front of the other and leave the rest to faith." Confirming the validity of her faith, she was able, with a little help, to complete the march.

At rest breaks during the march, I often saw Sergeant First Class Henry G. (Hank) Leerkamp of Company L, 34th Infantry Regiment, 24th Division, from Chester, Minnesota—the man who had headed the burial detail for Lieutenant Thornton. Hank had enlisted in the army in 1939, and he saw action during World War II in the Armed

Guard Transport, an organization whose mission was to protect ships from attacks by enemy submarines. May 1950 found Hank at age twenty-nine in Japan, just in time to be among the first American soldiers sent to fight in South Korea after the North Korean attack. The American attempt to stem the Communist advance in July 1950 had been a disaster. There was not enough of anything: trained and willing men or working equipment. The situation in combat had been chaotic; when the firing started, many men dropped their weapons and ran toward the rear, leaving those like Hank exposed to capture and death. Hank told me that the soldiers sent to South Korea were not the best in the first place, that they had been further softened by the "easy life" of occupation duty, and that in the heat of battle in South Korea "few stayed to fight."

Only gradually did we become aware of the full gravity of the situation we faced. Reality was again being filtered to make it more tolerable, just as it had been in the death cell. We grasped at wild ideas of possible rescue: American paratroopers might drop at any moment; sudden peace might come; the International Red Cross might be permitted to take care of us.

I became aware of things outside of myself as I walked along. My mind had options: I could think of the beautiful or the ugly. Sometimes the ugly seemed so powerful that it took an act of faith to turn my back on it. Yet from time to time, I saw the beauty of nature in a fleeting way. I even sensed that under different circumstances, this would be a beautiful place. One mountain followed another up the Yalu River, and each was covered with lush stands of green pine trees. It was possible to see beauty when all cause for joy was gone. Soon however, my mind was busy with the business of survival, programmed into my instinct, and all other stimuli were soon rejected. But for a moment, there was beauty.

The Korean weather was another matter. One would think that Korea would not have extremes in its climate, surrounded as it is by water on three sides. But that is definitely not the case. Temperatures can climb above 110 degrees in the South during the summer, and hover in the forty-below range in the North during the winter. "Korea still has aspects of unsurpassed beauty, but no non-Korean has ever been heard to say a good word about the weather."[5]

The mind plays strange games. I compared my situation with that in the death cell, where I had been told that I would be executed at any moment and had no way of knowing when they might carry out that threat. On the Death March I at least had a chance to do something that might prevent my death. Not only that, but my executioners were here with me and to some extent were sharing my hardship. In the death cell, all decisions on whether I lived or died had been made by unknown, faceless people.

Bill Evans, the American gold-mining engineer, was becoming more unstable on his feet, and it soon became apparent that he would need assistance. When Danny Dans was asked to help, he noted that Bill was carrying an old shirt with the sleeves tied up to form pockets. "Bill, I'm happy to help you, but if we are going to be a team, I think I have the right to know what you are carrying," Danny said. Bill didn't say a word, but taking the old shirt from across his shoulder, he emptied the contents on the road. They were rock specimens that Bill had picked up as we walked!

"You never know," Bill said somewhat defensively. "When this is all over, I may have the opportunity to come back here and do some mining." He threw the rocks away, however, and never picked up any more as far as I know.

Bill was a colorful figure who had been born and educated in Japan. His father was an American doctor and his mother was Eurasian; the combination gave him a slightly Oriental look. After graduating from Tokyo Imperial University with a degree in mining engineering, Bill had been drawn to Korea because of his special interest in goldmining. He told us that at one time he had the largest piece of mining equipment in Korea. By his own admission, he had made and lost several fortunes.

Bill also had a special interest in aviation and in 1931 had assisted Clyde Pangborn to become the first man to make a trans-Pacific nonstop flight from west to east. Japan at that time was ruled by a very militaristic government that had just sent its troops to invade Manchuria. Clyde Pangborn and Hugh Herndon, his navigator, were accused by the Japanese of flying over military installations. To make matters worse, the *Kempei Tai* (secret police) operated a Black Dragon Society in Japan at that time, some of whose activities were intimidation, terrorism, and political assassination. The Black Dragon Society had been accused of stealing Pangborn's flight maps and charts from his hotel room. Pangborn could not make the long flight to the United States without proper maps, but given the climate of hostility and suspicion that prevailed in Japan at that time, he found it impossible to get replacements from the Japanese. Bill Evans stepped into this emotionally charged situation and, through speaking the language and knowing the right people, was able to obtain the required maps, thereby making the flight possible.

The amount of fuel that could be carried was also critical, because the flight was to be made in a single-engine Ballanca. To help compensate for the weight of extra fuel, Pangborn threw out his lunch and boots. Then, just before closing the door of the plane, he also unfastened his belt and gave it to Bill. (Bill wore that same belt on the Death March.) Pangborn took off from Samushiro Beach, near Tokyo, and landed on October 5, 1931, in Wanatchee, Washington, a distance of 4,600 miles. Bill's invaluable assistance was confirmed to me by Pangborn in 1953, after my release.

Not wanting to leave Korea at the outbreak of World War II, Bill was ultimately arrested by the Japanese *Kempei Tai* and spent the entire war in prison. He had almost starved to death from that experience as well and proudly showed us the additional holes he had punched in the Pangborn belt as he lost weight. Following the Death March we saw him take a nail and punch another hole in that belt. "The Communists have starved me more than the Japanese did," he announced.

As the march continued, Kris developed a problem of balance that necessitated his being helped. He was strong enough to walk alone, but his problem was flat feet. Kris had lost the special shoes that compensated for his foot problem and was now wearing some old military shoes that were much too small for him. Moving through Manpo the night before, Kris was unable to walk straight and had wandered off the road and fallen in a ditch, receiving abrasions on his face and nose. Walking with him the next day, I could feel his tug and pull as he tried to retain his balance. He compared his situation to that of walking on stilts.

Later that day, I was assigned to help Sister Mary Clare, an Anglican nun. In Kosan she had fallen from an upper berth and had injured her back; as a result, she had difficulty in holding herself erect. At her suggestion, I had placed my hand on the middle of her back, exerting considerable pressure, and she held on to my arm at the same time in order to remain in an upright position. If I relaxed the pressure on her back for an instant, the upper part of her body would become bent.

Bertha Smith was able to keep up in spite of her age. A native of Missouri, she had come to Korea some forty years before as a missionary of the Methodist Church. Before the war I had seen her almost every day in Kaesong, where she lived a spartan kind of life even by missionary standards. She walked to most of her appointments in the area, even though she could have had the services of a jeep and a driver. Very thorough in everything she did, she confided to me on one occasion that she chewed each mouthful of food 100 times. In prison, she groomed her jet black hair with whatever comb was available. These were disciplines that would help her survive her three years in prison. She walked unassisted most of the time on the Death March but on occasion would team up with Helen Rosser. Even the Communists were impressed by her because she had taken the trouble to learn the Korean language really well.

Later that day, some of the Catholic POWs requested that Bishop Byrne give them general absolution. It was agreed that this would be done just as we resumed march after our next rest stop. I then observed Bishop Byrne kneeling by the side of the road for the entire rest period. When the order was given to resume march, he could not get up. Helping him to his feet, I asked, "Are you all right, Monsignor?"

"I'm all right, Larry, but I have a great burden," he replied.

The distribution of food was always a problem on the Death March. I'm certain that the local people had been given strict orders in advance to prepare food for a certain number of people, an order that no one would dare to disobey in a police state like North Korea. There was probably sufficient food at each stop, but there was never enough time for everyone to eat it. The Tiger was in such a great hurry that once most of the POWs had been served, he would give the order to resume the march.

We spent the night near a farmhouse on the top of a small hill after having come about twenty miles. One room of the farmhouse was given to the diplomats and the other to the families. The rest of us were obliged to spend the night outside.

Because we had all been captured in the summertime, no one was dressed for the cold. In an effort to stay warm, several of us followed the example of the Russian prisoners in stuffing our clothes with straw and tying a rope around our pant legs at the ankles. Throughout the period of the Death March and until January of the next year, I wore only a pair of seersucker slacks, a shirt and a lightweight coat given to me by the Koreans at Jui-am-nee. The American military prisoners were equally ill prepared for the cold with their fatigues and light-weight coats, though thanks to the kindness of the North Korean quartermaster at Jui-am-nee, most of them had warm fur hats.

That night, the wind was blowing moderately from the north, and I could not escape from it no matter where I went. At first I lay down between the farmhouse and another building with some of the others. But the wind was so strong and the ground so cold that I got up and began moving around. I soon discovered that Danny was having the same problem staying warm. The two of us spent the night on our feet.

All the POWs and civilian prisoners slept on the knoll of the small hill that night. It was possible to move around to some extent without bothering the guards, most of whom who had been withdrawn to form a perimeter. The remaining guards had built a fire at the top of the hill, and a number of POWs had come to it to try to get warm. The guards did not seem to object to the presence of the POWs at the fire as long as they could find places for themselves. Whenever one returned from a round of inspections to discover that he had been squeezed out, he would use his rifle butt to batter his way back to the fire. Those he knocked out of the way would crawl back to the fire as soon as the guard had cleared a path for himself. This scene was repeated over and over throughout the night. Each time we saw a guard returning to the fire, Danny and I would try to persuade some of the men to move out of his way, but it was no use. Even at the risk of being struck on the head with a rifle butt, no one was willing to give up his warm place.

Danny and I stood about ten to fifteen feet away from the fire, too far to benefit much from the warmth but close enough that we could talk with the POWs. About five o'clock that morning someone said, "Boy, I shore would like to be back in Arkansas about this time. Mom and Dad would be cookin' up bacon and eggs and hot coffee. I can smell it cookin' right now." The young man from Arkansas carried an unhealed wound that he took with him to his death some time later. Others joined the conversation with examples of breakfasts back home, some of which were truly extraordinary.

"At my home we had steak and pie for breakfast, along with gallons of coffee," said one.

"What?" someone else interjected. "What kind of home did you come from?"

"I came from a German home, and we ate like that every morning." I couldn't help believing that their memory of what breakfast had been like was highly colored by the hunger they felt at the moment. All of them spoke of finishing breakfast back home with "gallons of coffee."

Death by starvation, except in its initial stages, is relatively easy and painless. My memory of the plight of those cold, hungry, desperate men trying to hold on to life against all odds is sometimes more painful to me than the thought of the large number of deaths that followed. Later, as death came to some 70 percent, it was probably easier for them to bear than what they had experienced that night.

Occasionally, I could stand the cold no longer and would turn and walk slowly among the sleeping POWs scattered about the hillside. Near morning, I stumbled as I stepped over a form lying on the ground, and my foot struck the leg of a POW whom I assumed was asleep. The form began rolling down the incline, turning over and over, finally coming to rest some ten feet farther down. On investigating, I discovered that the man was dead. When I reported what had happened to those gathered around the fire, one of them replied, "Shoot, a little while ago I woke up and tried to move Bill. Me and Bill had been sleepin' under the same blanket, and Bill was dead. He was already cold."

Dawn was breaking when I suddenly realized that I had not slept at all that night or the night before. In fact, I had not slept during our last night at Manpo either, though I had managed to catnap the next afternoon in the warmth of the sun as we awaited the arrival of The Tiger. I found out that day what the body would do when denied sleep for a long time.

When the sun made its appearance bringing light and warmth, I felt that I could make it through another day. The harassment of The Tiger made our days on the Death March terrible, but the cold made our nights worse. To this day, that bitter cold in North Korea is more deeply etched in my memory than is the face of The Tiger. It is like the cold of no other place in the world as far as I know. It must have imprinted itself somewhere inside of me because even now, my friends laugh at me in the wintertime for overdressing when I go out. In prison I came to terms with hunger, but I never got used to being cold.

In the mountains there is usually a great difference between the daytime high temperature and the nighttime low. Commissioner Lord once spoke of the universal tendency of peoples all over the world who live in mountains to be sun worshipers. I find that understandable. I have more memories from North Korea of blessed sunrises than of any other time of day. We spent countless mornings standing outside in the freezing cold awaiting the life-giving warmth of the sun. Mr. Moon followed a specific ritual when the sun rose each morning: he would stand straight, legs wide apart, face the rising sun, and move his arms up and down in a kind of conditioning exercise.

At last the time came that morning for those who were lying down to get up. When all who would ever stand again were on their feet, we could see the huddled forms of about ten POWs who had not made it through the night. Eight more were so ill and weak that they were unable to march. Breakfast was a corn or millet ball. It wasn't bacon and eggs, but all of the POWs were at least given time to eat.

The Tiger ordered everyone to begin the march and then spoke to some village leaders who had come to see us off: "Bury the eighteen, and don't leave any mounds." Commissioner Lord, who had been instructed by The Tiger to remain by his side to translate in case any difficulties developed, heard that order exactly as it was given. Eight of those who were left behind were alive when we departed. "Don't worry," The Tiger had told us earlier that morning, "the wounded and the ill will be carried by oxcarts. Those who are unable to travel will be taken to People's Hospitals."

We were on the road that November 2 at an early hour and were at once ordered into a fast pace. Up ahead, the guards were beating with rifle butts any GIs who lagged behind. We discovered the advantage that day of pairing different people from time to time, matching strength to need. Not all the stronger people were of equal strength, and not all those who required help had the same degree of need. I began the morning supporting Sister Mary Clare, but after approximately two hours I found myself with Dr. Kisch.

Halfway through the morning as I warmed up from the sun and the exercise, I found myself growing very sleepy. I regained my thoughts at one point as though I had just been awakened. I asked Dr. Kisch, "Can you sleep and walk at the same time?"

"Yes," he answered, "if you are tired enough." I must have been tired enough. I dozed several times that morning for a few seconds, perhaps for a minute or so at a time. Doctor Kisch told me after one such instance that he knew I was asleep because I began to stray off the road to the left. Later in the afternoon, when I was with Kris, I caught a few more very brief naps.

Another man I often saw at rest breaks was Cpl. Wilbert (Shorty) Estabrook of B Company, 19th Regiment. Shorty was born in Houlton, Maine, in 1930 and enlisted in the National Guard in 1947. He told me that the men had had no combat training in Japan prior to coming to South Korea to fight. Everything and everyone was in poor condition: "Weapons were about 60 percent serviceable. Ammo was old and scarce. Many of us lived off post with Japanese girlfriends. We were soft and untrained." But Shorty was a great asset to our group in prison because even in our worst moments, he tried to cheer us up with his jokes. Life would have been much more difficult without him.

Monsignor Quinlan and someone else were assisting Father Charles Hunt, the Anglican priest. A very large man with foot problems, he found it difficult to keep up with the fast pace of the march. Monsignor and his partner were supporting Father Hunt's upper body, while the lower lagged behind by about three feet. This unnatural position placed an added burden on the two carriers. Father Hunt wore excellent shoes, but either they didn't fit him very well or else they couldn't fit because of gout. I remembered his problems with gout as far back as the schoolhouse in Pyongyang. When I asked him about it on one occasion, he sarcastically replied, "I always blame such things on that tomato juice I drank last night."

The only time so far in our prison experience that we had had anything close to a balanced diet was at Manpo. Father Hunt, however, had not been able to eat the dried fish supplied to us there. To have missed the relatively good diet during that one month at Manpo was to place oneself at added risk when the diet degenerated. The fast march coupled with the poor diet and inadequate rest was fast depleting the reserves of the best of us.

Walter Eltringham was also having difficulty keeping up. We had noticed that Walt had not eaten his entire food ration for some weeks. He had eaten well at the schoolhouse in Pyongyang, but after that time he would give part of his food away. When anyone asked him about it, he would reply, "I can't eat anymore; it chokes me." At Manpo he gave his entire sugar ration to the French nuns.

During the afternoon more members of the group began to lag behind. The French consul and his staff carried Mother Béatrix for a time until they could go no farther. Finally, the guard permitted her to continue at a slower pace. Mother Eugénie had almost worn herself out trying to ensure that Mother Béatrix would not be left behind.

Several of the elderly Russians had dropped behind and required the assistance of others. Tihinoff, the old Russian gentleman who had so expertly helped us install the cooking pots in Kosan, was just barely able to keep up.

A problem had developed that afternoon. Several of the more seriously wounded POWs had died as they were being carried, but their bodies could not be discarded until nightfall. The Tiger's order on this matter was clear: no one must be left behind. Commissioner Lord approached The Tiger with what he considered to be a humanitarian plan. According to that plan, Dr. Alexander Boysen, U.S. Army, or Dr. Kisch would be summoned to examine any person thought to be dead. If either doctor certified the death, the body could be left by the side of the road. The Tiger accepted the idea—with one change: "Don't trouble yourself about sending your doctors to certify to a man's death. If you think a man is dead, notify one of my guards. He will shoot him through the heart to certify the death. Then you can leave his body by the side of the road."

We walked past several American POWs that day as they stood or sat by the side of the road. "What is going to happen to you?" someone asked. "They told us that they would bring us by oxcart later," replied one of them.

Later that day we heard gunshots from time to time. "What's all that shooting about?" someone asked.

"I suppose they are shooting the dead," someone else answered.

"Yes, and they may be shooting the living," Kris commented. Kris may have been vocalizing what we were all thinking but were afraid to say out loud. We were aware that some POWs were dying every day of old wounds and general neglect, but others were simply disappearing.

That night The Tiger addressed us concerning the subject that was uppermost in our minds. "Don't worry about your friends who could not keep up today. They are being looked after in People's Hospitals." We remembered The Tiger's words that morning with reference to the ten dead and eight wounded who had been left behind: "Bury the eighteen—don't leave any mounds." It was then that we understood what it meant to be sent to People's Hospitals.

We also understood more about our own standing with The Tiger after his speech. He was not only exceedingly cruel but also deceptive, which indicated that he knew the ramifications of what he was doing. His order to the village leaders that morning to bury both the dead and the living and "not leave any mounds" indicated that he was trying to hide the evidence of his crimes. He knew that the U.S. Army might one day capture this area and would demand an accounting of those who had disappeared from our group. Clearly, we were in for more hard times, but we didn't know that our troubles were just beginning.

Comparing our circumstances with information on the Bataan Death March in Stanley Falk's book, I think that the situations were similar in at least three respects. First, like the Japanese, the North Koreans did not take into consideration the weakened condition of their prisoners, or didn't care. Second, in both cases the prisoners had to be moved quickly: on Luzon, it was necessary to clear the small area of Bataan in order for General Homma to begin his attack on Corregidor; the Communists wanted to move us out of the area to prevent our possible rescue by advancing United Nation forces. Third, in both instances, plans to feed the POWs did not take into account that they could not cover the required distance each day in their weakened condition.[6]

In the Korean culture there is a socially approved formula by which one person may communicate his dissatisfaction with the actions of another. It begins something like this: "It is difficult to speak to you about this, friend, sir, honorable teacher, etc., but . . ." Then the first person proceeds to inform the second of his concern. Commissioner Lord used this technique to communicate our displeasure to The Tiger at having to sleep outside each night. The Tiger didn't respond, at least not right away.

After traveling more than twenty miles, we stopped for the night at a small schoolhouse. When we had finished our meager meal, The Tiger called the group together and made a brief announcement. "You have been complaining about having to sleep outside. Tonight you will all sleep inside." That was all. He made no attempt to defend what he had done before, and for once he placed no blame on the American bombers for our hardship. On inspecting our sleeping quarters, however, we were all struck with one unanswered question: how can 800 people sleep in this small space?

We didn't know it, but The Tiger had a plan. The diplomats were given one small room, the women and children another, and the rest of us were quartered in the one large room of the schoolhouse. We civilian men were ordered into the room first and told to remain standing until all the POWs had been admitted. After the room was filled to capacity by any normal standard the guards continued to push in more people—and still more people. Finally, when the guards decided to call a halt, there were still some people left outside. The Tiger then made his appearance in the doorway and ordered us to sit down. We all hesitated for a moment, knowing very well that there would be even less space when we were seated. But The Tiger repeated his order in a much stronger voice, and we knew that we had to obey.

I found myself sitting on my tailbone with no other part of my body touching the floor, my knees pressing against my chest. In this position I was not only in pain but I had no balance, flopping either left, right, front, or back depending on the pressure from my neighbors. Someone on my right would push against me and I'd fall to my left, pushing my neighbor to his left, and so on like human dominoes. When the wave of humanity reached the wall, the action did not stop. Those against the wall were on the bottom at this point. But they had one advantage: by pushing against the wall they could gain the momentary relief of causing the human wave to flipflop back the other way. This had dire consequences for those who were next to the opposite wall. They, in turn, pushed against their wall and the process was repeated, causing great discomfort to all. Discomfort finally gave way to acute cramps in my legs. There was absolutely no way to ease the pain. I was so tightly compressed that I could not stand on my feet.

After about thirty minutes of this madness, someone screamed from somewhere in the darkness. The efforts of others to quiet him met with no success, and soon others—possibly some of the wounded—also began to scream. Suddenly the door was thrown open by a guard wielding a submachine gun, and by means of Lord's translation we were warned not to make any more noise. For a brief period there were no screams. When the guard was required to return the second time, he was obviously angry at our disobeying his order. Nevertheless, the screaming soon broke out again. At the guard's third appearance there was a difference: "This is my last warning. You must be quiet. If I have to return, I will open the door and fire into the room with my weapon." He slammed the door shut, leaving us alone.

Major Dunn, senior ranking American officer, spoke up from somewhere in the near-total darkness. "Men, you have heard what the guard said. I order you to be quiet for your own sake. Do any of you have any doubt that this guard means what he says? Let Commissioner Lord tell you what he thinks about it."

"I agree! This guard is under orders from The Tiger, and you all know what he did to Lieutenant Thornton. We have got to be quiet," concluded Commissioner Lord.

Major Dunn spoke again. "I don't know where the officers and noncoms are in this room, but you must be scattered all over. From now on, when anyone screams, he is to be picked up and thrown outside."

For a time there was quiet in the room, but after about thirty minutes someone cried out. Following Major Dunn's orders, those around the offender picked him up and passed him overhead to the door. Probably a total of two or three were ejected in this manner. Those who were thrown outside were not punished by the guards; they simply had to wait out a very cold night with those who had not been made to fit into the room in the first place. Again, there was quiet inside for a short time.

The next person who cried out did not want to be thrown out in the cold and fought back. From the darkness came the sound of blows, followed by a shout: "Now throw him out!" When the offender had been ejected from the room, there was some whispering in one corner. "That officer hit this man," someone spoke up. Immediately, the quiet of the room was broken by a loud clear voice stating name, rank, and serial number and adding, "If anyone ever wants to make anything out of it before some board of investigation after the war, then go ahead." There was no response. No one else cried out.

There followed a brief, subdued discussion in another section of the room concerning the 1946 report of the Doolittle Board. General Jimmy Doolittle had been appointed by the secretary of war to head up the newly created Board on Officers/Enlisted Men Relationships, whose job it was to make recommendations for improving the way that officers and enlisted men relate to one another. Some of those who were talking seemed to feel that the breakdown in discipline we had just witnessed could be attributed to the recommendations of the Doolittle Board.

I later asked Dunn what he thought about the Doolittle Board. "It was a twenty-four-karat disaster! It destroyed the discipline of the army. Ask any infantry officer." Major Dunn's remark seems typical of those I have heard from service personnel old enough to have a firsthand opinion about the military before the Doolittle Board. Many officers and senior NCOs contrast the largely unquestioned loyalty that they received from the lower enlisted ranks in World War II with the situation in the U.S. military during the 1950s and later.[7]

The people of the free world were fighting a combination of terrible evils during World War II, and everyone was committed to doing his or her part, even if it meant tolerating without complaint an autocratic sergeant or officer. Those who felt victimized waited until after the war to air their grievances against the military system—which they did: the Doolittle Board was formed to address complaints from the lower echelons against those above them in rank. Questioned later about the board he had headed, General Doolittle said, " 'The public was fed up with the military, fed up with war, fed up with discipline.' "[8]

Those who spent the night in that small schoolhouse were miserable with the crowding, the odor of dysentery, and the lack of oxygen. After a while I didn't notice these things. I had not slept in two days and nights except for the brief catnaps while walking on the road. Yet the mind was slow to let go, even though I needed sleep so badly. I lay in that torturous position for perhaps an hour. Gradually the sounds of coughing around me faded, and my cramped legs were not hurting anymore. I realized that I was running down at last. Little by little, I was removed from my body and that room by the soft mercy of sleep.

During the night, I was partly awakened several times by the shifting from side to side, but I would quickly drift off again. Possibly I slept so well, even under those seemingly impossible conditions, because of the warmth given off by hundreds of bodies in that relatively small room. For the first time on the Death March, I was warm at night!

The next morning the door was thrown open to reveal the smiling face of The Tiger. It was the first time he had ever come to wake us up. I was certain that he had a special reason for doing so. "Everyone stand up!" he ordered. That must have been the one and only order from The Tiger that we ever disobeyed without being punished. With the exception of perhaps six men, we simply could not stand up. Those next to the door fell forward and crawled slowly out on their hands and knees. The next row followed in like manner until all of us had crawled through the door.

The Tiger was standing beside the door to greet us as we crawled out. He had not responded the day before when Commissioner Lord had told him of our complaints about sleeping outside. On seeing his obvious enjoyment at watching us emerge from the schoolhouse on all fours, however, we knew The Tiger had given us his answer—in deeds, not in words.

After a minute or so, we were able to stand on our numbed legs. Once breakfast was out of the way, we were informed that The Tiger had a speech to make. He explained the humanitarian concern of his government for our welfare and said that any who could not march that day would be given transport; those who were ill would be sent to People's Hospitals. Knowing what People's Hospitals really meant, we wanted to avoid that fate at all cost.

When the order was given to begin the march on this November 3, the women were told to wait for transportation. Some of the weaker ones had had great difficulty the day before, even with the help of the entire group. Nevertheless, I remember that we had some misgivings as we marched away, leaving only Commissioner Lord to look after the women's group. At noon we were ordered to move into a field to wait for the women to catch up. Looking down the road, we saw a group of people moving in our direction but thought little about it at first because we were expecting to see our group arrive either by truck or by oxcart. Finally someone shouted, "Those people are too tall to be Koreans!" Instantly, we all knew that he was right and went running down the road to assist the women.

It had been a terrible morning for everyone, but especially for Nell Dyer. She had been made a leader of the women's group by order of The Tiger; she was already a leader by temperament and dedication. Leadership is generally regarded as an honor, but on the Death March it could cost you your life. That was exactly what had happened to Lt. Thornton. Nell had tried to keep the group together and had overextended herself in personally assisting those who could not keep up. The attempt to help the weaker ones at the expense of the stronger clearly had its limitations.

Two French nuns plus Madame Funderat and Commissioner Lord were still missing. Soon Mother Eugénie appeared on the road all alone except for a guard. She was extremely distraught at having had to leave Mother Béatrix behind, but the guard had ordered her to do so when Mother Béatrix fell far behind the group. Arriving in Korea in 1906, Mother Béatrix had devoted her whole life to working with the poor and the aged. She was seventy-five years old.

Not long after that, we were greeted by the strange sight of Commissioner Lord assisting Madame Funderat by means of a rope tied to each. Lord was exhausted, and I wondered how he could go on, considering his heart problem upon our arrival at Manpo in September.

When Commissioner Lord was first arrested, he was a very heavy person. After his four years as a prisoner of the Japanese during World War II, he had been released in a very weakened condition caused by malnutrition and, by his own admission, had overeaten ever since. "I made up my mind after getting out of that Japanese prison that I would never go short again. My favorite time to eat was at night. I loved to go downstairs and raid the refrigerator after everyone else was in bed," he told me.

But on our starvation diet he had steadily lost weight and was now a shadow of his former self.

When we resumed march after the noon meal, we were forced to leave Madame Funderat behind with the promise that she would be looked after. Neither she nor Mother Béatrix was ever seen again.

Normally, two people would have had no difficulty assisting a third, but all of us had been on a starvation diet for about a month. Although our bodies had not yet wasted away as much as they would later on, we were little more than living skeletons. Our bones were covered with cracked, dry, dirty skin; we had scruffy beards and long, dirty, matted hair. Our ragged summer clothes and hollow eyes completed the testimony to our depleted condition.

Little clusters of people from our various groups were scattered up and down the road for miles that afternoon. Monsignor Quinlan and Father Crosbie were trying to assist the oldest member of our group. Father Villemot, who had come to Korea in 1892, was eighty-two years of age on the Death March. Not having teeth, he could not eat the half-cooked corn that the local villagers prepared for us. As the old man's strength failed, Bishop Quinlan and Father Crosbie were required to carry more and more of the burden. Slowly, these three men dropped behind and were soon out of sight. At one time Father Villemot begged to be left to die in a farmyard. Finally, he was permitted to ride in an oxcart that was provided for Madame Martel after Perruche made a strong appeal to The Tiger.

Madame Martel's son Charles was chancellor of the French legation in Seoul before the Communist invasion. Mother and son marched side by side on the Death March until she began to fail. A strong family, the Martels were proud of a name that had first become famous in 732 A.D. when Charles (the Hammer) Martel, in one of the decisive battles of history, defeated the Saracens at Tours. His victory halted the expansion into northern Europe of Moslem forces operating from Spain.

Toward evening, more POWs fell out of line, unable to keep up. As we walked past them, we tried to encourage them to keep walking as long as possible. Some did make a new effort, but others remained by the side of the road. Later, we heard many gunshots behind us; we knew what was happening.

On this particular afternoon I noticed something different. The guard who marched by my side was not like most of the others. My burden became greater near nightfall, and I was obliged to fall behind rather than abandon the malnourished, weak, and frail Anglican nun by the side of the road to die alone. The main body of marching prisoners was miles ahead. Darkness was fast approaching, but this guard stayed by my side, offering encouragement. As other groups of two fell behind—one stronger, one weaker, but together trying to trade a little time in exchange for a life—each couple was assigned a guard, and the decision was his whether to tolerate the delay. Many did not. The sound of the gun was heard in the gathering darkness.

When we finally arrived at our destination for the day, we found that friends had saved our small food ration for us. Had the guard's friends done the same for him? We were given a new delicacy that night, a type of emergency ration that was issued to the North Korean army in the field. Consisting of ground and roasted grain, it could be eaten either dry or with water. The older members of our group could eat this ration quite well. It was unfortunate that it had not been given to us all along.

The civilian group spent the night in a church that was a part of a large compound, presumably a former mission station. In addition to the church, there was a school where the POWs were quartered.

Again, there was not enough room, and the attempt to assign sleeping spaces on the floor was only partially successful. Several of us had to take turns sitting with our backs to the wall to allow others to lie down. I spent part of the night lying in very cramped quarters on the floor and the other part in a half-sitting position. Again, it was a miserable might. Besides the physical discomfort, The Tiger's latest words to us kept turning over in my mind: those who had fallen behind on the march that day, he said, had been sent to the People's Hospitals.

9. THE FOURTH DAY AND BEYOND

WE were awakened earlier than usual the next morning. Looking out the door of the church, Kris, Monsignor Quinlan, and I contemplated what might be in store for us that day. Till then, the weather had cooperated, with comfortable daytime temperatures, though the nighttime temperatures were low enough to form thick ice on the rice paddies. Early that morning, however the weather signaled a change for the worse. Light snow was falling, and a strong north wind was whipping dust across the road.

Kris said, "I'm afraid we are going to have snow today. If we do, the mountain roads will become slippery. It's hard to walk in the snow, and if you fall and break a leg you won't be able to walk at all." To the northeast the ribbon of road on which we were to travel rose and fell as it stitched itself into layer after layer of mountains, rugged enough to be likened to a sea in a heavy gale. We had been warned by the guards that we had to move out early and travel quickly that day before snow blocked the summit over which we had to march.

"If there is a lot of snow, I'm afraid that some of us are not going to make it," I said to no one in particular.

"Larry, me boy, you're right," Monsignor Quinlan answered with his characteristic Irish expression. He continued, looking me dead in the eye, "But the Good Lord will give them a better welcome in heaven than the Communists have ever given them in this unhappy land." The phrase "this unhappy land" was characteristic of Monsignor's references to North Korea. He had known this same land before it had become a Communist country and was now able to see what the new regime had made of it. We did not have much time to think about what Monsignor had said. The order was given to move out. There would be no breakfast that morning.

The man who was really having trouble during this march was Major Dunn. I'm surprised that he was not shot, given The Tiger's policy of holding leaders accountable for the behavior of their groups.

Maj. John J. Dunn, in charge of regimental S-3 (plans) for the 34th

Regiment, was born in Rome, New York. After enlisting in the army in 1934, he performed heroically in combat in World War II, winning the the Distinguished Service Cross. And in South Korea in July 1950, when Americans were racing south in disorganized retreat, "in an extraordinary display of leadership, Dunn turned the whole mass around and headed it back north to reoccupy its positions."[1]

But his efforts and those of other men in South Korea were not enough, and they were overwhelmed by the superior North Korean army. In the fighting Dunn had been wounded in the jaw and neck so severely that he lost consciousness for a time from loss of blood. After being taken prisoner in that condition, he was lucky to have arrived in North Korea alive. Dunn's job of trying to look after his men was always thwarted by the North Koreans, who refused to observe international law in their treatment of prisoners. But he did what he could with great courage and determination.

We were positioned in the usual formation that day: the POWs in the lead, followed by the South Korean politicians, the diplomats, and finally, the civilian prisoners. Bishop Byrne and Kris had been selected to lead the civilian group because their pace was moderate. We hoped that the guards would be a little more tolerant if we all stayed together as a group, even though we might drop behind the others. To some extent, the strategy paid off. At one time that day we were some three-quarters of a mile behind the POWs, whom The Tiger was pushing at a killing pace in an effort to reach the summit of the mountains before it was blocked by snow. The diplomats were only slightly ahead of us, giving us reason to suppose that they had understood our delaying tactic and were playing the same game.

We had marched for approximately an hour when I saw the first indication of what the day might bring; it was not reassuring. With the snow continuing to fall and building up on the road, the task of walking became more difficult. We had marched the first half hour through a broad and relatively level plain. Soon after that, the grade of the road began to rise as we reached the foothills of another mountain range.

At first, I had been assigned to Sister Mary Clare, but after about an hour I was asked to drop behind and pick up Dr. Kisch. He had been marching without assistance about a quarter-mile to the rear of the main civilian group. When I reached him, I saw that he was hobbling along slowly, taking very short steps in the snow for fear of falling. Sagid, a seventeen-year-old Turkish boy, walked slightly behind Dr. Kisch lugging a suitcase full of clothes for his younger brother, Hamid. Sagid was the oldest of six children belonging to the Salahudtin family.

All were on the Death March, and all of them walked except Hamid, who was not yet a year old. The family had been traders in Seoul before the war and had lived in the Orient for a long time. Most of them spoke several languages well enough to get along: Korean, Japanese, English, Turkish, Russian, and Chinese.

Because of the weight of the suitcase, Sagid tied a rope around it and pulled it behind him over the snow. The guard urged us on. Little by little we closed the distance between us and the main group. By the time Dr. Kisch and I had made our way to the front of the group, the road had steepened, and I could see switchbacks ahead.

We had marched around a steep curve when we heard a sharp sound like a single gunshot. Perhaps twenty seconds later I saw four or five guards and one officer walking back to the main road from a small canyon. One of the guards said something to his companion, and they both laughed. The officer turned slightly in the direction of his men and smiled also. They soon disappeared, running around the next bend of the road. We were lagging far behind the POWs; we could no longer see them, but I believe we had heard the first execution of that day. There would be many more.

When I saw red streaks in the snow I did not at first recognize them as bloody footprints. They belonged to Bishop Byrne, who was walking with Kris about ten feet in front of me. One of the bishop's shoes had a hole in it which exposed raw skin to the snow-covered road, reminiscent of winter at Valley Forge. On that day the blood of many men would stain the snow red.

Bishop Byrne and Kris had been paired together for a special reason. Kris had his problem of balance, but he was otherwise strong enough to keep up and even to help others. Bishop Byrne had good balance but was getting too weak to continue without help. Together, they made a good team.

A change was made, and I found myself assisting Sister Mary Clare again. Although her back seemed to be stronger, she was having more difficulty in keeping pace with the march. Soon we began to hear shots ahead of us, and not long after that I saw a pool of fresh blood by the side of the road. At this point the road on which we were marching had been chiseled out of the side of a mountain; it ran along a precipice that dropped several hundred feet. Although no one commented on his own thoughts at this time, I think we all knew what was happening. The deep canyon made a very convenient location for disposal of the bodies of prisoners who had been shot.

Presently, we came upon a POW sitting in the middle of the road unable to walk another step. A guard was standing nearby, waiting for us to march past. A minute or so later we heard the crack of a rifle shot. I looked back to see the guard rolling the body over the snow toward the side of the road.

I had seen the first of many American soldiers to drop out that day because they could not keep up with the grueling pace through the snow. For a moment the realization that these young men would soon be in the presence of God filled me with awe and almost succeeded in converting this barbaric scene into one of tranquillity. Then I was brought back to reality: someone was dying—someone was responsible for this outrage.

It is impossible for me to describe my reaction to what was occurring. We had known for some time that prisoners who could not keep up had been executed, but this was the first time that we had seen the horror firsthand. There was such a searing of sensitivity that no one spoke for a few minutes. Then from somewhere behind me someone said, "They are shooting those boys." Kris turned partway around and shouted, "Yes, and they will shoot us too if we don't keep up."

In the face of such jarring reality, I was out of touch with my own feelings for a time. I had never felt this way before because I had never seen anything like this before. The feeling came across as a nausea in the pit of my stomach and a weakness affecting the entire body. There are no words. Feelings don't even have a name. Soon we came upon other young men who could not go any farther. They were awaiting execution as soon as our group had passed them. I could tell by looking into their eyes that they knew what was coming. I looked back a second time at the sound of another shot to behold the same wretched scene as before. I didn't look back anymore.

My mind seemed to float after a time. I seemed strangely out of touch with my body. I didn't have to make any concerted effort to remember what happened yesterday or the day before that—it was all there, instant recall in bold relief. As if looking through a camera with a wide-angle lens, I could see it all.

There was no physical pain as I walked along. The pitiful sight of those hopeless men, younger than I, lying by the side of the road awaiting their own execution took away all feeling of fatigue, hunger, and cold. There were a million things to think about, but my mind refused to make a choice—perhaps because any choice would involve pain. One young man, as his last earthly act, was singing "God Bless America" as loudly as his weak cracking voice was able. Tears were streaming down his face as we marched past. There were tears on our faces as well. I was staggered by feelings of hopelessness and grief.

Those young men were in the prime of life, but the abuses heaped upon them since their capture had weakened their vitality. With nothing but summerweight clothing, no medical attention for the ill and wounded, and little food, they were no longer able to meet the test of mere survival. One POW later remarked, "We just didn't have anything left to fight with. That was our situation just before we were captured in South Korea too."

Approximately 100 feet ahead, four emaciated American prisoners struggled to carry one comrade. In spite of all they could do, they continued to fall farther behind their group. The guard ordered the four men to put the wounded man on the ground and leave him. Suddenly Maj. Newton W. Lantron appeared and picked up the man lying on the ground. He threw him over his shoulder and moved swiftly forward to rejoin his group. I wondered how long his strength would last.

Some of these young men were so stunned that they were not fully aware of where they were or what would soon happen to them; others were not so fortunate. We were horrified not only by the thought of what these young men were facing but also by the look in their eyes, the sound of their voices, what they said, and what they asked for. They were not asking for very much, but it was beyond our ability to deliver. One young man sitting by the side of the road asked for a cigarette. Another American soldier, waiting to be shot, asked for a speedy death at our hands: "Will someone please hit me in the head with a rock?" he pleaded. We heard this request over and over, from the time we came within hearing range until we were out again.

We marched by them all. Some in our group tried to say words of comfort to them. I didn't. I remember making a conscious effort to think of something appropriate to say, but to no avail. I even went so far as to repeat over to myself the words that others had used. It was no use. Knowing that it would be the only thing I would ever be able to do for them, I still couldn't come up with anything appropriate.

Up ahead, one POW had fallen behind to help a buddy who could no longer continue on his own. They were urged on by the guard, but at last the weaker one fell to the ground and remained there. After a few moments, the guard shoved the stronger man away and motioned for him to go on by himself. The young man stood for an instant, then turned and went running up the road. He was barefooted. After a few paces, he stopped and returned to his fallen comrade. He knelt down, removed the shoes from his friend, and, holding them in his hand, ran forward to rejoin the group. The man sitting calmly on the ground made no effort to stop his friend from taking his shoes, and neither did the guard. At that moment his action seemed cruel to me. Thinking about it now from the vantage point of many years, I am not so sure that it was. I expressed my disapproval to Sister Mary Clare. She did not answer. Most of our group was saying very little at that time.

Walking just in front of me, Kris almost fell in the snow as he wiped tears from his eyes. Kris had learned, as we all had by that time, just how much grief he should allow himself to express at any given time, measuring it very carefully so as not to be overwhelmed by it. Catching up with him I asked, "Are you all right, Kris?" He didn't answer my question directly.

"I just hope that some day I have the time to sit down and have a good cry over all this."

"How much time will that take, Kris?"

"More than we'll ever have, I'm afraid."

That was only the second time that I had seen Kris cry. The first was back in the death cell at Pyongyang when he had become aware that he had placed me in a very dangerous situation by hiding empty brass cartridge shells in my basement after the battle of Kaesong.

Most of the civilians were on that Death March because they had chosen to remain behind when the South Koreans evacuated their cities. Kris was caught because of me, and I felt bad about it. "Kris, I'm sorry I dragged you into all this," I shouted.

"Larry, if there is anyone else here, I belong here," he replied.

Later I compared that answer with the one I had received in the schoolhouse in Pyongyang when I had apologized to Kris the first time. At that time he had said, "Listen, Larry, some day when this is all over we will sit down and have a good laugh about the whole thing." The "whole thing" had still been humorous in the schoolhouse—but not any more. The tenor of his reply had changed with our circumstances. We never did manage to get together for that laugh, and I don't know whether he ever had the time to sit down for the good cry that he spoke of. Circumstances denied me the opportunity of keeping our first appointment, and for myself I found that one good cry was not enough.

The snow continued falling and building up on the road. My lightheadedness was swept away by a torrent of anguish at the sight of another exhausted POW lying in the road awaiting his execution as soon as I marched past him. One thought constantly remained in my mind: can I make it through today? I reasoned that the answer would be determined by future conditions over which I had no control: if the speed of the march is not increased, making it impossible to keep up; if the debilitated person who I am supporting remains conscious. We rotated "burdens" often. Those burdens represented human faces, and they were not all the same. Some were older, weaker, sicker; they deserved to live as much as I.

Even the face of the enemy changed from time to time. At one moment, the enemy was the killing pace; at another, an armed and angry man walking behind you; at another, the snow building up on the road and becoming slippery. I became concerned about falling and perhaps injuring myself. Trying to be careful, I'd walk more slowly, concentrating on each spot in the road where I would place my next step.

Here the strategy for survival was up against its toughest opponent: trying to save other people's lives places one's own at greater risk. Clearly, it was not an option for all. Then there was the added realization that I might do all that was humanly possible and still fail. The alternative was worse. My strategy was to walk as far as possible, taking someone with me, and to say my prayers on the move.

Sometimes even the man with the gun changed, and I found myself walking with someone I could relate to as a human being. If he was patient and nonthreatening, I wondered what must be going on in his mind.

I learned to walk for great distances with tears welling up in my eyes, for there was no time out to cry. Everyone at one time or another had his own time for grief, and no one tried to talk him out of it. It would not have been a friendly thing to do.

We began to see items of discarded clothing lying on the ground. Bill Evans threw away a coveted blue wool blanket of high quality. It was immediately picked up by Father Booth, who carried it until his release from captivity some three years later. We realized that those who discarded prized objects of so little weight must have been very desperate.

Nearing the crest of a mountain, we saw The Tiger and a group of North Korean soldiers standing in the road looking down at us. We supposed that this was the long-awaited summit that The Tiger had been willing to kill twenty-two young men that morning to reach. Some of the group were more fortunate. The Tiger had provided an oxcart for Father Villemot, Madame Martel, and Sophia, one of the Turkish women. By this time the snow had stopped falling, but it had reached a depth of five to six inches.

On arriving at the summit, we noted that the attitude of The Tiger had improved considerably. In fact, he appeared to want to be friendly, but we held our distance. Having absorbed a certain amount of outrage from your captors, you never want to get close to them again. Apparently, The Tiger did have a timetable that he was willing to do anything to keep. With talk of a possible rescue attempt by the U.S. Army, The Tiger was probably afraid for his life if he did not succeed in moving us quickly out of the Manpo area. We didn't know at the time of Kim Il Sung's broadcast statement that anyone could be shot on the spot for being a traitor—and in the insane atmosphere that existed in North Korea in the fall of 1950, anyone could be branded a traitor if he didn't carry out orders. The fear we all felt may have been part of the overall plan under a Communist government. "Fear permeates everyone in such a society, from the ruler down to the most abject subject. The Reds arranged their environment in such a way that fear is always present." [2]

The descent was not as easy as we had thought it would be. For some of our very weak members, going down the mountain road proved to be as hazardous as going up. When Mother Thérèse became unable to walk on the slippery melting snow, Father Crosbie and I helped her. But the snow had stopped, and an almost mild wind was blowing. The sky began to clear, and the sun broke through for a short time, giving us renewed encouragement that there would be no more snow for that day.

The Tiger told us as we neared the city of Chasong, that we could rest the remainder of the day and part of the next. We were taken to a schoolhouse where we were given straw to sleep on—more than we had dared to hope for! When we were all inside, Commissioner Lord and Monsignor Quinlan stood in front of the group and expressed their thanksgiving that we were still alive. There was a collective feeling of gratitude to God that we were not lying somewhere back on the road.

When The Tiger came into the room later, Commissioner Lord and Monsignor Quinlan pleaded for transportation for the weak. Apparently still in a humanitarian mood, The Tiger indicated that he would arrange it, and still later that day the children, the women, the old men, and five ill POWs were driven away in a bus and a truck. After that demonstration of concern on the part of the authorities, we felt a little better about our situation.

We departed from Chasong the next afternoon with the main body of POWs. A smaller group of American prisoners was allowed to proceed at a slower pace behind us. We traveled for about ten miles and spent the night of November 5 in another schoolhouse. Trying to find water to drink, I went to a small pond by a well and found that I had to break the ice with a rock. Filling a small rice bowl with water, I heated it on one of the many small fires that the guards had built inside the compound, hoping to kill the germs.

The next day we were able to travel about ten miles. Even though this distance represented only about half the daily amount required by The Tiger earlier in the march, he never harassed us about it, and that night we slept on a heated floor. The Russian prisoners were given the room next to the firebox because they seemed to like more heat than anyone else. .

We spent the next night in yet another schoolhouse. The end of our march being near, The Tiger had some bookkeeping to do. He called Commissioner Lord, Major Dunn, and Dr. Kisch to his room, where he drew up a list of all those who had died or had been killed. After the name of each person was a column listing "Cause of Death." The Tiger made it known that the cause of death for all ninety-eight names would be listed as "enteritis." This was duly translated to Dr. Kisch, who was then ordered to sign the false document.

Dr. Kisch informed us later that he had been required to do similar things by the Nazi authorities of the Hitler regime in Buchenwald and Dachau. He had no choice; to have refused to sign such a document would simply have added another name to the list of those who had died of enteritis. He later explained to me that enteritis is a relatively mild form of inflammation of the intestines and is rarely fatal to anyone except babies.

We arrived in Chunggangjin on November 8, having departed Manpo on October 31. The distance of the march had been variously estimated at 110 to 120 miles. It is difficult to compare one death march with another, but there are certain similarities between the Bataan Death March and our own. Stanley Falk lists four principal reasons that made the Bataan march so tragic, and they apply to ours as well: the very poor physical condition of the American POWs, the unprepared-ness of the captors to handle so many prisoners (North Korea was so devastated at this point that looking after 800 prisoners represented a severe strain on their resources), the cruelty of individual soldiers, and the failure of the leadership of the host nation.[3]

In Chunggangjin we were quartered for a week in an old school-house, where we were met by the women and the elderly who had been transported by bus and truck from Chasong. Helen Rosser came up to inform me that Sister Mary Clare had died after she arrived at Chunggangjin. She placed in my hands a familiar folded light blue object—the sheet that had belonged to Sister Mary Clare: "Here, Larry, Sister Mary Clare would have wanted you to have this," Helen said. There was a kind of unwritten law in our group: once two people had been teamed together on the Death March, the survivor fell heir to anything that had belonged to a deceased partner. I took the sheet from Helen and kept it for more than a year before it wore out.

The temperature was growing colder each day with the arrival of winter, and our march had taken us to higher elevation and away from the sea. At Chunggangjin we vainly attempted to heat the old schoolhouse with a large wood-burning stove, but day and night cold air poured through large openings between the floor and the walls. Dr. Kisch warned us not to sleep with our heads next to the wall because of the increased danger of pneumonia from the cold air. People tried as best they could to stay away from the wall and the inrushing arctic air, but with so many people in the room, it was not always possible to do so. Two or three days after our arrival, I was discussing this matter with Bishop Byrne. "I'm worried about that too, Larry. I've slept next to that wall for the past two nights." I then noted that Bishop Byrne's face was very red.

We drew up a roster of firemen in order to ensure that the stove in the middle of the room be kept burning throughout the night. One night when it was Walter Eltringham's job to keep the fire going, he was supposed to turn over the job to the next man on the roster at midnight. The next morning when we all woke up, we saw Walt seated by the stove, keeping it fired as hot as he could. He had stayed awake all night in order that someone else could sleep. Walter was that kind of person. We rearranged the schedule after that so that Walter's shifts began at midnight; that way, we could be sure that he slept at least part of the night.

Walter's face, like Bishop Byrne's, was beginning to look very red, a possible indication of pneumonia. I asked him one morning how he felt, and he replied, "If I could drink about a half-gallon of coffee, I think I would be all right."

"But Walter, you may need medicine. You don't look well to me," I said. We both knew that there was no medicine available. His black eyes pierced me for a few seconds before he answered.

"Listen Larry, I have talked it over with the Creator, and it's all right." His stare was impossible to read, and his remark was ambiguous. I wanted to know what he really meant by it, but I was reluctant to ask.

The morning after our arrival at the schoolhouse in Chunggangjin, we were ordered to fall out and exercise in the below-freezing weather. The Tiger believed in exercise as the cure for our health problems. That first morning, Commissioner Lord and Monsignor Quinlan tried vainly to persuade one of the Communist officers that exercise under such conditions was madness. The argument was still going on when The Tiger arrived on the scene. It did not take him long to make his point: he pulled his pistol and placed it to the head of Commissioner Lord.

At first, The Tiger ordered everyone to exercise. He would show up every morning to see that all the civilian prisoners at least made their appearance in the courtyard. After that he would walk to the POW compound and personally supervise the American military prisoners in their exercise.

The first morning of the exercise, Father Villemot was carried out into the freezing cold, even though he could not stand on his feet. After everyone was outside, The Tiger permitted Father Villemot, Mother Thérèse, and Mother Mechtilde to return to the schoolhouse. But Fathers Antoine and Julien Gombert, though both very ill and in their middle seventies, were required to remain out in the cold and go through the motions of exercising. We could not convince The Tiger that they should be excused.

The Gombert brothers were French priests who had arrived in Korea around the turn of the century. When I had first met them at the schoolhouse in Pyongyang, I was struck by the fact that they spoke Korean even to each other.

Father Villemot died on November 11. He was followed two days later by the Gombert brothers, who had wanted to die at exactly the same time. They almost made it—they died within twenty-four hours of each other.

The French nuns came into captivity better prepared than any of us. When they were arrested in July, they had been instructed to wear as many clothes as possible. Some of them arrived in North Korea wearing as many as five petticoats. They were always making items of clothing for someone else from the extra cloth the petticoats provided. Every morning one could see them with their backs against one wall sewing feverishly to make socks for others. Concern for their own welfare did not seem to be a part of their agenda.

Mother Thérèse came over to me one morning with Monsignor Quinlan as interpreter. "Monsieur Larree, why are you not wearing socks?" she asked.

"Mine have worn out," I told her.

"Then we will make you some right away."

"That is very kind of you, but there are others here who need them more than I do. You can wait a little while about making mine."

"I have to work quickly because I haven't much time."

"What do you mean, you haven't much time?" I asked. I was a little suspicious of her answer.

"Because I'm not going to be here much longer," she replied. Then turning around and pointing to the French nuns busy with needle and thread, she added, "And they may not be here very long either." I didn't say any more. About twenty-four hours later, I was given a beautiful pair of padded socks to wear through the long winter. I regret to say that she was right: she did not have much time left.

One of the worst jobs at that time was the task of bringing water from the Yalu River, about half a mile away. The job fell to the POWs, and we civilian prisoners were not allowed to help them. I recall on several occasions seeing men arrive at our camp pulling an oxcart containing a barrel of water. Many of them, wearing summerweight clothing with a thin jacket and worn-out shoes, were wet to the skin. Yet these men were often joking and laughing in spite of it all, in an attempt, perhaps, to keep up their courage in the midst of a desperate situation. I was surprised months later to see some of them still alive and as healthy as anyone else.[4]

The town where we were located was attacked from time to time by F-51 Mustang fighter aircraft firing machine guns and rockets. The Koreans were so afraid of American aircraft that they ordered us to evacuate the schoolhouse and spend each day in the nearby hills. Everyone complained to the officials about such a prospect, and in one of those few times when we won an argument with the Communists, our view prevailed. I suspect that even they hated the thought of spending the entire day out in the cold.

On November 16 we were told that we would be moved soon, but not how far we would go. After much confusion, Danny, Father Crosbie, Ahmet the Turk, and I were told to go into an abandoned house and wait until we were notified. Walter had been given the option of remaining in the schoolhouse to await transportation, but he elected to go with us. We waited through most of the day, but nothing happened. By that time the weather was growing colder, and we realized that we would very probably make the trip under cover of darkness.

When we entered the old house, Walter had walked over to the far end of the room, turned around, and emptied his pockets of everything they contained.

"I've been a damn fool," he said.

"Why? Because you have come this far and are still alive?" some-

16 Nov 1950

one asked. No one made any effort to pick up what he had thrown on the floor.

"Walt, you had better keep those things; you might need them later on," someone else added.

"I won't need them," Walter replied with a note of finality. No one wanted to press the matter further. We gathered up the items on the floor and placed them in a pile in one corner of the room. Walter lay down and went to sleep; at least we assumed that he went to sleep. He never woke up again.

We had waited in the little room for most of the day when the order came to leave immediately. The thought of marching off again to some unknown destination, especially at night, frightened us. When Danny was unable to awake Walter and we realized that his unconscious state was something more than sleep, we contrived a makeshift litter out of a blanket and carried him outside. It was our intention to carry him back to the schoolhouse, where he could await the promised transportation. There was utter confusion everywhere.

In the gathering darkness, we could see civilian prisoners and POWs marching toward the east. Turning in the direction of the schoolhouse, we found ourselves bucking the traffic. We didn't get far. A captain armed with a submachine gun demanded that we turn around and go with the others.

"But this man is very ill. He is in a coma, and will only get worse if we have to carry him far," we explained. Until that moment, the weapon carried by the captain had been casually pointed nowhere in particular. He suddenly leveled the submachine gun and swung it back and forth in our direction.

"Then carry him until he dies," came the final order.

The captain who had given the command had been trained well. He was the deputy of The Tiger, named by the POWs "Burp-gun Charlie." We turned around and began our march to the east just as darkness was falling. Walter was too tall for the short litter, and his head hung off the end, bumping the ground occasionally. Bishop Cooper appeared and took up the task of supporting Walter's head in his hands.

Very soon we found ourselves alone except for the one guard. In spite of the starvation we had all suffered, Walter was still a very heavy man, especially to us in our weakened condition. We could carry him for only 300 yards at a time before we were totally exhausted. The guard was one of the better ones, but he was very concerned that we were falling so far behind the main group of prisoners and would not tell us how far we would have to march that night. When we asked, he would only say, "Hurry on, it's not much farther."

Soon Walter began to show some sign of movement; he appeared to be trying to get up off the blanket. While two of us supported him, Walter stood on his bare feet and slowly began to walk. We couldn't believe it. His head hung limp, drooping forward over his chest. Although he could not speak, he could walk! Moving slowly forward in the darkness, however, he would suddenly stop from time to time. Even when we tugged at him, we couldn't get him to move. The first time it happened, I didn't know the cause until I felt a slight pull against my left foot. I was standing on Walter's bare right foot on the frozen earth! He never displayed any sign of pain. When I removed my foot, he resumed walking as though nothing had happened.

Walter's ability to walk when he was by all appearances unconscious will always remain a mystery to those of us who were there.

We marched through the night at a very slow but steady pace and finally arrived at our destination. When we caught up with the others of our group, they were standing outside in the cold while guards ran from one Korean house to another, shouting and making preparations. We must have waited about three hours before we were finally permitted to enter our quarters. Fifty-one of us were assigned to a house with three rooms, each about ten feet square. Twenty-seven men were divided between two rooms; twenty-four women and children were placed in the room next to the firebox to give them added warmth. We had arrived at the village of Hanjang-ni.

10. WINTER AT HANJANG-NI

WHEN we entered our new home, we noted that the floor was still warm. Apparently the former occupants had been required to leave suddenly in the middle of the night.

Walter showed no sign of consciousness as we laid him on the floor. With the aid of a small oil lamp, I could see that his eyes were closed. He remained alive until the next afternoon. His breathing was very heavy at first but became progressively quieter just before he died.

A very complex man, Walter was someone you didn't get to know right away. We were all aware that he had deliberately gone hungry in order to give part of his meager food ration to others, and he always did more than his share on every work detail. His outward manner might give you the impression that he didn't care about anyone or anything, but that was only a front. His language was what one could call "salty"; except in the presence of women, he used so many expletives that he could not be quoted directly. But he did communicate three things to those of us who knew him: he was a man of faith, he was a very caring person, and he loved his wife deeply.

When Walt drew near to death, the crowded room became silent. Monsignor Quinlan suddenly spoke up: "What religious faith is Walter? Does anyone know?" There was no answer. "It doesn't matter," he concluded as he made his way over piles of people in the room to reach the dying man's side. In a few minutes it was all over.

Danny removed a plain gold ring from Walter's finger and handed it to Monsignor Quinlan. "There is something written inside that ring. What does it say?" Holding the ring up to the dim light of the oil lamp, Monsignor read and translated aloud three Latin words: "*Mors Non Separabit:* Death Will Not Separate."

Walter was buried the next day about 300 yards south of the village public well, a location that became the burial ground of the civilian prisoners. The POWs were usually buried some 300 yards south of the civilian site. We positioned Walter's grave so that he faced the south—

the direction of the nearest non-Communist land. We buried all of our dead in this configuration with the exception of the Russian prisoners, who requested that their dead be turned to face the east. True, it was only symbolic, but symbolism becomes important when it is all you have left.

The next morning we were ordered out early and marched about a quarter-mile to the village schoolhouse. All prisoners were present: the POWs, the diplomats, the Korean politicians, and the civilians. The Tiger was waiting for us. He seemed unhappy about something.

Walking to the center of the group, The Tiger made quite an impressive figure with his erect military bearing and his jodhpurs. "Please be seated," he said, meaning that we would be required to sit on the frozen earth. Through Commissioner Lord, we indicated that we would prefer to stand if permitted to do so. "Sit down!" The order carried a note of finality. We sat down.

"You are under the protection of the Korean People's Government, and it is our intention to look after you. But you are not cooperating," he continued, coming to the main point of his speech. "Last night, American soldiers were quartered in this school building to get them out of the cold. But they did not appreciate what we had done for them and went to the bathroom inside the building. Americans must be the dirtiest people in the whole world."

The speech became a real chauvinistic diatribe after that, running the gamut from the American bombing of North Korea to the defeat of the American Army in the South. We listened as we were required to do, sitting on the frozen earth. The temperature was well below freezing. It was a long speech, even by Communist standards, but it contained nothing new. I am certain that the speech was intended not to instruct but to punish. It did. Incidentally, since all prisoners had been locked in their rooms on our arrival at Hanjang-ni the night before, those with diarrhea could not wait. But you didn't tell such things to The Tiger.

When the speech finally concluded, we were marched back to our house and given instructions concerning our own housekeeping. We were to cook our own food, draw our own water, and keep the fires going only at night. The wood for our combined cooking and heating would be supplied. The authorities wanted no smoke coming from chimneys anytime during the daylight hours; such was the fear of American aircraft.

We drew up work details and quickly set about trying to make the place livable. Our captors gave us a small hand broom made from the heads of maize stalks. It was decided that the two men with families would be the cooks. Ivan Kilin, his wife, Maria, and three children were Russian; Salim Salahudtin, his wife, Faiza, and six children were Turkish. A rotating work detail was set up to carry water from the public well about 100 yards away.

The keeping of the fire in the kitchen was handled by Dimitri Verosiff, a Russian who was handy at everything. I suspect that at first he didn't believe that the Europeans and Americans could do the job without him. He was difficult to get along with at times but a hard worker who always did more than his share.

The job of fireman was made more difficult because we had to use green wood brought in by the local villagers. When Dimitri became ill, Father Crosbie and I volunteered to rotate the work between us. The task of building a fire took so long that we were obliged to get up at least three hours before sunrise. To check on the approximate time, we observed the position in the western sky of the three stars in the belt of the giant in the constellation Orion. Our job was to get up when temperatures were as low as forty below zero and build a fire without matches, from the few live coals left over in the fire box from the night before using only green wood. At first we were permitted to build a fire only very early and at night.

The ever present guard was there to watch or help if he felt that the job wasn't being done properly. On one occasion, a guard grew exceedingly impatient at my futile attempts to get a fire going. Handing me his rifle, he knelt down and built the fire himself. I wondered how some other guard would have reacted had he entered the kitchen at that exact moment and seen me holding a rifle.

The daily death count began to climb. It was not possible to bounce back from the effects of the Death March on our starvation diet. The weeding out of the weaker ones that had begun during the march continued at an accelerated pace. Nor were all the ones who died among the weakest; some of the POWs were fortunate enough to be quartered in homes with heated floors while others, through no fault of their own, were placed in the schoolhouse. Those who had to live in the schoolhouse with inadequate heating had a much more difficult time of it.

There was medical treatment of sorts, but it was never enough. While returning from a bathroom call one night, Father Crosbie was challenged by the guard on duty who had apparently been sleeping on the job. It was the rule that we tell the guard each time we went to the toilet. When Father Crosbie went out of the house, the guard was probably asleep and woke up just in time to catch him returning. The guard couldn't admit that he had been asleep, of course, so he ordered Father Crosbie, half-dressed, to stand out in the cold as punishment for about thirty minutes. Father Crosbie contracted pneumonia as a result of that exposure and was in very serious condition for a long time.

He was lucky. The only shipment of real antibiotic drugs that we ever received as prisoners arrived just after Father Crosbie became ill. Treated by Dr. Kisch with this medicine, he made a slow recovery. Those who came down with the same ailment when no such drugs were available usually died.

Doctor Kisch had a theory that a great part of our problem in this area was caused by the fact that North Korean medical personnel did not know which illnesses were contagious, or they may have felt incompetent to make an accurate diagnosis of a particular disease. Like everyone else in that village, nevertheless, the medics had to answer to The Tiger for all they did. If they allowed a sick prisoner to remain in a room and contaminate others, they would be held accountable. Faced with such a prospect, they played it safe, assumed that everyone who was sick was contagious, and moved all who were sick to "hospitals" in the village.

The North Koreans had set aside certain houses as "hospitals." I use the word with caution, because about 99 percent of those who were sent there died. They were simply isolated places where ill prisoners were taken to die away from the others.

One such hospital was located about fifty yards from our house. I do not know about the others, but this one was a dilapidated old house with the floor partly caved in. Having no floor, the hospital could not be heated; the ordinary Korean house is warmed by the heat from the kitchen fire that cooks the food. Normally we were not permitted to visit the hospital and give ordinary home care, but whenever we found a guard who would agree to escort us, we would go and do what little we could for the dying. Such visits were infrequent, either because the guards didn't want to be bothered or because they were afraid of exposure to those who were ill.

Food could not be cooked at the hospital, given the condition of the floor, so it was brought from somewhere else. By the time it arrived, it was usually cold and a little short, having passed through so many hands. For some in the hospital, a short supply of food didn't matter. On one of the few occasions when Monsignor Quinlan and I were allowed to visit the hospital, we noticed POWs sitting around not eating their food. When we inquired about it, they answered, "Leave us alone. We know what we're doing." I suppose they did know. They were in the process of escaping from their brutal circumstances in the only way that was available to them. We tried to talk to them, but they pretended not to hear us; after a time they refused to look in our direction.

Knowing what the hospital was like, we tried to hide those who were ill from the authorities. A North Korean officer would come to our house each morning, throw open the door, and demand to know how many were ill and how many had died during the past twenty-four hours. We were successful at hiding our sick for a while until the authorities began to inquire about those who were lying down. Bishop Byrne, Father Canavan, Father Coyos, and Bill Evans were caught in this trap one morning and were ordered to go to the hospital.

Knowing that to send these men to the hospital would be like sending them to their death, Commissioner Lord and Monsignor Quinlan pleaded with the medic, who at length relented and went on his way. But the danger had not passed: a few days later another medic came and again ordered these men to the hospital. The hour being late, Monsignor Quinlan suggested that the transfer wait until morning, but this time the Korean doctor prevailed. In the bitter cold night, Bishop Byrne was carried and the other three walked to the hospital, where they were to lie on straw mats with a straw mat for covering. A single straw mat served as a door, offering so little protection against the cold that the walls of the room were covered with a thick layer of frost. Such conditions would have been sufficient to make most well persons ill.

We were allowed to return to the hospital to take the men a little food from time to time, but the condition of Bishop Byrne and Bill Evans grew worse, and we realized that unless we were liberated soon, it would be too late. Bishop Byrne had spoken of that possibility before he was taken to the hospital. He asked me once if an American aircraft could land on the nearby frozen Yalu River, and I assured him that such a thing was possible. Even in the hospital he clung to the hope that a dramatic rescue might be in the offing. I went with Monsignor Quinlan one night when he took some soup to the bishop. With our support, he was able to sit up long enough to drink most of it. When we laid him back on the straw mat, he remarked that he was waiting for that aircraft to land and rush him to a hospital in Japan, where he would be looked after. The night before he died we found him unconscious and talking senselessly. But occasionally he spoke of already being aboard a medical evacuation plane bound for a hospital in Japan.

The next morning, November 25, Monsignor Quinlan got up early to check on Bishop Byrne. When he returned a few minutes later, he called out through the closed door to Father Booth, "Will'm, Pat's gone to heaven."

Later that morning Monsignor Quinlan and a few of us buried Bishop Byrne in one of the last few graves that we were able to dig in the fast-freezing earth. The Monsignor had earlier placed a light cassock with metal buttons on the body, which he hoped would make it possible to identify the remains at a later time. After conducting a brief funeral service, he turned to me and asked, "Larry, do you think you will ever be able to remember this place?"

I stood up and looked around me. "Monsignor, I don't think I'll ever be able to forget it."

Those contemplating writing a tribute to the life of a great man would be well advised—or so I tell myself—to consider the matter carefully: are you in possession of the pertinent information regarding his life, and do you have the consummate skill to put it on paper? If not, then you had better leave that task to others. Yet it is unthinkable at this point in my story not to observe the passing of Bishop Patrick Byrne with some small note of tribute, however inadequate. The one comment that I will allow myself—the only one I can make with some authority—concerns his pivotal role in addressing our most obvious defect as a group: our lack of unity. In spite of all that happened, he held us together—American, British, French, German, Austrian, Russian, Swiss, Korean, Turkish, Australian, Irish. When Bishop Byrne died, we became splintered, and remained so for some months.

Father Coyos, Father Canavan, and Bill Evans returned from the hospital after a few days, but they were not well yet by any means. Alfred Matti, the Swiss hotel manager from Seoul, and Mother Thérèse died and were buried on November 30. That date sticks in my mind, as it was my birthday and also the last day we were able to dig through the frozen earth. Even then, we were required to spend hours burning several bundles of millet stalks on the surface of the ground in an effort to make the digging a little easier. We labored throughout the day to dig the grave. The guard was so afraid that he came no nearer to us than fifty feet. I regret to say that from this date until the spring thaw, we were not able to bury any who died. All we could do was cover them with snow.

Three other men were not to be with us for long: Father Charles Hunt died on November 26, Father Frank Canavan on December 6, and Bill Evans on December 12, 1950. Ignoring our protests to the guard, Father Canavan, as he was being led away to the hospital for the second time, turned around, waved his hand, and shouted, "This is nothing. You should have seen what the English did to the Irish!" I never saw him alive again. We had attempted to keep up his morale by reminding him that we were going to eat Christmas dinner in the free world. "I'll have my Christmas dinner in heaven," he replied.

After the deaths of Father Villemot and the Gombert brothers, the three remaining French priests began to spend more time with each other. On two or three occasions, conferences among the French priests and nuns were held in a corner of one of our three rooms. They all seemed to participate in these discussions. Sometimes there would be a few tears. They were discussing their chances for survival and sharing their thoughts in general. Conditions in Hanjang-ni in early December 1950 gave little reason for hope that anyone would survive the winter. Indeed, if there was any hope at all, it necessarily had to rest on something other than our living conditions.

I do not know what decisions were reached at those meetings, but after one such conference Father Joseph Cadars stood up, threw back his shoulders and called to Father Joseph Bulteau in a surprisingly loud voice. "Father Bulteau, how does a French soldier die?" The reply came in a thin, crackling voice, "Bravely, Father, bravely."

This dialogue was repeated each morning until Father Cadars died on December 18. Father Bulteau died on January 6, 1951, leaving only Father Coyos of the original six French priests. A Frenchman can cry without having to account for it to anyone; he can also die bravely.

We faced enemies of many kinds in Hanjang-ni that first winter. This may be a delicate matter to some, but if the story is to be accurately recorded, then it should include some mention of the problems of diarrhea and lice.

Our ration of grain that first winter was 600 grams of millet per person per day, or approximately one average water glass full. When cooked properly, it swells to about three times its normal size. About twice the size of a pinhead, each individual grain is surrounded by a hard shuck; hence, cooking millet thoroughly enough for human consumption is difficult. If diarrhea is to be avoided, it must be well cooked so that the shuck is split open by the swelling of the grain inside. Improperly cooked millet caused great problems for us during that first winter. The excessive diarrhea caused us additional weakness at a time when we were being starved by the poor diet. We had no way of knowing how many people died because of diarrhea.

Getting up off a heated floor that was sometimes too hot and going outside to answer a call of nature when the outside temperature was forty below zero was very stressful. Just how often did we have to go outside? For me the average was from six to twelve times each night. I hasten to add that this relatively large number of bathroom calls was true of the first winter only. After we had gained more experience and had better control of the firewood, the problem was not nearly so great. We simply added more water to the grain and cooked it longer.

Dr. Kisch told us that our digestive problems were aggravated by the fact that we had little else to eat in addition to the millet. The vegetable ration during the worst part of the first winter was as little as one frozen head of cabbage for about thirty-five people. We made soup from bean paste (made by a process of fermentation), water, and cabbage. Each person received approximately one small bowl of cooked millet and the same amount of watered soup per meal. During the first winter, we were not allowed to cook during the day, so extra food had to be prepared at breakfast for the noon meal.

One can perhaps visualize how lice could spread through the group in a ten-foot-square room containing ten people. They multiplied so fast that we were overwhelmed by them before we realized that we had a problem. We set aside part of each day to delouse by the light of the morning sun shining through the paper door on the south side of our room. Delousing was simply a matter of taking off items of clothing, one at a time, and searching the seams thoroughly. When you found a louse, you mashed him between your fingernails. We spent about two hours each morning searching for lice when their infestation was at its worst. But there were those who were too sick to delouse every morning, so we were continually fighting the battle. It was not until the coming of spring that we were able to gain the upper hand. Later, when we were able to boil the clothes in hot water and kill the lice eggs, we got rid of them completely.

I suppose the worst problem caused by the lice was one of morale. Those who were very ill were tormented all the time. This added still another problem for anyone who seriously questioned whether it was worthwhile to continue the struggle to survive. For some, the demands of survival were too great.

Perhaps another matter not sufficiently understood is the role of morale in keeping one alive on a starvation diet. The officers and men of the POW group told me that this was particularly a problem among the younger men. We had all arrived at the point where we were no longer hungry—you get that way if you live on a starvation diet for a long time—and prisoners with low morale found that by skipping their evening meal they could ensure themselves a more comfortable night of rest: they could significantly reduce the number of trips to the latrine. Not being really hungry anyway, they found it easy to take this option. Some played this game innocently enough; others became seduced by it. There were many ways to die in our prison camp if there was no will to live.

How does a prisoner will his own death? One method is simply not eating his small ration. Some came to look upon the missing of a meal here and there, and eventually not eating at all, as a way out of their misery. After seeing some of their buddies die the easy death of starvation, they made a conscious decision not to eat anymore. To some of the prisoners the thought of such an apparently peaceful death became very attractive. In the final stages of death by starvation, the individual goes to sleep or into a coma and does not wake up. Once a person was in a coma, he was beyond our ability to help. We had no provision for intravenous feeding. When Walter was in a coma, some of us brought up the idea of pouring food down his throat, but Dr. Kisch rejected the plan: "He does not know to swallow and you will only kill him faster," he said. We never mentioned the plan again when others were dying.

For a time, Kris was losing strength and going downhill rapidly, finally reaching the point where he could not eat all of his pitifully small ration. One day as we stood outside the room, Father Booth asked Dr. Kisch about the condition of various members of the group. The doctor quickly went through the list, coming at last to Kris: "Jensen will not last much longer. He is not eating all his food." About five seconds later the door was thrown open and out hobbled Kris.

"So you think I won't last much longer, do you? I'll show you! From here on I am going to eat everything they give me." Kris was as good as his word, and though it was a struggle, he survived.

What did we think about during that worst winter of 1950? For one thing, we didn't have as much free time on our hands as one might suppose. On starvation diets, we slept much more, upward of eighteen hours out of every twenty-four. Dr. Kisch explained that our excessive need for sleep was a means of preserving energy. Later on, when we were given more food, our need for sleep diminished to a normal level.

In addition to the everyday details of eating, delousing, bathroom calls, and housekeeping duties, we spent most of our time talking, praying, and thinking about home. We often spoke of our identification with the Jewish people in their long history of captivity in Egypt and Babylon. We had a few thoughts about the future but more of the past. We did not care to dwell on the present, and the future might be denied us, but there were always beautiful memories. During that winter of 1950 we relived those memories over and over. There were many thoughts of home which by that time seemed so far away as to be in another world. But often our prayers and daydreams would be cut short by the simple act of falling asleep. Lying on the floor of our room in our weakened condition, we seemed to be living in a kind of twilight zone between sleep and wakefulness most of the time. Unless we were on our feet or actively engaged in conversation with someone, it was next to impossible to sustain a train of thought for very long without drifting off.

I believe that the body reaches a certain saturation point of pain beyond which any increase in those factors that cause pain are not felt in the same order of magnitude. The fact that we were starving to death and not responding to anything in a normal manner would only serve to strengthen my theory. We experienced pain, of course, with each new deprivation and insult to the senses but not to the same extent that we would have felt it had we been living in relative comfort. That proved to be a blessing in disguise. With ten people crowded in a ten-by ten-foot room, of necessity we slept partly on each other. Yet going to sleep was never a problem. Even having to get up and go to the outdoor latrine as often as a dozen times a night did not greatly decrease our amount of rest. When we returned to our room and lay down, we were asleep almost at once.

A starvation diet and one with almost no protein does strange things to the body. The skin becomes dry and hard and has the consistency of parchment. If you pinch it together on the back of your hand, the skin forms a crease, called "tenting," that remains there for several hours. When you rub your hand over your face and neck, you find no oil, even though you have not bathed in months. Dirt has little to cling to on a body that secretes no oil—another blessing.

During the winter at Hanjang-ni, we had very little medical attention. But as Dr. Kisch was quick to point out, without adequate diet even the right medicines would not have saved some of our group. For example, the blisters we all developed on our feet on the Death March were with us for a very long time. Without adequate protein, according to Dr. Kisch, the body does not rebuild tissue. A diet of millet will provide energy to keep you going, but it will not repair the body. The blisters on my feet did not heal for six months. That was also the case among the other prisoners. Father Cadars had fallen during the Death March and cut his hand on a piece of glass. When Dr. Kisch examined the wound a month later, he attributed the lack of healing to a diet with inadequate protein. Father Cadars's death was at least in part due to the injured hand that would not heal, according to Dr. Kisch.[1]

Each of us experienced his own emotional cycles at Hanjang-ni. When someone was down, the others in the room tried to make things easier for him. Sometimes there was an obvious reason, the most apparent of which was excessive diarrhea. At other times, the reason was not easy to pinpoint. For most of us, these periods of depression did not last more than two or three days. If the duration was longer, then the health of that person would usually begin to decline. Should it continue long enough, the individual might not be able to eat all his food, a certain cause for concern. There were obviously many reasons for the death of prisoners, but one could not hope to survive if he did not eat all his food.

I always ate everything given to me, but even so, I reached a point in my general health at Hanjang-ni where I was no longer hungry. There was no doubt in my mind that I was "over the edge," as we called it—a condition to be feared because it was always associated with the latter stages of starvation. The only thing I could do was to keep eating my ration, even though I was not hungry. The crisis passed in about a week, and I found myself in the strange position of giving thanks that I was suffering hunger again.

There were times at Hanjang-ni when survival was just a matter of luck. In our group there were not very many young men who were able to work. Father Crosbie and I usually alternated with Ahmet, Danny, and Sagid in carrying water from the public well. One morning I awoke with a high fever and realized that I should not work that day. Father Crosbie, Danny, and Ahmet were also ill, leaving only Sagid available for duty. But carrying water required two men, since the only container we had was a barrel slung beneath a ten-foot pole. About midmorning the door was thrown open and a guard asked, "Where are the young men? We need water in the kitchen." Commissioner Lord explained that all the young men except one were ill. The guard looked across the room until his eyes fell on me. Pointing his finger straight at me, he shouted, "You! Out!"

Getting to my feet and putting on my coat, I heard some of the women in the next room calling through the open door, "Don't go, Larry. Tell him you are too sick to go out in the cold." I didn't have to think about an answer. "Don't tell him anything," I said as I left the room. "Do you think I want to be sent to the hospital?" Being sent to the hospital was the fastest way to die.

I walked out into a temperature far below zero, but I was so feverish that it felt good. We found that the well bucket could not be used because of the build-up of ice on the sides of the well, so we had to wait there out in the cold for about an hour while the guard chipped away the ice with a piece of metal attached to a long pole. Sagid and I carried water for another hour or so, but I never felt cold. When I returned to the room, Dr. Kisch told me to lie down on the warm floor and cover up for a while. The fever left me in about three days. One could not expect to be that lucky all the time.

The very high death rate among the American teenage enlisted ranks has been the subject of many studies. In one prison camp it was found that the deaths among the very young had been highest at first, possibly because of their higher metabolic rate, and then dropped in the spring of 1951. At the same time, the death rate among the officers, who were older, soared to a new high: "When the last officer's death occurred in August, their percentage had exactly equalled that of the enlisted men."[2]

The Turkish POWs, who suffered no losses among their 229 men, are often held up as an example. It is true that they did what they were supposed to do, and they gave an excellent account of themselves. But the Turks were older professionals, and half of them were not captured until April 1951, by which time the worst was over for all prisoners. The survival rate for U.S. Army POWs captured during that same month was more than 87 percent. Another significant point is that one group of American POWs might have a survival rate twice as high as that of another group captured just a few days before or after.[3]

Morale was extremely important in survival. The British discovered after the war that the units with great traditions of military glory had the best survival rate. The British also found that faith in God gave a soldier an even better chance to survive: "For it was those who believed in Nothing who died squalidly of Nothing at All."[4]

There were some who stole food from their starving buddies, but they were a small minority. And it should be pointed out that those who helped others did not always put their own lives at risk in doing so. Nevertheless, "it was the helpful ones who in the end stood the best chance of survival. No one is sure why."[5]

There are many factors, some of which the individual does not control, that determine whether he or she will survive in a situation such as we experienced. Where every moment of life is pain and death is never far away, motivation becomes crucial: the prisoner without the strong will to survive is not going to make it. Physical size is important: the very large man requires more food to live. Another factor is age:

both the very young and the very old are at a disadvantage. One's sex is significant—women can survive on less food—as is one's general health when taken prisoner. Luck plays a role as well: the temperament of those responsible for your capture, under what circumstances it occurred, what season of the year, and what kind of clothes you were wearing—you might not be given any more for a long time. And your chances are diminished considerably if a guard decides that he just doesn't like you for some reason.

When one is suffering from malnutrition, ordinary illnesses such as flu can be deadly. Many POWs died in a flu epidemic that struck the camp during the middle of the winter at Hanjang-ni. According to Dr. Kisch, the virus had attenuated to some extent by the time it reached the civilian group. Even so, it knocked us out for a week.

The kind of genes that one is born with has to be important in withstanding malnutrition. For example, we learned through experience who and in what order the people of our group would first show signs of beriberi when the food situation deteriorated each winter. The ones who were most affected died very early. Of those who survived, Monsignor Quinlan was usually the first to show the symptoms of swollen feet, face, and wrists. Nell Dyer was never far behind. I was usually the eleventh to show such symptoms.

And then there is another important factor—the inner strength of the individual. In prison we learned to identify this quality in others, but I'm not certain that we can see it in ourselves. It may be in part inherited, it can certainly be taught, and I believe it can be cultivated. I'm going to step out on a limb here, but in my opinion this inner resource for survival should include at least your faith, your values, your goals, and your loyalty to someone or something beyond yourself. This one factor will not save your life if the other forces operating against you are too strong, but it is a great plus.

This inner coping mechanism, however it is defined, is useful in all circumstances of life; one need not be a prisoner to take advantage of it. I have to agree with Agnes Keith that it is the individual who makes the important difference in a situation of stress: "In the end I learned that it isn't the outward circumstances which determine what one can endure, but something in ourself which either breaks, or stays intact, under stress. It isn't the strain, it's the difference in the tensile strength of people."[6]

Social graces can be a poor substitute for character. The veneer of civility may be very thin indeed and, once scratched, may reveal a totally different person underneath. I have seen that thin veneer of civilized behavior scratched away by hunger, cold, pain, and fear. You may come to understand why a particular person does not measure up in a crisis; you may even come to look upon that person with compassion, but you do rejoice whenever you meet someone whose character is sterling; even in the greatest of stress, it remains the same. We came to refer to it as integrity.

We lived on the edge of whatever life we had at Hanjang-ni. The only hope we had in this world was our belief that, in the words of the Psalmist, "I would have fainted, if I had not believed that I would see the goodness of the Lord in the land of the living." If you do not know where the land of the living is, then you must not have lived in the land of death. Sadly, there are many lands of death in this world other than North Korea.

At Hanjang-ni we discovered that Lt. Donald S. Sirman, U.S. Air Force, had brought a Gideon New Testament with Psalms into captivity, the only one we ever saw in prison. At first, we could not understand why it had not been taken away from him. He explained that when he was shot down in his F-80 Shooting Star, the North Koreans were so busy beating on him that they never got around to searching him thoroughly. Somehow two Catholic prayer books and an Anglican Book of Common Prayer had also been retained. Don generously shared his New Testament with us and others. He discovered, however, that one had to be careful about lending anything made of paper, which was in very short supply. The New Testament came back with pages missing from time to time; We were told that some of the prisoners had removed those pages to use as cigarette wrappers.

I am alive by choice. Perhaps I should say that I chose not to die, insofar as I had anything to do with it. For some, there was no will to live. I wondered about those who did not want to live at all. Was I to pity them more than those who fought heroically to survive, only to discover that it was not enough?

For others, there was so much concern for self that little or no thought was given to others. There were some alternatives in that place that I did not like. I think that I witnessed the logical limits of the survival instinct during that winter at Hanjang-ni. I wondered about the humanity of those who had paid such a high price to become a survivor. We lived among a few who had been given much in life but were willing to share very little. From their example, I concluded that to accept and not share is an act of betrayal; to accept much and then consciously choose not to share is the ultimate betrayal.

Here the strategy for survival was clear-cut: to live as peaceably as I could with my neighbors in our crowded room, to do what I could for the group, and to make every day count because it could be my last. In a place where human life appeared to be so cheap, even a simple gesture of kindness by either friend or foe could be a noble act. We were made aware of the sincerity of such acts by the great risks they involved. The thought that someone had enough humanity to put his life on the line for our sake kept us going when all was darkness.

One sometimes felt the guilt of not doing more to help others. At times some of us felt the stigma of being alive. In looking out at the nearby hospital where skeletons with a thin layer of flesh walked out naked to relieve themselves in the below-zero temperature, I felt a sense of guilt at being merely a witness. I wondered if being an observer to all this made me guilty. We were restricted to our house and could go nowhere without a guard to escort us, but that fact did not make me feel any better about what I saw taking place. Then I considered an even more disturbing question: how many steps removed is the observation of a murder, one that you know in advance will take place, from the act of murder itself? I was observing someone about to die because others had not done their duty—those in overall authority for causing this outrage in the first place, and some of the prisoners for permitting their friends to die by default.

Some of the deaths were preventable by the Americans. "There were G.I.'s who would give up a day's food for one cigarette rolled in old newspaper, and—I am sorry, it is true—there were G.I.'s who bought food at the price of another man's life. There were those who worked in the cookhouse and stole their comrades' food. There were those who stripped their skeletic, dying companions, hours before they died."[7]

The types of behavior displayed by various American POWs in North Korea were not new. During the Civil War, Americans in Andersonville prison fought with one another over food. German POWs held in Russian prisons in World War II became listless and died. American and British prisoners in Japanese camps withdrew into unreality, and some became informers.[8]

I suspect that soldiers all over the world are inclined to feel that "if that bullet has your name on it, there is nothing you can do." Fatalism can be a comforting philosophy—it certainly was so to me in the death cell in Pyongyang, where I was expecting to be executed every day. But in that bleak winter at Hanjang-ni where "giveupitis" became a fact of life for many, fatalism turned ugly. Perhaps fatalism is a two-edged sword—it cuts both ways. Perhaps this is too simplistic, but I believe that fatalism and giveupitis may be two sides of the same coin, and they may feed on each other. Fatalism can sometimes enable you to move ahead when your reason tells you that your life is incredibly dangerous.[9] But fatalism can also cause you to give up when all you meet with is defeat. "What's the use of trying? I'm not going to live anyway," was a remark that I heard often in the hospital where people were sent to die.

And they died! They died in peaceful silence, the manner of their death contrasting sharply with the violence they had learned to expect in prison. They drifted away by degrees, the human body being no match for the evil of humankind. Their appearance did not change when they became aware that their own death was near. Only death held the power to remove their suffering.

In such a place, life itself became a holding action. The line between life and death became blurred, as did our emotional response to that which it separated. We shed few tears for those defeated by death. We experienced precious little joy for the victory of life. Daily existence was just you and your witness against whatever they and nature and circumstance could throw at you.

They didn't have to die, not all of them. Some died because their buddies stole their food. Others died because they were not given what we could call ordinary home care. Some were left alone to die because they were unpleasant to be around, not being able to go to the latrine on their own. Many of these deaths were due to the failure of the human spirit. And for some, death became a conscious option in a seemingly hopeless situation.

It is true that the survival instinct is ever at work, but there are other instincts as well. There are times when I thought that I should either rectify the terrible situation in this place or else die trying. The fact that I was still alive proved, in my own mind, that I had not done all that I could do. If I had done everything possible, then either they wouldn't still be dying or else I wouldn't be alive. At times I blamed myself for watching outrages take place and not being able to do anything about them. I was guilty as long as they were still dying.

I was beyond the expression of grief at Hanjang-ni. If we who survived are still compelled to relive those memories even today, perhaps the reason may not be difficult to find. It may well be that during the winter of 1950 our very capacity to accommodate grief was overwhelmed to saturation. We simply could not cry enough to keep pace with the pain. Perhaps the subconscious credited our sorrow accounts with an excess grief, to be withdrawn and expressed at a later date. Powerful emotions lie there, not too far from the surface, needing only the right word or mental picture to cause a flood. We may well be paying the price still for the grief that we could not adequately express back then.

The guards had taken my wedding ring, and my small photo of Frances had been lost. I remember my first wedding anniversary on November 19, 1950. Surrounded in my crowded room by the blackness of death on that anniversary night, I thought, "This must be the lowest. There is nothing more that they can do to me that will be any worse." But my bitterness was tempered somewhat by the gratitude I felt that Frances had escaped from Seoul.

Having to go to the public well every day, we often met the POWs, the diplomats, and the South Korean politicians. We always shared what little information we had concerning the status of the war. Philip Deane, Norman Owen, and George Blake always gave us very interesting rumors. Owen repeated his "Home For Christmas" motto until Christmas Day!

Until some time in December, we often heard sounds of mysterious explosions in the distance. We were unable to decide what they meant, hearing them was strangely comforting, helping us maintain the naive belief that our rescue by the U.S. Army was near.

Our fervent hope for rescue held one glaring error. We did not know, fortunately, until after our release in 1953 that any such attempt by the U.S. Army or anyone else would have greatly jeopardized our lives. A standing order had been issued to all commanders of the Korean People's Army that all prisoners were to be killed if there was any possibility of their being rescued by the enemy. There is now ample evidence that the order was generally carried out.

Only Nell Dyer had considered that such a thing could happen to us, on the basis of her experiences as a prisoner of the Japanese in the Philippines during World War II. In Jui-am-nee, when the rest of us were dreaming about our immediate rescue, only Nell took a negative view. She told us that it had been necessary for the American forces liberating the Philippines to take swift action as they neared the prison camps to prevent Japanese guards from shooting the American prisoners. To preclude such an outcome, American forces made a dramatic rescue at Los Baños on February 23, 1945, involving paratroopers and sea, land, and air units.[10] Some American POWs were shot by North Koreans, but I don't think any of us believed at the time that we were in that kind of danger at the hands of the Communists.[11]

Major Dunn and Dr. Boysen were escorted to visit us from time to time, and through these contacts we were able to keep abreast of the condition of the GIs. They tried to reassure us, but the cart loaded with corpses moving past our hut each morning told a different story.

To be a leader under The Tiger was one of the most dangerous jobs of all. One day The Tiger ordered Commissioner Lord to confess his crimes. Not knowing what his crimes were, Lord refused and was placed in a cold room. When the Communists demanded that you confess your crimes, they were really ordering you to submit totally to their discipline. It was a little object lesson in humility that could be played by anyone in authority at any time. In order to prove to them that you were sincere, you might even have to confess to crimes that you hadn't committed. In playing this game, both sides got something in return. They received your recognition of their superior position over you: your confession implied that you were willing to continue the relationship as before but with renewed commitment on your part. If they accepted your confession as heartfelt (you didn't have to be actually guilty) and granted you their forgiveness, your position was reaffirmed.

Of course, should they wish to get rid of you, they could use your confession of guilt to accomplish their purpose. The process that brought all of this about was so traumatic and placed the prisoner at such added risk that he gratefully grasped the forgiveness offered. The captors ended up feeling reaffirmed; the prisoner ended up feeling grateful. There was, indeed, something in this deadly little game for everyone. "Fear permeates both sides in the Communist confession ritual."[12]

Commissioner Lord understood this system only too well and refused to submit himself to the litany of alleged crimes. For several days The Tiger played a kind of cat-and-mouse game with the commissioner. To help make his point, The Tiger resorted to one of his favorite learning techniques: he drew his pistol, placed it on a table, and demanded that the prisoner confess. "I will confess when you tell me what I have done wrong," Lord responded. Such an attitude was regarded as arrogance and insubordination by the Communists.

Finally, through the intervention of the deputy commandant, called Mystery Man (because he never wore any insignia or rank), Commissioner Lord learned what his crimes were supposed to have been. They were errors having to do with an alleged lack of proper discipline in the civilian group. After taking all of the valuables in Commissioner Lord's possession, Mystery Man said that he would try to appease The Tiger. Whether he actually helped Lord's case is unclear, Commissioner Lord was allowed to return to the group a few days later.

When Lord had been hauled away to the cold room he was not wearing a hat, and Father Booth decided to do something about it. The cold room was only a short distance away, and Father Booth found it easy to slip a hat to the commissioner after dark. The next morning, Mystery Man noticed that Lord was wearing a hat and asked him where he got it. When Lord refused to tell him, Mystery Man came to our house and demanded to know the identity of the guilty person. At length, Father Booth stepped forward and was taken outside and lectured by Mystery Man for several minutes. The punishment ended with Father Booth being kicked in the rear a few times.

There were always those who could manage a smile in the midst of adversity. I went to visit Helen Rosser one day and discovered her in deep thought. "Helen, I think we may soon be going home." She seemed to ignore me at first, but finally, looking at me with a weak smile, she asked, "Which home, Larry, this one or the next?"

With the approach of Christmas, the North Koreans told us that they would do their best to help us celebrate. They informed Commissioner Lord that we would not be permitted to engage in group singing unless we followed the rules. Lord was told to prepare a list of Christmas carols, with Korean translation, and submit them in advance. I recall seeing the commissioner sitting in the room for two or three days preparing the list. Everyone in our group wanted to celebrate. I remember Sagida saying, "We are Moslems, but we would like to sing too, if that would be all right." The Russians in our group, members of the Orthodox Church, also wanted to participate, even though their Christmas does not occur until January 7.

On Christmas Eve some Korean officers came to the house to observe our celebration. We sang until we had used up the prepared list. When informed why we could not sing anymore, one of the officers instructed us to sing any Christmas carol we wished as long Commissioner Lord told him the words in Korean.

The Korean officials seemed to enjoy the singing, but they monitored it carefully. The first time the French group sang, one of the officers recognized that the sound was not the same and asked Commissioner Lord why. When told that the song was in French, they laughed and requested Father Coyos and the nuns to sing some more. Prisoners and Communists alike were enthusiastic when they sang the traditional French carol "Gloria," familiar in America as "Angels We Have Heard on High."

When we had exhausted our repertoire of Christmas carols, the officers requested us to sing other songs we knew. They were puzzled by one religious song that made reference to the nail marks in the hands of Jesus: "What did that song say about Marx?" asked one of them. The officials were in no hurry to stop us and allowed us to sing as long as we wished. What brought the concert to a close was our weakened condition. It was a strange gathering—atheistic Communists celebrating Christmas with Moslems, Russian Orthodox Christians, Catholics, a Jew, and Protestants.

There was peace at Hanjang-ni that Christmas Eve; for a few golden moments we shut out the wickedness of that place. The light shone on those of us who sat in darkness and in the shadow of death.[13]

Was The Tiger an aberration among North Korean officers, given the maniacal climate that existed in North Korea during his tenure? I can't answer that, but I believe that there were certainly other officers who were capable of doing what he did. During the Death March, Capt. Vyvyan Holt once remarked of The Tiger, in typical British understatement, "He's not a man who listens to reason."

Major Dunn told me that he may have had a hand in getting rid of The Tiger. Two inspection staff officers from the central government had questioned Dunn in mid-December 1950 about The Tiger. "I had learned by that time that in the Communist system you don't share your information with others. So I told them exactly what The Tiger had done to us. I knew they wouldn't tell The Tiger what I said." After the two inspecting officers had departed, The Tiger called Dunn into his office and inquired, "What did they ask you?" Dunn replied, "I told them that you were doing the best you could under very difficult conditions." The Tiger smiled and offered Dunn a cigarette. In about two weeks The Tiger had been replaced.

We didn't know it at the time, but we had said goodbye to The Tiger. At first, we refused to believe that he was really gone. (He did come back to our camp for a very brief visit after the first of the year, but he was not the same. He carried no pistol, the real badge of his authority, and he appeared distant and preoccupied.)

What is there to be said about The Tiger? He took life. He caused pain. He destroyed dignity. Under his control we lost our respect and our pride of membership in the human family for a time. Beyond that, he took from us only what we had ceased to value.

11. CHANGE OF COMMAND

THE new commandant came to us in January 1951 carrying no pistol, which was the first indication that he might be prepared to help us; I think he did try. He restricted to some limited extent the beating of POWs by the guards and made an inspection of the entire camp several times each week. Certain problems would remain beyond his control—the starvation diet, woefully inadequate medical service, the lack of warm clothing—but he always gave us the impression that he was trying to keep us alive under difficult conditions. He even gave us lightly padded clothing, but it was not enough to withstand the brutal cold.

The first attempts by the Communists to indoctrinate us at Hanjang-ni were not very sophisticated but did improve as time went on. It appeared to me that Communist propaganda as we knew it at that time should have been divided into two classes. First, there was information—that is, misinformation—about how bad living conditions were in the United States and the rest of the free world; this was for consumption by people living behind the Iron Curtain. Second, there was information for dissemination to the free world concerning how good living conditions were supposed to be in Russia. It would seem unwise to mix up the two classes: you couldn't get anywhere by telling the Russian people how good their living conditions were in 1950, or by telling the Americans how bad theirs were. To have any chance at success, the Communists needed to supply you with information that you might not believe but could not disprove.

The Communists should have known better. They spent days telling the POWs how bad things were in America. "We understand that you enlisted men cannot own automobiles," they said. This brought a roar of laughter. "Why do you laugh? Don't you care that you cannot own a car?" they continued, unmindful of the trap they were in. When told that most of the enlisted men had owned automobiles, the Communists simply did not believe it. They were obviously using propaganda that had been designed for consumption behind the Iron

Curtain. What they needed but did not have at that time was propaganda about good living conditions in the Soviet Union. (There was obviously no use in trying to convince the POWs of the good living conditions in North Korea!) But that kind of information, though certainly false, was months away. In the meantime the Communists blundered ahead, using what was available. They did improve in their manipulative techniques, however, as we later came to know.

The Communists discovered that they were on safer ground when they took up discussions of Marxist-Leninist theory. Most of the POWs had not studied the writings of Marx, nor were they familiar with the terrible living conditions of the working class of nineteenth-century England, where he formulated his economic theories.

A Communist officer who identified himself as Mr. Lee, a former schoolteacher in South Korea, was in charge of teaching Marxist-Leninist theory. Mr. Lee was a soft-spoken intellectual who often came to our group to lecture. He was always very polite and proper; therefore, we tried to show him the same respect—until the question-and-answer period. Then, having been encouraged to be candid, we became rather pointed in our questions. "How can you justify your high-sounding theories with the way we are being treated?" we asked. "Y-e-s-s, we understand that your living conditions are not good at the moment. We understand that you are not getting an adequate diet," Mr. Lee responded. Then, as though to demonstrate that he was knowledgeable about nutrition, he outlined the basic elements of an adequate diet. I don't think Mr. Lee made any converts, but he was one of only perhaps two or three Communist officers whom we did not mind coming to our house.

One of our captors who apparently retained the unqualified right to beat prisoners was Mystery Man, the one who wore no sign of rank or insignia on his uniform. (The POWs called him "Gooseneck" because his neck was long and slightly cocked to one side.) He continued to beat and generally abuse POWs from time to time even after the departure of The Tiger. On one of his visits to our room I asked him about the welfare of Sergeant Tex Kimball; I had heard that Tex had been badly beaten by M.M. Reacting to my question, M.M. turned quickly in my direction and shouted, *"Kimpall cha-ill cho-tow nigh."* A mixture of bad Korean and Japanese, it means, "Kimball is the very worst of all." So saying, he turned his back and walked briskly away.

Before the war the South Koreans held in prison those suspected of being Communists; the North Koreans arrested those suspected of harboring any ideology other than Communism. As the North

Koreans captured each town in their attack on South Korea at the beginning of the war, they opened the prisons, and the former inmates became instant heroes. One guard (I'll call him "Kim"), had shown kindness to me on the Death March—a very rare display of humanity from a North Korean. Given the climate of hostility and paranoia that existed in the land, showing any concern for the enemy was a very dangerous thing for a North Korean to do. In fact, no guard was left with us for very long because of the fear of ideological contamination from the prisoners. But I suspect that Kim had already been "contaminated" by someone else.

Kim had been a political prisoner in the South Korean city of Kaesong before the outbreak of the Korean War, and there he had come to know Rev. Lyman Brannon, who had lived near me in Kaesong. One day during the Death March, Kim told Kris and me that he had met Brannon often in prison, where the clergyman had conducted weekly worship services and taught Bible classes for the inmates. When I told Kim that the Reverend Mr. Brannon had officiated at my wedding in Seoul seven months before the outbreak of the war, he became even more interested.

In Hanjang-ni I had not talked with Kim for several weeks when late one day he appeared at our house escorting a young American soldier known to us only as Charlie from Louisiana. Charlie had requested permission to visit us, and Kim had graciously agreed to escort him (Charlie would not have been permitted to visit us on his own). As we talked with the guard, Charlie noted that Dimitri was having difficulty lighting a fire in the kitchen to cook the evening meal. Without dry wood, we always had a hard time getting a fire started.

Koreans normally gather their winter wood supply in the summer and early fall to give it sufficient time to dry properly before it is used. When we arrived, the authorities ordered the local villagers to supply us with wood. Not wanting to deplete their own fuel supply, they cut green wood in the nearby forest. The first few days after our arrival, we had pulled dry pieces of wood to use as kindling from the little privacy fence that surrounded our house. The Tiger had put a stop to that, and all prisoners had been warned not to take wood that belonged to the inhabitants of the houses in the village.

Either Charlie had not heard about the order or didn't think Kim would mind if he helped Dimitri out with a piece of wood from the fence. Kim had his back turned to Charlie as he talked to us, so he didn't see what Charlie had done. But Charlie was observed by some North Korean guards who were doing close-order drill in a nearby field. "Look at that!" they shouted to Kim. "What are you going to do about it?" Kim seemed stunned at first and hesitated for a moment. The other guards continued shouting for him to punish the offender; they had, in fact, stopped drilling and were all standing and looking in our direction.

Had Kim refused to act decisively, he would most certainly have had to answer for not doing his duty. In the maniacal atmosphere that existed in North Korea at that time, he had to demonstrate his loyalty by acting resolutely. He took the stick away from Charlie and beat him severely across the head and back. When the ordeal was over, Charlie could hardly walk. Kim helped him back to his quarters, but Charlie died within three days.

About a week later, a group of us were standing on the west side of our house trying to keep warm in the afternoon sun when we saw Kim approaching. At first he merely greeted us and then walked slowly about the house and nearby storage buildings, as though he had other business. We later realized that he was making certain no other guards were around. He then came back to our little group and asked how we were doing. We had a standard answer to that question; we said we were doing all right.

Kim quickly changed the subject. "I'm sorry I had to beat that American soldier last week. But he was observed by others disobeying the rules, so I had to punish him." So saying, he looked at each of us in turn. No one said anything. We could see pain written on his face as he continued: "If the other guards had been near enough, they would have punished him. They expected me to do the same. What else could I do?" He paused again, as though to give us a chance to say something in return. We didn't know how to respond.

What do you say to a man who has beaten your friend to death? The country he represents has made you his enemy, and he says he is sorry for what he had to do. Does one try to make it any easier for him by offering forgiveness? Kim obviously wanted some word from us that we understood. I think that we should have said something, but we didn't. We had become so traumatized by the actions of irrational people that we couldn't respond properly to a person who was desperately trying to establish some kind of communication with us. He turned to me, spoke some kind words about Rev. Lyman Brannon, and left. I don't recall seeing him again.

We thought a long time about what we had just witnessed and decided that for one thing, the good people in this country didn't have a chance. No one there felt secure enough to show any dissent. In that unhappy land, one had to learn to expect abuse from the zealot and the uncommitted alike. And we thought of Charlie, the innocent victim, a captive in a country whose citizens were suspect for displaying basic kindness. And we thought of those Charlie had left behind. Would it make any difference to them to learn that Charlie had been killed by an unwilling enemy? We could not decide. We thought of Kim as well—a young man on the wrong side in this war, tortured by conflicting ideologies.

Soon after my return from North Korean captivity, I shared part of this story with Lyman Brannon in Headland, Alabama, where he was living in retirement with his wife Myrtle. Brannon remembered the young man that he had visited in the Kaesong prison before the Korean War, but he couldn't recall his name. I didn't tell him the bad part of the story—the part dealing with Kim beating Charlie to death; I was afraid that it would make him sad. But now I wish that I had told him the whole story before he died several years ago. Under Brannon's teaching, Kim had probably become a Christian. Then, perhaps without intending to do so, he had killed a helpless man in order to protect himself from charges by his peers of being soft toward Americans. It was a tragic turn of events, but one that I think the clergyman would have understood.

Around the middle of January some of our group began to notice swelling around their wrists, ankles, and eyes. Dr. Kisch immediately diagnosed the ailment as beriberi, a vitamin deficiency disease: "If you don't get adequate vitamin B-1, this condition may get worse." The condition did get worse for some people. Doctor Kisch told some of us privately that the swelling could cause death when it reached the heart. We never had much confidence in the Korean medics, but we showed them the evidence of beriberi on their next visit. They painted all the swollen areas of the body with iodine and prescribed aspirin. Doctor Kisch was outraged: "Can you imagine treating a vitamin deficiency disease with iodine and aspirin?" he demanded.

The next day, however, some Koreans arrived with soybeans and instructed us in the best way to prepare them. After soaking the soybeans overnight, we ground them on a stone grinder. This operation gave a thick creamy mixture which, when mixed with water and boiled for forty-five minutes, produced a very fine soup. To the surprise of almost everyone, the swelling caused by beriberi began to disappear overnight. From then on we resolved to beg, borrow, trade for, or steal soybeans at every opportunity, and we were able to trade part of our grain for them from time to time. Later, we discovered that the milk from the soybeans could be curdled and made into cheese. When allowed to stand overnight, a bowl of soybean milk would develop a top layer of something resembling cream. The soybean became a necessary part of our ration. We could not sing its praises enough, because we felt then, as we still do, that it saved our lives.

We continued to exchange rumors (there was very little real information) with the POWs, diplomats, journalists, and South Korean politicians at the public well. Good news of any kind was hard to come by. On one occasion we were told that Philip Deane, the journalist from England, had been very ill. At another time George Blake and Norman Owen, both from the British legation in Seoul, shared some so-called information that cheered us up: Blake told us that peace talks to end the war had begun and that we would be going home soon. This same news was given to us a few days later by a North Korean officer. Not until years later did I learn that peace talks in Kaesong, and later Panmunjom, were still months away.

There is no way of knowing whether the North Koreans actually knew that their information was false. One might speculate that the local North Koreans, alarmed at the death rate in the camp, put out that false rumor to give hope to the prisoners. American guerrilla forces operating behind Japanese lines in the Philippines during World War II had similar problems: according to Philip Harkins, they could not rely on most of the news that was brought in by the Filipinos. "And to find out it isn't true is quite a letdown. Moral: don't listen to rumors."[1]

I wouldn't go quite that far. I think rumors helped some people keep fighting to survive when there was precious little else to keep them going. But the prisoners had to walk a fine line here; to believe too much too soon was to set ourselves up for great disappointment. "Perhaps we could not have lived without these false hopes, but we lived miserably with them."[2]

Some people in our group were always saying that we would be released by some arbitrary date and that if we were not, we would all be dead. Then they would become very despondent when the predicted date arrived and we were still in prison. "We lived at high tragedy level because we expected release to come, the war to end, or ourselves to be dead, quite quickly. We could not conceive of living in these conditions for years."[3]

There were often disputes within the group, coupled with hurt feelings. Our greatest source of friction concerned living space. Our allotted spaces in the room were marked on the ceiling, not on the straw mats on which we slept, because they were constantly shifting. I have seen grown, rational men argue over encroachment to the extent that they would resort to the use of a crude plumb bob strung from the ceiling. It would be unrealistic to expect people to live under so much stress for so long without some conflict, which always remained verbal. Considering our circumstances, I am surprised that there was not more. The reason may have been in part that because of starvation, we had so little strength left at that time; it takes energy to argue. Moreover, then there comes a realization on the part of most prisoners after a time that strife is counterproductive. "One thing only bound us to comparative peace: the lesson that life was hideous if we surrendered to our hatreds; more livable only when we tried to be decent."[4]

Every nationality would occasionally have its own problems. We Americans and Europeans sometimes had difficulty getting along with the Russian prisoners, particularly if we accidentally stepped on or even touched them at night during our coming and going in the very dark and crowded room; when this occurred, they communicated their displeasure not so much in words as by kicking. I accidentally touched Kijikoff's foot one night as I returned from a bathroom call, and he gave me a terrific kick that landed just behind my knees. The blow knocked me off balance, and I fell backward right on top of him. He didn't say a word. Perhaps he was too surprised to respond, or he may have thought that for once his colorful vocabulary was not equal to the task.

But the Russians didn't always live peacefully among themselves either, and their disagreements produced far more fireworks. While Kijikoff could be irritated by almost any word or act from an American, Briton, or Frenchman, it took another Russian to make him really lose his temper; he would fill the air with Russian expletives for a full minute without repeating himself. But his greatest anger seemed to be directed against inanimate objects that stood in his way: a button on his own coat that refused to cooperate was summarily ripped off and then replaced; a stick that tripped him up outside the door was not simply tossed out of the way but beaten into small pieces with a large rock; a nail that projected just far enough from a doorway to snag his pants was pounded with a hammer so thoroughly that even the head could no longer be seen. Kijikoff was quick to anger, but like all the Russian prisoners, he did forgive. Poor Smirnoff was often picked on by the other Russians to the point of tears; if things went too far, he would go for the nearest weapon, usually a stick, knife, or ax. But it was always a standoff, pure posturing. No one ever won; no one ever lost.

On February 2, 1951, the diplomats and journalists were taken away by a group of North Korean officials. We assumed that they were on the way to better prison conditions because of their relative importance. We later learned that we had been incorrect in that assumption. The Communist officials then decided to move part of the civilian group into one of the rooms vacated by the diplomats. Six of us were selected for this honor: Commissioner Lord, Danny Dans, Dr. Kisch, Father Crosbie, Smirnoff the Russian, and me. The selection was entirely that of the North Koreans: we could never determine how they arrived at it. But the move did enable everyone to have a little more room.

In our new location I had an experience one night that caused me to appreciate Mr. Moon. The South Korean politicians lived in the same house as we did, occupying the middle room (oddly enough, the authorities had permitted an old Korean man and woman to remain in the first room of this same house next to their kitchen). One night as I was returning from a latrine call, I was challenged by the guard. I suspect that the same thing had happened a few weeks earlier to Father Crosbie: the guard had been asleep when I left the room and simply did not hear me when I shouted out where I was going. Not being willing to admit his error, he charged that I had not told him what I was going to do. He ordered me to stand outside in the cold as punishment. The floor on which we slept was so hot that we never wore very much in the room, and most of us simply went out to the latrine wearing our indoor clothes. That proved to be a mistake for me on this occasion. Standing there in the below zero-temperature, I shouted for Commissioner Lord, who dressed and came outside to see if he could help. The guard wouldn't talk to him.

After a few minutes, however, I heard someone stirring in the middle room. Then Mr. Moon appeared and addressed the guard; he continued to talk even though he received no response for several minutes. Mr. Moon was smart enough not to tell the guard what he suspected had happened. We had often found the guard asleep when we went out. Instead, Mr. Moon said that I had forgotten to shout out my intention as I left the room. Finally the guard permitted me to go back inside, after I told him that I was sorry.

In our down moments at Hanjang-ni we fought daily battles with ourselves. Such inner struggles covered everything that was important to us. The following are a few that I fought.

If you ask me if there is a God, I can answer, yes. I talk to Him from time to time, and He is always present in this place. He is not always present in the free world.

If you ask me where the free world is or if it exists at all, I cannot tell you except from memory. Sometimes the memory grows dim. I do not hear from the free world. If it acts on my behalf, I am unaware of it.

I don't know whether the people I love are alive or not. In any case, the separation from them is complete as far as this world is concerned.

I look out at the people who call this home and I see misery, poverty, and death all around. They must feel what I feel because they suffer as I do. Do they get used to it? Do they have other resources for coping with this madness?

Cut off, isolated, manipulated, starving, and deprived of freedom, I no longer respond to anything in a normal manner. But the survival instinct works whether you think about it or not. What can one do to live? How does one go about prolonging life in a place where life means so little to those who have the power of life and death over you? What does life mean in the Land of Death?

It is said that you have hope when all else is taken away. But before hope there must be faith in something.

I wonder if I am going to live. If not, then I would have been better off to have been executed in the death cell in Pyongyang. There is more honor in dying when you are still living and thinking like a human being. I do not so much resent their taking my life. But I do resent their requiring me to live like an animal in order to live at all.

I make promises to myself about what I will do if I am ever free again. But will I be able to keep them? What is the nature of those promises? In the main, they have to do with time and what I consider to be important. Those you love become closer to you. They are important. Will I be able to keep these promises? Are some of them really all that important? Some of them are magnanimous, but others are frivolous.

You have no value in the eyes of this land. To look and see an armed man deliberately walking in your direction is to be made aware of your own mortality. Every person who approaches you has the power to do you harm. Even the common citizen can abuse you. The soldier can beat you, and the officer has the power of life or death over you. A frown on the face of any person in authority is at best a cause for concern, at worst a reason to say your prayers.

The job that we dreaded more than all the others was that of going to collect our food rations. There were two reasons: one, waiting for more than an hour in the bitter cold; and two, watching the guards abuse the American soldiers as they also waited in line. Some POWs were struck occasionally with a rifle butt; others were sometimes kicked, often until they fell to the ground.

Watching the North Koreans sport with the Americans was one

thing; standing by helplessly as some of the POWs cooperated with their enemy in humiliating themselves was another. The guards knew what to do; they would often throw down a cigarette butt and watch the POWs fight over it. Some who were thus wrestling on the ground were so weak that they could not stand by themselves. The American officers were powerless to do anything because they were being held in separate huts.

Even in our depleted condition, we were able to give an account of ourselves against the ideological attacks of the Communists. Father Booth, especially, delighted in looking for chinks in the armor of their reasoning; they were not hard to find. Near the end of one lecture given by a Communist official, we were asked to raise questions. Father Booth jumped at the invitation.

"Do you mean to say that all your Communist theories are perfect?" he asked.

"No, some of them are not. But we have the means to make them better," the instructor replied.

"Well, do you mean to say that all capitalistic ideas are bad?" Father Booth pressed on.

"Of course not. There are some high ideas in your system. But they cannot be made to work because of the greed of Wall Street."

"Well, there are some pretty low ideas in your system," Father Booth lashed out, visibly angry.

"Yes—but you must understand that the lowest Communist idea is still better than the highest capitalistic thought." All of us laughed out loud, and the lecture was immediately concluded. There was even a slight smile on the face of the Communist teacher as he turned and left the room.

Commissioner Lord used a very effective technique on several occasions to break up abusive antireligious lectures. "Honorable teacher, some of the founders of Communism were very great men," Lord would begin, making them feel proud.

"Thank you for those words. It is very kind of you to recognize the greatness of our leaders," the Communist officer would reply.

"Then how can you say that such men as Marx, Engels, and Lenin [he didn't mention Stalin] have died and have been put into a hole in the ground like a dog? Do you mean that there is no other life for such great men?" He was taking issue with the traditional Communist teaching against life after death. At about this time there would always be a slight pause while the Communist official thought of an answer. He was plainly on the defensive.

"Well . . . yes . . . that is all true, but such great men will live on through their teachings and influence." So saying, the teacher would usually bow low and take his leave.

To make the time go faster, we continued to share personal experiences, subjects that we had studied in school, and general information. One day I asked Dr. Kisch if he would tell us the story of some well-known opera; he must have known all of them almost by heart. He agreed but added that he wanted to wait until after dark; later he told us that he was too embarrassed to sing opera if we could see his face. It was an arrangement that worked out in a wonderful way. Night after night we were treated to the sounds of the arias of famous operas; *Tristan and Isolde*, *Carmen*, and *Faust* seemed to be his favorites. He would include narrations between the arias to keep us abreast of the story.

In addition to Walter, who had already died, there was another man in our group for whom personal survival was not always a major consideration. Monsignor Quinlan would sometimes try to give away part of his food ration on the grounds that he was not hungry. Most people refused his offer because they knew what he was doing. Father Crosbie and I made it a point to be nearby when the Monsignor ate. We couldn't prevent his making the attempt to give his food to someone else, but we did make the recipient of that gift feel so ashamed that he would not accept it again.

"Honorable teacher, it is very difficult to talk to you about this, but we prisoners are worried about our welfare here when the spring thaw comes." So began Commissioner Lord's speech to one of the Communist officials who had come by our house one day in late March 1951. "Many bodies are buried under a few feet of snow near here," Commissioner Lord went on. "That snow will begin to melt in a few days. Our situation could become very unsanitary if we remain here much longer."

The Communist officer looked at Commissioner Lord as he answered, "You need not trouble yourselves about this matter. We are well aware of it. We are perfectly capable of looking out for your welfare. Lay your mind down [don't worry]. We are responsible."

Apparently we were in complete agreement with the authorities on this matter. Previous to this discussion, in fact, we had observed guards shooting at dogs in the neighborhood. One of the guards had told us that no dogs were permitted in the area for fear they might disturb the bodies of the dead.

We departed Hanjang-ni on March 29, 1951, in a totally different mood from that in which we had arrived the previous November. We had come in the middle of the night, exhausted, frozen to the bone, starved, and half-carrying Walter Eltringham. Now, we had mixed feelings. We were leaving behind most of our group in shallow, unmarked graves of snow, but for some reason we felt optimistic. There was a great confidence on the part of everyone that we were going to something better. One reason might have been the weather: it was a glorious springlike day. Even though snow still covered the ground everywhere except on the road, the air was clear and warm, giving a promise that spring was near. I think all of us felt that if we could make it to the spring, then we would be able to survive what followed.

First the POWs were moved out and headed southwest, in a direction that took them back down the Yalu River toward Chunggang-jin. Their deteriorated condition pained us as we observed their ragged clothing and hollow-eyed look. Some of the weaker ones were stumbling along on their own; others were being half-carried. But they too reflected the optimistic mood.

The civilian prisoners were told to bring up the rear. Father Crosbie and I were assigned by one of the guards to walk last to assist any who might drop out. None did. The pace was very slow, and we were not hurried by anyone. We stopped and looked back several times as we marched away from the village, and I tried to think about what we were leaving—the bodies of 200 to 250 people, most without proper burial—but my mind went blank. I wanted to move ahead to our new camp, wherever it might be.

The sun was shining on the white snow that lay all around us. Melted snow was trickling across the narrow road that had been made mushy by the rising temperature.

Even though we were still losing people daily, our departure from that terrible place seemed a sign that we would one day see the land of the living. Any change has to be interpreted as a change for the better when one has so little else to go on.

12. DIGNITY AT AN-DONG

OUR march took us through Chunggangjin and back down the road that parallels the Yalu River in a southwesterly direction toward Manpo. We had seen it all the previous autumn on the Death March, but even the most pessimistic of our group did not believe that our present trip would be as long or as bad. After walking for about four miles, we turned to the left and followed a road that led up a relatively wide valley. About two miles farther along we could see our destination on our left, an old Japanese army camp from pre–World War II days.

The camp was built in the shape of a square with large, sturdy wooden buildings located around the perimeter. The central area was open except for one small building. The entire complex, roughly 800 by 400 feet, was surrounded by a barbed wire fence only about five feet high. Obviously the North Koreans felt confident that they could rely upon their guards, the weakened condition of the prisoners, and the great distance from the front lines to discourage any escapes. It was a confidence that proved to be well-founded.

There are many reasons why more Americans didn't escape in North Korea. To begin with, most American prisoners had been marched many miles to POW camps near the Yalu River—hundreds of miles from the front lines—and usually arrived so starved that they had difficulty walking on a level road. The average POW may have been wounded before capture or by that time so severely beaten by his captors that setting off to cross the mountains of North Korea was out of the question. The steep mountains covered with thick undergrowth made movement by night—the only time an escapee could expect to travel—exceedingly difficult.

In addition, North Korea was an enemy country made up of people who didn't look like most Americans. One could identify Americans in North Korea from a considerable distance just by their size and manner of walking. Forged documents, even if we could have gotten them, would have been no help.

Escape is difficult if one is not among friendly nationals. Allied airmen shot down in France during World War II could expect the French to offer them food and a safe haven; many were moved by the French resistance to the safety of neutral Spain. American prisoners were given invaluable assistance in escaping the Bataan Death March by the Filipino people, at great danger to themselves.[1] But the American POW in North Korea could not count on such help, or even on acquiring good footwear or adequate clothing to protect him if he tried to escape.

There were some Americans in Korea who escaped just after their capture near the front lines. Also, almost 100 U.S. airmen who evaded capture eventually gained freedom after being shot down behind North Korean lines.[2] One of these was Captain Clinton D. (Clem) Summersill. Though badly injured in the crash of his aircraft, he and his observer, Wayne Sawyer, began their trek south in the direction of the front lines in snow and zero temperatures. After incredible hardships, and with the assistance of a friendly Korean family, they finally reached safety. Both of Clem's feet were frozen and had to be amputated; by special order of General Hoyt Vandenberg, Chief of Staff of the Air Force, Clem was allowed to remain on active duty, however, becoming the only double amputee in the Air Force.[3]

To put all this into some kind of perspective, it should be noted that only one German POW escaped from the British in Canada during World War II. He was able to cross the Canadian border to the then neutral United States and eventually rejoined German forces.[4]

Once inside the buildings of our new quarters, the Russian prisoners were pleased to discover that large woodburning stoves were used for heating. No sooner had we moved into our room than the Russians built a roaring fire in spite of their constant bickering over which of them was most qualified to do so. In fact, throughout the remainder of the cold weather, there was always at least one Russian seated by the stove both to stoke it and to discourage anyone else from opening the stove door. Anyone who might be brave enough to try to add wood to the fire was greeted with the shout, "Shut the door!" For the remainder of our stay in that compound, the rest of us never had to worry about fire-building detail. The Russians had a monopoly on it.

March 31 found us standing outside in formation to receive instructions and food rations. During a lull in the proceedings, we heard a faint roar of aircraft and saw about nine B-29s flying northward at moderately high altitude, perhaps 12,000 to 15,000 feet. They had just passed directly overhead when we saw something black streaming out from underneath each aircraft. At first we did not know what to make of it, but soon we could see the black stream break up into individual objects. "Bombs!" someone shouted. "They are dropping bombs!" There was no panic; everyone could see that the bombs were moving rapidly away from us. Presently we heard the same "swishing" sound that we had heard at Pyongyang when it was being bombed. The bombs disappeared behind the high mountain to the north. In a few seconds there was a continuous rumble of explosions. "They are bombing the bridge across the Yalu River at Chunggangjin!" someone shouted.[5]

Late that afternoon, some POWs returned to camp with the information that they had been in Chunggangjin with a guard to pick up food supplies when the bombing occurred. They told us that part of the bridge had been destroyed and that three POWs and a guard had been slightly injured in the bombing. The guard had been struck on the side of his face by some object hurled by a bomb blast.

The injured guard was returned to duty in a day or so. One could see that though the injury was not serious, it must have been painful. That particular guard was always inclined to be short-tempered and nasty, one to be avoided whenever possible. A few days later we were awakened by the sound of gunfire and discovered that during the night Lt. Donald S. Sirman, the Air Force F-80 pilot who had shared his New Testament with us, had been shot and killed. The story around camp was that Lieutenant Sirman had been shot by the same guard who had been injured in the bombing of the bridge at Chunggangjin. With the exception of Capt. Dave Booker, a U.S. Marine Corsair pilot, Lieutenant Sirman had been the only flyer remaining in camp. There had been several flying personnel a few months earlier, but to my knowledge they were no longer around; whether they had all died or had been taken away by the authorities, I do not know. In any case rumor had it that Lieutenant Sirman had been killed as an act of revenge by a guard who bore a grudge against flyers.

Our stay at the camp at An-dong provided the first real opportunity for POWs and civilian prisoners to get to know one another. At Hanjang-ni we had been able to talk to the POWs only at the public well, and then only if the guard permitted it. We in the civilian prisoner group wanted to learn more about the kind of war they had fought in South Korea and the circumstances of their capture. Seated on the ground inside our compound in the warming spring sunshine, we whiled away many leisurely afternoons in long conversations. The memories of those talks are as pleasant as any I have of prison life. We spoke of home and food and freedom and friends; there was ample time for all to express their views on any subject. Our collective memories were the only sources of uncensored information that we had available, and we tried to make the most of them.

Our common experience was that our own memories of the world as we had known it immunized us against the false information supplied by the Communists about that world. In a peculiar sort of way, we were better informed of general conditions in the free world than the Communists were. Some stories given out by the Communists were so absurd that we simply would not believe them; the Communists did believe them and were therefore misled in many areas. We did not know specifics concerning what was going on in the outside world, of course, but our reason told us when those propaganda stories got too far out of line.

All news supplied by the Communists had to be treated as suspect. Their reports depicted a world that was totally alien to us. They told us, for example, that people all over America were rioting in the streets, that millions were starving to death, and that thousands of American soldiers in South Korea were deserting their units. Had the Communists been more skillful and not exaggerated so much, they might have been more successful at fooling us into believing some of their lies.

We thoroughly enjoyed our conversations with the American POWs, but some of what we heard was disturbing. Invariably, they told of weapons that did not work properly, of walkie-talkie radios that could not be used for lack of batteries, and of an almost total absence of information about the strength of the Communist forces.

The first criticism I heard concerned the combat performance of the M-1 Garand semiautomatic rifle, which had been the standby of American GIs in World War II. Some of the prisoners stated that they had gone into combat with their M-1's still covered in the heavy grease that was applied to such weapons prior to shipment to prevent saltwater corrosion. Others indicated that their personal weapons were clean and should have worked properly but did not. Stories were told of firing the M-1, then hammering the breach mechanism open with a trench shovel, and then firing again. "We could have done better with slingshots," one man said in disgust. Oddly enough, I heard universal praise for the Browning automatic rifle, a relatively complex weapon, or so I had been led to believe in my own basic training days. "We never had any trouble with the BAR," some soldiers reported.

All the POWs I talked to complained about the lack of adequate intelligence concerning the strength and location of North Korean forces.[6] Major Dunn said that in his intelligence briefing in Japan, just prior to being sent to Korea, he was informed that he might confront a few obsolete tanks. Then he told of lying in a ditch by the side of the road at night in South Korea counting some thirty to forty modern T-34 tanks as they moved past him. I heard the same comments from many of the others: "The tanks just kept coming; we never had anything that could stop them." One GI said bluntly, "Our bazookas wouldn't even knock the paint off those North Korean tanks."

Those far more qualified than I have already investigated these monumental mistakes and, presumably, have learned lessons from them. I am in no position to pass judgment or recommend corrective measures. Finding myself a prisoner among those who had to pay dearly for whatever mistakes were made, I feel that they deserve to be heard; I can relate to their frustration.

There were tragedies aplenty at An-dong but none more poignant than those we brought upon ourselves. I refer to the practices of trading food for tobacco and gambling for food. Tobacco would have caused no problem in our group if there had been either none at all or an ample supply. Instead, there was just enough floating around the camp, given out by guards to their favorites, that men were willing to trade their lives for it. The practice flourished in spite of the efforts of Major Dunn and the other officers and noncoms to put a stop to it.

Some of the POWs gambled with their food at a time when they were starving to death. Some of these men who were gifted at gambling had won so much food that they could not accept delivery of all of it at one time and were obliged to keep a calendar. On any given day, the winner would inform the loser that he wanted delivery of the food he had won. Together, they would march into the mess hall and sit next to each other at the table. The winner would eat his bowl of millet very quickly while the loser would pretend that he was not hungry. Then they would switch bowls.

I recall many times being seated in the mess hall and observing POWs walking outside just before the food was served, each one occasionally looking through the window to locate someone who owed him a ration of food. If he was successful, he would rush to take a seat next to his debtor victim.

There was really no way to know how many men died because of gambling and selling their food for tobacco. Major Dunn told me that many died from such practices. When one was so near death from starvation, it was difficult to calculate just how much food he would have to miss to be pushed over the edge. At a time when we were dying for so many other reasons over which we had no control, even one unnecessary death was too many.

Although some of the heavy-handed Communist tactics were laughable, I must concede that they were extremely successful in at least three significant areas: their extensive use of informers; their ability to divide the American prisoners, particularly through informers; and their skill in evaluating an American prisoner. After only one or two interrogations, they could determine with considerable accuracy who was most likely to give in: to collaborate, inform, sign propaganda documents, and make propaganda speeches.

The chief weapon of the Communists in dividing the prisoners was the informer system. It was the plan of the North Koreans to know everything that was going on in the camp, and in that they were fairly successful. When you find yourself being punished by the authorities just a few minutes after you have met with a small group of prisoners to plan something illegal, you begin to wonder who you can trust. After one or two such unpleasant experiences, you conclude that your best plan for staying alive is to trust no one. You may be convinced that even though most of your fellow prisoners are loyal and trustworthy, you must still go it alone. Doing otherwise is simply not worth the added risk. Even if there is only a handful of informers in the entire group, you don't know who they are. Hence, every person you meet must be considered someone who can hurt you.

Such a conclusion has at least one more effect: you decide that it may be safe to talk to anyone about food, about the thousand and one menus that everyone is writing and sharing with everyone else, and about your first act on reaching freedom; you won't get into trouble for sharing such trivial things. But you will refrain from discussing those things that could be considered illegal by the authorities: locating extra food outside the barbed wire, obtaining the latest news about the progress of the war from a nearby farmer who has a radio, and assisting someone who wants to try to escape. Yes, such committees to plan escapes and other activities were formed and did operate for a short time, but the informer system soon broke them up.

The fate of those informers and collaborators who were identified was sad. To protect themselves from self-appointed vigilantes, they were obliged to withdraw from the group and spend most of their time in the library, a large room in the camp set aside by the authorities for propaganda material. (It was the only room in the camp where a twenty-four-hour-a-day guard was maintained, necessitated by the fact that prisoners would otherwise take the propaganda material and stuff it down the toilet.) Only in this environment did the "Library Gang" feel relatively safe. They would wander out in groups of two or more on occasion during the day, but they spent most of their time in the library. At An-dong there were approximately twelve of them.

Well after midnight on one occasion, I witnessed the initiation of another member into the Library Gang. Several of us in one room were suddenly awakened by the sound of loud shouting. "Ah, there you are! We know all about you, you—! You've been working for your red points [collaborating with the Communists], have you?" someone screamed out. For light the vigilantes had only a small oil lamp, but they had found and identified their man. The victim protested his innocence until the beating began. No one tried to stop what was going on. It was all over in a few seconds. The next morning I watched as the visibly marked man arose from his place on the floor and walked out the door in the direction of the library, dragging his dirty, worn-out quilt behind him.

To be branded as a collaborator was permanent. There was no higher court to hear your case, even if the sentence was unjust. Two of these collaborators told me that they wanted to return to the group, that they were fed up with the Library Gang. They had made only one mistake, they said, and it had marked them for life. But in a life-or-death prison existence, there is no such turning back, no second chance. At some later time, perhaps those who slept on soft beds in comfortable houses, those who ate a balanced diet and were free of fear and possessed the wisdom of Solomon, could determine who was really guilty.

After the indoctrination began in earnest at An-dong, one of the first moves of the Communists was to undermine the rank structure of the American military prisoners. This they tried to accomplish by dividing the POWs into mixed groups composed of officers, NCOs, and lower ranks and placing handpicked enlisted men in charge. "We are all of equal rank here," they would say in response to those who protested such an arrangement.[7]

Unless chaos was what the Communists had in mind, this procedure did not always work out to their own advantage. The Communist-picked leaders did not have the respect of the group and were therefore unable to maintain discipline. Nor were they able to control the men long enough to march them to the lecture hall for the indoctrination program. After each lecture session began, guards were obliged to move around the compound rounding up stray POWs who had managed to slip through the net.

With the rank structure destroyed, it was not long before discipline in the camp had become unbelievably chaotic. There were other contributing factors as well. Now somewhat limited in their practice of physically abusing prisoners, the Communist officials were not able to keep order for a time. We concluded that the change in the treatment of prisoners was the result of two considerations by Communist authorities at the highest level: first, the recognition, perhaps for the first time, that prisoners had trading, propaganda, and hostage value; and second, the realization that extreme physical abuse would be counterproductive in their indoctrination program. Such restraints on their treatment of prisoners was probably new to the Communist prison authorities. Their training, after all, had been in dealing with their own North Korean criminal prisoners, for whom such humanitarian considerations were unnecessary and irrelevant.

In a more normal prison environment, discipline can be at least partly enforced by the withholding of privileges. But short of the privilege of existing on a starvation diet, there were no privileges in our camp. The Communists now held the stick, but its use was limited, and they didn't have the carrot at all. Our physical treatment changed for the better at An-dong, but our food ration, medical attention, and clothing situation did not improve.

The Communists did have some very useful skills going for them, however, in their ability to evaluate the POWs and quickly determine who was potentially weak. This talent was very useful for an interrogator facing some 300 prisoners. He had to decide, after talking to someone two or three times, whether that person could be useful. Those POWs who were judged to be weak in their loyalties and convictions were marked for special treatment. This special treatment was not something one would desire; it meant being interrogated more than the others. On getting to know some of these men whom the interrogators had chosen, I came to realize how accurate their selection had been.

That is another reason why playing games with the interrogator was a very dangerous thing for a prisoner to do. Pretending to go along was an open invitation for still more interrogations, probably even more severe ones. The best strategy for the prisoner in this situation was to blend into the background as much as possible. You could not become known for any unusual characteristics. Speaking too little or too much in interrogations or indoctrination sessions marked you as someone different. If you were merely seen out by yourself, you could give them ideas. We stayed out of their way and out of sight. We tried as much as possible to look and act like the majority of the group. This was no time for showing off. Such actions could cause problems for you; it could even mean your death.

The general anarchy caused by our new situation was fun at first, but after a time we saw that it was also dangerous to us. The house-keeping duties of the camp had to go on. Food had to be prepared. The wounded had to be looked after under very difficult conditions, and various work details had to be organized each morning. The leaders who had been selected by the Communists were not able to get all these jobs done. Slowly, Major Dunn was able to reassert himself as the senior ranking officer, and the camp became less chaotic.

The Communists knew many ways to manipulate the POWs. With the coming of spring, we kept requesting permission to go to the nearby river under guard to bathe. The authorities never gave us a yes or no answer but merely put us off. Finally one morning they an-nounced that our request was approved. We lined up near the gate, as instructed, and awaited the arrival of the guards. When everyone was in place, the guards gave the order to move out. On arriving at the main gate, we were halted in the customary manner to make certain that all was in order before proceeding. Standing there, I noted an unarmed guard walking toward the gate from the commandant's shack in the center of the compound. It was obvious from the smirk on his face that he would not permit us to go. "We have just received word from South Korea that the ill-bred Americans have killed six brave North Korean prisoners in one of their camps. Therefore, you will not be permitted to go to bathe this morning. You can blame the Americans," the guard announced.

A young American POW standing close to me called out, "Damn those Americans! It's their fault that we don't get to go!" I don't know whether he was trying to be cute or not, but everyone walked away from him.

But there were others who made you proud. One such man who will always stand tall was Sgt. Billy Knowles. On one occasion we were ordered to report in formation to go on wood detail. When Knowles continued to talk after the order had been given to remain quiet, a small North Korean officer ordered him to come forward. After Knowles had been made to kneel on the ground, he was kicked repeatedly about the face and head. All through the punishment, Knowles wore a smile and continued to do so even as he was ordered to return to his place in the formation. Later I asked him why he took such a beating when nothing really seemed to be at stake. "Why did you keep smiling at him as he kicked you?" I asked. "You know that made him mad."

"I don't want these people ever to get the idea that they can get the best of me," he replied. I had thought that no issue was involved; it must have been the price that he had to pay for his own self-respect. His demonstration of courage and spunk, though not something I could recommend to everyone, was one that I shall never forget.

It is one thing to work around the sick when you have all the medicines and conveniences that modern society affords. It is quite another to find yourself trying to look after sick, wounded, and starving men with little or no medicine. Dr. Kisch believed that on our starvation diet, many of our group would still have died even if adequate medicine had been available. One of the factors that makes pain and illness tolerable to some extent is the hope of getting better. Those with major wounds were already gone by the spring of 1951. To languish for nine months in a prison camp with what would have been a relatively minor wound in America is a deplorable thing. I still wonder how people like Dr. Boysen, Jesse Sizemore, and countless others who worked with the ill under such conditions—so little to work with and so much to do—were able to keep going.

At An-dong two different philosophies of survival were formulated. Dr. Boysen, the Army doctor, counseled moderate exercise; he advised that everyone who was able should go outside every day and walk. Dr. Kisch, on the other hand, was of the belief that on a starvation diet we should "conserve our strength," as he put it. He argued that one should expend no more energy than absolutely necessary; he discouraged going out to walk even on a good warm day and spent much of his own time lying in the room or standing by the doorway looking out. Fortunately, most followed Dr. Boysen's advice. I don't remember that anyone survived by following Dr. Kisch's direction to the letter—though of course it would not be accurate to say that following Dr. Boysen's advice was 100 percent successful either. There were some who fought hard to survive at An-dong and did not make it.

In the main, however, the overwhelming evidence favored taking moderate exercise each day, and many people could be seen every evening after supper walking up and down the long length of the compound with Major Dunn. I recall Lt. John Fox walking without shoes; he never seemed to have shoes that were large enough for him. Also, there were Frederick Stumpges, Earl Colby, Waddie Rountree, Charles Minietta, Charles Napier, and many others. It was a valuable lesson that we continued to use throughout the prison experience.[8]

The Communists loved to plan activities that would involve the entire community. The first of several "command performances" was held soon after we arrived at An-dong. The idea, as we understood it, was to provide entertainment for everyone, and in that the Communists were at least partly successful. Everyone was expected to contribute. Whether you could actually sing or not was beside the point. When Major Dunn was called upon to sing, he would enlist the aid of the audience. This was permitted by the authorities. Commissioner Lord would always break into "It's a Long Way to Tipperary." Sagida, the teenage daughter of the Salahudtin family, was the favorite of the troops by far. She could sing songs in several languages. Danny Dans was a good singer, having been an entertainer at an earlier time in his life. Irish songs were led in turn by Monsignor Quinlan, Herbert Marlatt, and Joseph Tarbuck. My contribution was "San Antonio Rose." Dr. Kisch was called upon to play the very out-of-tune piano. Although he did not know modern popular music, he played the classics very well.

One task that most of us were happy to participate in was wood detail. Almost every morning, "The Whip," an old North Korean sergeant, would round up two or three hundred men and women to march to the nearby mountains for firewood. The guards would assemble us on the parade ground and then march us out the gate. We would turn left immediately on the main road and move in an eastward direction for some three to five miles. Other guards—given such names as Iron Pants, Road Runner, and Pig—would accompany us and The Whip on this detail. Yes, Pig knew that he had been so named and seemed to enjoy it. We were provided with a few axes and sickles for this occasion, but most of us had to make do with picking up branches that had already fallen to the ground. Two or three oxcarts were usually provided to haul the wood back to camp.

It was on these occasions that we often saw burial details at work in the field just east of our camp. Digging graves was relatively easy in this field because it had been used for agriculture. (For the record, I would estimate that this burial site was located between 500 feet and a quarter-mile due east of the camp. Approximately 100 to 150 people were buried there.)

It was in casual conversation in the early spring of 1951 that I made a million-to-one discovery. Capt. Marion (Pappy) Green, stationed in Japan at the outbreak of the Korean War, had been ordered a few days after the Communist invasion of South Korea to prepare coffee and sandwiches and take them to the nearby port of Fukuoka. A Norwegian freighter, the *Reinholte,* was due to dock at the port carrying some 700 Americans and other refugees from Inchon. Green's job was to provide support to the Red Cross, who had established a location at the port near where the *Reinholte* would dock. Green told of watching as those 700 refugees, almost all women and children, came ashore with little more than the clothes on their backs. He then spoke of seeing two women rush up to the Red Cross tent and inquire about two American men who had driven to the 38th parallel the day before the Communist invasion. I jumped when he said that. "Pappy, what did those two women look like?" I demanded.

"Well, one was shorter. The other one was tall and thin," he responded. I couldn't believe what I had heard. That would have been the exact description of Maud and Frances—Kris's wife and mine!

Following that encounter, Pappy's unit had been sent to Korea, where he had been captured, taken to North Korea, and placed in a prison camp. The mathematical odds of the two of us ever meeting and discussing this incident must have been exceedingly small.

Commissioner Lord had seen our wives leave on a ship from Inchon at the very beginning of the war. Now, Green had confirmed that they had arrived safely in Japan. I went running to tell Kris the good news. That was one less burden for us to worry about.

Others may dispute my claim, but I think that I made the very first iron needle in our group at An-dong. Needles are a very necessary tool in a prison camp. Quite a few had been made earlier from soft copper wire, but a copper needle has to be large in order to give it sufficient strength.

After a few weeks at An-dong, everyone seemed to be at work doing something. Whittling was a very good hobby if you could make a knife. The solution was to find a worn-out iron cow shoe on the public road. The two-piece iron shoes made for a cow's split hoofs could be fashioned into excellent knives.

A very useful hobby was raiding the food storeroom. The POWs found new and creative ways of diverting the guard's attention while others broke in and made off with bags of rice, corn, and beans. One technique was starting an argument near the point where the guard was on duty. When he left his post to investigate the disturbance, someone else would break in. In another instance, I saw a POW with a slingshot trying to kill a bird near the food storehouse. The guard became interested as well and left his post to see whether the POW would be successful in his hunt. Other prisoners were waiting nearby to seize the opportunity.

After a time all such tactics became known to the authorities. But the POWs were not through yet. What proved to be the best and most enduring method of stealing food from the storehouse involved no breaking and entering. If the Communists saw someone sneaking around, they knew that he was up to no good. Therefore, the best way to steal from them was to do it right out in the open—the more brazenly the better.

Each morning the guards would round up ten or so men whose job was to march across the parade ground to the food storehouse and bring back the rations for that day. When the ration detail marched by a certain building and were out of sight of the escort guard, an extra man would join them. His duty was to enter the storehouse with the others and pick up whatever he could. On one such occasion, I saw the extra man pick up a fifty-kilo bag of beans (just over 100 pounds) and walk across the parade ground to the kitchen, greeting the camp commandant on the way. He was seen by perhaps fifty or more guards. No one said a word. The Communists never caught on to this trick as far as I know.

The morale of the men began to improve, and with it their resistance to the Communists. Increasingly the POWs became willing to stand up to the authorities, even if it meant punishment. The Communists were pretending to be friends, so out of concern for their indoctrination program, their punishment did not involve killing a prisoner unless the offense was very severe. Those who were punished might be kicked repeatedly. Some were made to stand at attention for hours just outside the commandant's office; in that position, they were considered fair game to the occasional guard who might walk by. A favorite sport of the guards was to walk up to a POW standing at attention, lift up his hat, and knock on his head with his knuckles—just as you would knock on the door of a house. That may seem a minor annoyance, but so many of the guards played this little game that the resulting punishment could be severe.

It was becoming increasingly difficult for the authorities to conduct their group indoctrinations—the POWs were simply not attending. To combat this truancy, the Communists sent out large numbers of guards to round up any prisoners they could find and take them to the sessions. The POWs responded by playing hide-and-seek in and behind the various buildings in the compound, tipped off by some of the other POWs, the children, and civilians. Considering all that we had been through, it was humorous to watch. The authorities were furious. Generally denied the use of the gun in such circumstances, they simply didn't know how to make the system work.

The Communists considered political indoctrination a necessary part of life for every citizen. Therefore, they did not believe that the American POWs had been sent into combat without such instruction.

Perhaps it was just as well: the Communists pretended to have nothing but contempt for the fighting ability of the individual American soldier; had they known the truth about his lack of psychological preparation before being sent into South Korea, they would have been even less impressed. Aware that I had been in World War II, they asked me if I had been given indoctrination at that time and appeared not to believe my negative answer.

It should be noted here that the vast political indoctrination programs that the North Koreans and Chinese Communists conducted for their soldiers did not keep them loyal after they were taken prisoner by UN forces. Following signing of the armistice, 83,000 Communist POWs chose to return to their homelands, but 88,000—with no indoctrination during their imprisonment—refused to go back. Of the 75,000 South Korean and UN prisoners held by the Communists, fewer than 15,000 could be accounted for. Of these, "12,760 were allowed to go home and, according to Communist tabulation, only 327 Koreans, 21 Americans, and one Briton were converted to Communism."[9]

The American prisoners were beginning to give a better account of themselves: to stand together as a team, obey their superiors, and keep faith with one another—something the Code of Conduct would have instructed them to do. But the code had not yet been written; that would not occur until 1955, well after the armistice in 1953. In North Korea, some American prisoners had to learn the lessons taught in the code the hard way, with incredible hardship and great loss of life. The wisdom of that code is obvious to me. I believe that it might have made a difference in the way some American prisoners conducted themselves during the Korean War—but I must concede that I am outvoted in that opinion by Major Dunn and other military men from our group. They seem to feel that many of the young men were simply not properly trained for their job as soldiers.

We civilian prisoners had been required to attend the indoctrinations at first but after a time we were told to stay away. Thereafter, the authorities would not even allow us to walk near the lecture hall. Then on May 10, 1951, the Communists came to us with long faces and spoke almost in whispers, displaying what they considered to be the gravity of the situation. "You people are old and religious. Therefore, you cannot appreciate the blessings of Communism. Moreover, you are working against what we are trying to do here. Therefore, we are going to separate you from the American military prisoners and place you in a camp of your own." Startled, we asked how soon this move would take place. The officers replied, "As soon as possible."

When the officials had departed, Kris spoke first. "What is that all about? Why are they separating us from the GIs?"

"I don't know, but I have an idea," Commissioner Lord replied. On sharing our opinions, we found we had all reached the same conclusion: they were trying to indoctrinate the GIs, and we were a "bad" influence. On any given day, in fact, all the civilian prisoners could be seen talking to many POWs. Just a few days before the announced move, Bishop Cooper had baptized Capt. Dave Booker, the Marine Corps Corsair pilot. Bishop Cooper summed it up: "Isn't it strange? Our greatest compliment has come not from our friends but from those who call us enemy. By separating us from the POWs, the Communists have given us the greatest compliment we could possibly receive."

We didn't want to leave the POWs, but we had no choice. Our new quarters though only about a quarter-mile away, were outside the barbed wire. Our isolation from the GIs was almost complete. Our only contacts after that would be on the weekly ration detail (and then we were not supposed to talk to them), in using the services of camp barber Carl Cossin, and at the occasional command performance.

13. A CHANGE FOR THE BETTER

AFTER our move from the main POW camp at An-dong on May 10, 1951, to a private house nearby, Mystery Man began visiting us on a regular basis. He was never a pleasant person to be around. His disposition was hostile, argumentative, and confrontational most of the time, and he was without reserve in kicking anyone in the shins for even minor offenses at any time. When he came calling, we responded to him with extreme caution. We had learned by that time not to discuss anything freely with Communist officials if we had any choice. The rule was, Never volunteer any information; be polite, be brief and answer only what was asked.

Mystery Man came to our room more frequently once he came to know Dr. Ernst Kisch better. At Hanjang-ni he had made fun of the nuns, priests, and Dr. Kisch because of their celibate life-style. Here at An-dong, he and Dr. Kisch engaged in long discussions, with Commissioner Lord serving as translator. Naturally M.M. determined the subject of these discussions, but most of them related to Dr. Kisch's boyhood in Austria where he had grown up between the two world wars. Listening, we all became interested in learning about an elegant world of music, art, and culture that has now largely disappeared. Mystery Man wanted to know about Dr. Kisch's extensive education, his parent's profession, and why he never married. He even became a bit crude on one occasion in his remarks to Dr. Kisch about his bachelorhood.

Apparently M.M. came to believe in Dr. Kisch's credentials because one day he asked to be given a physical examination. On hearing such a request, Dr. Kisch grew excited and asked, "How can I give you an examination? I have no laboratory, no X-ray, not even a stethoscope."

Mystery Man would not be thwarted. "I think I can get you a stethoscope, and I'll be back tomorrow." True to his word, he returned the next day with the stethoscope.

Dr. Kisch instructed his patient to strip to the waist, at which point the rest of us decided that it might be prudent to leave. Mystery Man reassured us that it was all right to remain.

When he had finished with what appeared to be a thorough examination, Dr. Kisch told M.M. that he could dress. "When you were young," he said, "I think you had pleurisy in your right lung. I believe you have recovered from it and have had no further complications. You appear to be in good health." That brought the first genuine smile that I had seen on the face of Mystery Man. Apparently the good news was exactly what he had been waiting to hear. He thanked Dr. Kisch profusely and left.

Later, Dr. Kisch began to fail physically. He had always seemed to be rather frail, possibly because of his previous imprisonment in Nazi Germany, and appeared to have more trouble with diarrhea than most of us. At that time our ration consisted of 600 grams of grain per person per day, divided equally between millet and rice. Of the two grains, rice is much easier to digest. Father Crosbie and I traded 150 grams each of our rice for a total of 300 grams of Dr. Kisch's millet ration. In that way, each of us would still have the same weight in grain, but Dr. Kisch would have all rice.

It soon became apparent that Mystery Man also was concerned about the health of Dr. Kisch, and he began to visit him more often. On one of those visits, discovering what Father Crosbie and I were doing to try to help, he indicated his approval of our actions and said that he hoped Dr. Kisch would soon recover. When the doctor's condition worsened, M.M. came one day and took him back to the main camp, where Dr. Boysen could look after him. Before he walked away, M.M. told us about his concern for Dr. Kisch's health and that he would try to look after him.

We saw Dr. Kisch a few times after that on ration detail but he seemed to be going downhill steadily. He died near midnight on June 28, 1951, one year after his arrest with me in Kaesong.

A week or so later, M.M. came to our hut again. It was the first time we had seen him since the doctor's death. He struck up a conversation, seemingly with no one in particular, but before long he turned to Father Crosbie and me and asked, "Why did you give Dr. Kisch your rice for his millet? Everyone knows that rice is better." We were stunned at the question and didn't know how to answer. How do you tell an avowed Communist about values and beliefs that his political system rejects? Finally we told him that our actions had been based upon our beliefs about life, trying to keep the explanation as short as possible. Mystery Man did not respond in any visible way. We thought that at the very least he would give us an argument of some kind, but he quickly took his leave and went on his way.

With Dr. Kisch gone, we all felt that M.M. would not visit anymore; in fact, we hoped that he would soon forget all about us. But he did return to visit from time to time. In addition, he affected my life once more in a confrontation that I would not have imagined in my wildest dreams.

Before we civilians had been moved from the main camp, I had taken the lining from an old padded jacket that I had worn and had made it into a shirt. We had been told to turn in all such clothing to the authorities, but I had neglected to do so. The shirt was contraband, so I dared not be caught with it. The small irrigation canal that ran through the back of our compound provided the perfect answer. Digging away the sandy bottom of the canal, I hid the shirt there. Knowing that we would be returning on a weekly basis for rations, I planned to pick it up later.

Soon after the death of Dr. Kisch, the time seemed right for me to retrieve my contraband shirt. Walking close to the secret location on our next ration detail, I dropped out of the marching formation and ran toward the stream. Grabbing the shirt out of the water, I wrung it out very quickly and shoved it under my old padded coat. By that time the group had reached the ration storehouse. I was aware that the camp commandant had seen me rejoin the group; I hoped that he had not seen anything else.

Rubber Neck had been given his name because of his bothersome habit of walking around the compound hatless with his head down, his long hair completely covering his face. On meeting someone, he would suddenly throw back his head to get the hair out of his eyes so that he could see; he did it so quickly that the name Rubber Neck seemed to fit. Although he was not as vicious as The Tiger, he was equally unpredictable and someone to be avoided.

Rubber Neck approached me swiftly and took hold of the front of my old padded jacket. Bareheaded as usual, he was not such a bad-looking person except that his eyes were a bit strange. I had never seen him that close up before. Taking hold of my jacket, he asked me where I had been.

"I've been to the toilet," I lied.

My old padded jacket was held together with one handmade wooden button attached with rotten blanket thread. With one sharp pull from Rubber Neck, the button would pop off and the contraband shirt would fall to the ground. Should that happen, I knew I would be in real trouble. He gave another tug with one hand while at the same time reaching back with his right hand for his pistol.

I don't think he actually planned to shoot me. All Communist officers had their own personal methods of meting out punishment, and Rubber Neck's specialty was pistolwhipping his victims. I knew that at the very least I was in for a beating about the face and head with a pistol. Worse yet, the beating might cause the wet shirt to fall out.

Seemingly out of nowhere, M.M. appeared and thrust himself between Rubber Neck and me, throwing up his hand and shouting in mixed Korean and English, "*Pyun-so* [toilet] OK, all right, all right!" Rubber Neck spun on his heel and walked briskly across the parade ground in the direction of his office, head down as usual. Apparently, if this was to be a confrontation, it wouldn't come from Rubber Neck, I thought. Without even glancing at me, M.M. walked off rapidly in the opposite direction. His line of march between two buildings ended with an abrupt right-hand turn at the barbed wire perimeter. He disappeared from view around the corner of the building. I looked back to see Rubber Neck continuing to walk toward his office. A crazy thought ran through my mind: when those two meet again, what will they talk about? No matter, it certainly won't be about me. The guards in charge of our ration detail stood immobile for a few seconds; they never took any initiative in the presence of high-ranking officers.

When I looked across the line of prisoners, my eyes met those of Monsignor Quinlan. He was alternately glancing at me and looking up into the sky, as though to heaven, and clutching his rosary. An even more impish grin than usual covered his face. I knew then that he had been praying for me when he saw that I was in trouble.

By all accounts, M.M. was the political officer of the camp as well as the deputy commandant. His wearing no rank insignia and his great authority would be consistent with such a position. Still, his action on my behalf placed him at considerable risk. Mystery Man had caused Rubber Neck to lose face in front of his own men, an action not to be taken lightly in the Orient. From the moment of that incident, I became a nonperson to M.M. He never spoke to me or even acknowledged my presence again. For a few weeks, I feared for my safety, but as time passed, I could only conclude that Rubber Neck was also afraid of M.M., and with good reason.

Was Mystery Man touched in any way by the attempt of Father Crosbie and me to keep alive the only person in our group that he ever seemed to care anything about? I don't know. I only know that M.M. saved me from a severe beating or worse, and I am grateful to him for it.

And what about M.M? Should he be punished in some way? I think the answer to that is yes. He certainly caused a lot of pain to many in our group. If he is still alive, however, he is probably having to live out his days in North Korea—a very severe punishment.

The death of Dr. Kisch was a great personal loss to me. Not having a family, he had lived with Frances and me for several weeks in Kaesong before the North Korean attack on South Korea. The other missionaries had planned for him to live with the Andersons or some other family, because Frances and I had just been married. But Dr. Kisch had his own ideas. He told me once in prison, "Larry, I wanted to live with you and Frances because I knew that I would have more fun there. You were a young couple and were always laughing." I didn't have to be reminded that as a Jewish survivor of Buchenwald and Dachau, he deserved all the laughter he could find.

Dr. Kisch had reminded me on several occasions during the Death March and the terrible winter at Hanjang-ni, "Larry, aren't you happy that Frances is not here?" His presence had made me count my blessings. I grieved that he had been denied his fondest wish—to be allowed to return to China and resume his medical practice there.

With the passing of winter, I resolved to try to become human again as soon as possible, a passion shared by all of us. There was much to be done. First of all, we wanted to get clean! The spring thaw and the breakup of the ice in the river enabled us to jump into the water for a few minutes at a time. Ice was still floating in the river, but we braved the low temperature many times. The pores of our skin were clogged with oil and dirt, giving the feel and appearance of sandpaper. Not having soap or hot water, we resorted to the use of ashes and a brush made from straw rope. The shock of the cold water and the irritation caused by the scrubbing made washing a real exercise in discipline. It took most of us about two weeks to remove the "sandpaper" from our skin.

At An-dong we faced a new problem of how to use our time constructively. In the past we had either been fighting a desperate day-to-day battle to survive, or were in a situation where we really didn't control our time anyway, or both. When our Russian and Turkish families began to discuss the problem of how to educate their children, we knew we had found our answer. The families were becoming increasingly concerned about what their children were learning at An-dong. What passed for wisdom in our prison camp consisted of a cunning sufficient to steal anything of value from the Communists, the art of deception and lying so well that falsehood became truth, and an audacity that permitted one to take the big gamble when the prize seemed to justify the risk. The basic tools of survival in a Communist prison camp could become the recipe for juvenile delinquency in the outside world. So when we decided to begin a school to teach the children, the Turkish and White Russian families were delighted.

The Communists had given us paper and pencils to use in taking notes during their political lectures; now we put them to other use. Strange as it may seem, from the time of our arrival at An-dong, we were usually given an adequate supply of paper and pencils. That was at a time when our basic food ration remained on a starvation level, and in fact, many of our people were still dying from malnutrition. We could only conclude that in the Communist lexicon of values, ideas and correct political thinking were more important than food.

Sagida, the linguist of our group, studied French with the nuns and proved to be an excellent student. I decided to see what I could do for Sagid, the oldest teenager in the group. First, I taught him physics, writing the textbook from day to day as we went along. Admittedly, much was left out, but Sagid quickly became the master of what I taught him.

After Sagid expressed an interest in learning geometry, I realized that we would need a real textbook, even if it was in Korean. Commissioner Lord borrowed such a text from one of the students in the village, and we set about the task of translating it into English. Commissioner Lord knew nothing about geometry, and my Korean language ability was not equal to the task; by working together, however, the two of us in time produced a very credible textbook in English, complete with crude hand drawings, theorems, and numbered pages. To construct the book, we used the paper that had been provided by the Communist authorities. Although it was of very poor quality—about one grade above American toilet paper—it could be written on if one was careful.

Our school was composed of ten children from three families: six Turks, three Russians, and one French. Unlike the Communist "schools," ours was willingly attended by students who were so eager to learn that they took notes in class, something I never saw anyone do at a political lecture. After each school session, there was never any shortage of tutors to assist the students in preparing their lessons for the next day.

Beginning in the spring of 1951, we were brought English-language newspapers from China and Russia. We also began receiving books by Russian authors that had been translated into English in Moscow.

Danny volunteered to read these books aloud to those in our room. It was a good arrangement, helping us fill our time and permitting Danny to practice his voice and diction skills.

The books were heavily laden with propaganda, but they were better than nothing. During the remainder of our stay in North Korean captivity, Danny read to us such books as *Golden Prague, Far from Moscow* and *Men with a Clear Conscience*. The writings of the Russian author Ilya Ehrenburg were featured prominently in the list of books and articles that we received. Ehrenburg had won the Stalin Prize for his book *Storm*, which meant that it had to toe the party line exactly.

We were also supplied selected stories and quotes from articles and newspapers by the American writers John Steinbeck and Mark Twain. Apparently the Russians were especially fond of Mark Twain's short pieces such as "Grief and Mourning For The Night," concerning the American involvement in the Philippines in 1898 during the Spanish-American War. Others by Mark Twain that I remember were, "As Regards Patriotism," "The War Prayer" and "The United States of Lyncherdom," the latter having to do with the lynching of blacks in America. By design, it was not a very uplifting list of reading material.

We were able to find new life during that spring and summer of 1951. The Communist authorities seemed chiefly concerned with indoctrinating the POWs in the main camp. Consequently, we were generally left alone in our house except for the presence of a few guards and an occasional propaganda lecturer. We organized wood details and walked the nearby mountains almost every day in search of wood and food. We found wild onions, mushrooms, grapes, and many kinds of berries in abundance. Our recovery from the ravages of the Death March and starvation was slowly brought about by our being permitted to graze on the mountainsides.

The living conditions were still very primitive, but they had improved. There had been no increase in our basic starvation diet or the medical and dental attention that some of the group so desperately needed. But we were very grateful for something: we had new freedom. For the first time in our prison experience we could walk to a spot in the mountains where we were out of sight of the man with the gun! At the start we had been required to have guards in attendance as we walked about the area, but this restriction became such a bother that it was dropped. In the end, we merely had to request permission from the guard on duty in order to leave the camp in search of firewood. We always took an ax with us to make it look authentic. It was certainly a far cry from what we had known before.

The North Korean civilians were not permitted to cut trees in the nearby forest for fuel, and the authorities had warned us of the same prohibition. However, we found as we walked the mountains that most of the small shrubs that we were allowed to cut had been taken already by the North Korean civilians. There were two choices available: either walk greater distances in search of wood legal size, or find some other way. We noticed that large clusters of pine and larch were abundant in the area, and in talking with the guards, we learned that the taking of trees was permitted if they were dead. Father Crosbie and I drew up a very simple plan: make some trees dead.

There was a medium-sized stand of trees on the side of a mountain about half a mile from our house. Each morning as we departed for the higher mountains in search of legal firewood, we would walk through that grove cutting one or two trees in the very center. The trees were so close together that one could not see from outside the cluster what we had done. This practice went on throughout the summer. Finally, when those trees that we had first cut were dry, we began hauling them down to our house. Once there, others would help us quickly chop them into smaller pieces. Both the prison authorities and local officials came around a couple of times to check on the dryness of the wood, which indicated whether or not it was legal, but they never said anything. I don't know whether they were actually fooled; in wartime North Korea they may have had other more important things to worry about. They did have the last laugh, however. We had cut this wood specifically for use in the coming winter; we had to leave it all behind when we were moved out in October.

With the passing of time, Kris suffered more and more from sciatica, a condition that made it difficult for him to walk properly. After we moved to our new location at An-dong, Kris began to walk in a slightly bent-forward position, using a long wooden stick. One day he came to me and pointed to the top of a mountain that rose up directly south of our house. It was a mountain that Monsignor Quinlan, Father Crosbie, and I had walked over many times in search of wood and food. "One of these days I am going to climb to the top of that mountain, and when I do, I won't need this anymore," he said, shaking his walkingstick as he spoke. At the time, I thought that such a thing was totally out of the question. However, wanting to encourage him, I told him to take a look on the other side of the mountain when he reached the top.

On the Death March, Kris had taken quantities of Korean-made aspirin in an attempt to fight the pain. The aspirin tablets—probably not as strong as those made in America—had been obtained from Dr. Kisch when we moved out of the quarantine station at Manpo; it was the only time we ever had so much medicine of any kind on hand. Before we departed from Manpo, Kris filled each of the pockets in his suit coat with them. I have a distinct memory of one morning on the Death March when Kris and I were walking together. I saw Kris reach in his pocket, take out something, and throw it into his mouth while holding his head back, as if he were eating peanuts. "What are you eating, Kris?" I asked, thinking he might have some food to share. He didn't say anything; instead, he reached into his pocket again and drew out a handful of aspirin.

Kris several times repeated this promise of climbing to the top of the mountain, both to me and to others. I don't think any of us took him seriously. But one morning we awoke to find him gone. The guard on duty told us that Kris was taking a walk; he was obviously not worried about Kris's getting very far in his debilitated condition. We didn't think much about the matter until after lunch; it was not considered normal for anyone to miss a meal if he could help it. Finally, late in the afternoon, we saw a tall figure striding down the side of the mountain. We could tell even from some distance that it was not a Korean, but we could not imagine that it was Kris. Soon we were shocked to discover that it was indeed Kris, and walking without the aid of his stick. He was moving at a moderately fast pace, carrying his walkingstick over his shoulder. When he arrived, he was hungry and wanted to eat the lunch we had saved for him.

He then told us of his slow and painful climb to the top of the mountain. It had become so difficult that he found that he could take only 100 steps before he had to rest—"rest and cry and pray," he said. On reaching the top, he was so exhausted that he lay down and slept for an hour or so. After waking up, he feasted on grapes and berries for a time and then started home.

"I had to do it," he exclaimed, "because we might have to go on another long march some day, and I wouldn't be able to make it. I don't have any more aspirin left to kill the pain, as I did on the Death March. For a long time I have been afraid of another long march, but now I won't be afraid anymore."

Given our situation of new freedom, it would be naive to think that someone would not make an attempt to escape. One day we all returned from work on the mountain for the noon meal to discover that Danny was missing. Commissioner Lord waited until almost nightfall to report his absence, giving Danny as much head start as possible. The authorities did not seem to be overly concerned. "He will be found," they said.

Danny had made thorough preparation—that is to say, as thorough as one could make under the circumstances. He had enlisted the aid of the POWs in obtaining extra clothing, boots, and dry roasted grain. He had a handmade backpack to carry his supplies. He had addressed every eventuality except the one he could do nothing about: he had no rain gear, and the heavy rains that fell every night soaked his grain supply at the very beginning. Danny was caught three days later and brought back to the main POW camp. The authorities were so pleased with themselves that they put him on display and told him to tell his story to the POWs. Obviously, this was good strategy on the part of the Communists. They wanted all to be made aware of the great difficulties involved in trying to escape.

Danny was kept in the POW compound for the remainder of our stay at An-dong. He explained to us later that his plan of escape was to keep off the main roads and walk only through the mountains in a southerly direction. Korea is a land of mountains; North Korea, especially, is a succession of one steep mountain after another separated by narrow winding valleys. The people live in these valleys along the streams and roads. No one lives high in the mountains. Being aware of this, Danny planned to stick to the high country, where the possibility of being caught was slight. Coupled with the prospect of becoming thoroughly drenched with rain each night, however, and eating wet grain that was soon to rot in his backpack, the mountains proved to be too much for Danny. Taking to the main roads, he knew he would not get very far. He walked about thirty miles before he was stopped at a village.

The authorities were always trying something new on us. Early one morning a new guard came to our door and told us to line up in the yard for calisthenics. "We exercise every day walking over these mountains collecting firewood. Why should we exercise now? Anyway, it's too early," Commissioner Lord argued.

"If you follow my instructions, you can live to be very old," the young man in his late teens announced.

"How do you think I have lived to be seventy-one years of age?" asked Bishop Cooper.

"That is irrelevant. Everyone is to line up in the yard for exercise now, now!"

This illustrates why you could never win an argument with a Communist. If your logic got the better of him, he could instantly nullify your victory by simply remarking, "That is irrelevant." Realizing that we had better not push the matter any further, we all left the warm rooms and lined up in the yard—all, that is, except Maria Kilin and her three children. She was taking her time in dressing herself and her children.

The eager guard went bounding to the door and ordered her out immediately. When she did not respond quickly enough, he pointed his rifle at her. "Go on," she said. "Shoot me and my innocent children. They are starving to death anyway. Here, I'll make it easy for you," and she lined up the children single file in front of her. "Now you can kill us all with one bullet. You are always saying that your country is so poor that it cannot give us enough food. Maybe your country cannot afford the extra bullets to kill all of us one at a time. Here we are. One bullet will be enough!"

This plucky Russian woman had a very powerful voice and spoke in Japanese to the guard. Instantly, he knew he was over his head and went running off in the direction of the POW camp. A few minutes later he was back with the commandant and about six more guards.

"You have caused a riot by not following the guard's instructions," the commandant told us. "That is not a very nice thing to do. Such actions do not contribute to peace and harmony. Please try to cooperate more in the future." Before leaving, however, the commandant turned and reprimanded the guard for exceeding his instructions.

He had accused us of causing a riot. In Communist thinking, you caused a riot if you refused to carry out an order. We caused only two "riots" while in prison; the other one had been at Kosan when a guard had threatened to shoot Commissioner Lord for refusing an order to clean up the area.

After the commandant had departed, we discussed our new situation as prisoners. The authorities who were in charge of us a few months earlier would have severely punished our entire group for such a breach of discipline. We could only conclude that for whatever reason, the abrupt change in our treatment had originated at the highest level. This incident was further proof that the central government of North Korea had become aware that prisoners had value.

Among the varieties of wild food that we were able to gather in the nearby mountains, we learned with the aid of Bishop Cooper, to select edible mushrooms, which grew in abundance. With their meatlike flavor, they were very much in demand. For a few weeks, Bishop Cooper walked the mountains with us, teaching us the difference between the good and the poisonous varieties. We had been on our own for another few weeks when there was an incident that demonstrated how much we still had to learn. We had found what we considered a good variety of mushroom, cooked them for lunch, and sat down to eat. Within five minutes we felt sick; in another minute or so we were very distressed and had to run outside to relieve ourselves of what we had just eaten. There were no lasting effects, but we had learned to be more careful.

The women of our group withstood the rigors of imprisonment at least as well as the men, if not better. They never received any special consideration, either bad or good, just because they were women. As far as I am aware, none of them was raped, although they were subjected to embarrassing searches at times. I do remember one incident when a young guard walked up to Lotte Gliese—the one German in our group—as she stood just outside the door of her room; he broached his subject directly: "Let's you and me make a baby." Lotte was so horrified that she started screaming in several languages. Another guard who had been standing nearby came and took the amorous one away. When they had gone, Lotte turned to me: "Larry, that guard is an idy-oat."

At the end of World War II, Lotte and her Korean husband—who was then regarded as a Japanese—were living in Berlin, where they witnessed the arrival of victorious Russian troops who killed, robbed, and raped. Together they had endured great hardships in making their way across Russia, to China, and then to Korea. Lotte compared the situation in Berlin with the incident at our camp: "At least this guard asked. The Russians in Berlin, what they wanted they just took!"[1]

The major concern of the Communist authorities at this point remained the political conversion of the American military prisoners. They had become aware that we civilians were not likely to change our political views and that we had only hostage value to them. That may account for the much less harsh treatment that we were receiving: as hostages, we had value only if we were alive. They did give us political lectures from time to time. On one such occasion, a new officer arrived at our house and requested that we round up all the civilians. The lecture that followed concerned the traditional Communist view that their world revolution would very soon circle the earth. "When that happens," he said, "you religious people will have to find something else to do."

Then, looking at me, the youngest missionary present, he asked, "And you, what will you do? I don't worry too much about these older people, but you are quite a bit younger. Can you work with your hands to make a living?"

As I thought about his question, I could see that he was eyeing me intently for an answer. "I think I could be a successful carpenter," I said. "There was at least one person of our faith who was good in that profession." I was referring to Jesus Christ, of course, who was a carpenter in Nazareth in his early life. Monsignor Quinlan almost collapsed trying to hide his laughter. Poor Commissioner Lord! He tried to hold a serious expression on his face as he always did when he translated. If the lecturer caught on, he never showed it in any way.

One day some of the children came running to the yard to announce that they had seen a large black car stop at the POW compound. Through the rumor mill, we learned that three Russians had arrived to conduct interrogations. One was a tall, thin, blond individual who had been given the nickname of Blondie. After a few days Blondie and the other two Russians came to our house to interrogate the Russians in our group and try to persuade them to return to Russia. Those sessions became quite bitter, primarily because the Russian prisoners did not want to live in Russia, China, or anywhere else behind the Iron Curtain. On one occasion, Ahmet and I sat in a corner of the yard about fifty feet from where Blondie was talking to Dimitri. Ahmet translated what was being said. "If you think I am going back to Russia, you are crazy. I would rather cut my throat right now than go back!" Dimitri screamed.

The exchanges between Blondie and the Russian prisoners were so heated that interrogations with other nationalities were mild by comparison. Blondie was good at what he did. He never threatened in any way but tried to put across his ideas by means of reasoning unique to Communist thinking: by definition, Communist ideas were superior to others and should be so announced to the world, by force if necessary. He knew how to put a person on the spot. I don't think he had any converts from our civilian group. Unknown to us, however, Blondie was also at that time interrogating George Blake, the former British vice-consul in Seoul. It may have been at about this time that Blake made his ideological shift.

About that time, although we were given very little in the way of medicine except aspirin and iodine, we each received an inoculation that was administered into the back just below the shoulder blade by means of a very long needle and a large, almost bicycle-pump-sized syringe. The dosage must have been at least four times what American medical practice would have allowed; it gave us fever for several days. The Communists told us that the shot was to combat the germ warfare that was being waged by the ill-bred Americans.

The time had come to leave An-dong. Unlike our joy at departing from Hanjang-ni, there was disappointment this time at the prospect of having to leave an area where we had done so much preparation for winter. Also, we regretted the likelihood of being separated completely from the American military prisoners.

The authorities ordered us to turn in all our old winter clothing, promising as usual that new clothing would be provided at our next location. Some of us decided not to trust their promise and wore our winter coats underneath our summer tunics. That decision turned out to be a wise one.

It was a sad time when we crossed the little stream for the last time and walked to the main gate of the POW camp. We had heard a rumor that we were going to be handed over to the Chinese. We all regarded this as a good sign, believing that the Chinese would look after their prisoners better than the North Koreans.

Eleven of us had to remain behind, there not being enough transport to carry all of us at one time. Our extra night at the POW camp was well worth the wait. During that night, POWs broke into the storehouses and liberated potatoes, corn, beans, and tobacco. We stayed awake well into the morning hours, enjoying the conversation and the food.

The next day, October 10, 1951, we boarded a truck and departed for Manpo in the company of two guards. We were greatly surprised to see Burp-gun Charlie and his wife join us in the back of the same truck. She was the most strikingly beautiful and well-dressed woman that we were to see in all of North Korea. As she had boarded the truck, holding a young baby in her arms, several of us noticed her likeness to a classical picture that we had seen before. "Bing, do you see what I see?" I asked Father Crosbie.

"Yes, she looks like the Korean Madonna," Father Crosbie answered. In the Orient as in other countries, the Madonna is recreated by local artists in accordance with the facial characteristics and dress of each country. It seemed incongruous to us that this woman could be married to someone like Burp-gun Charlie.

We spent the night in a village about halfway between An-dong and Manpo. All of us slept on a heated floor and were given two good meals of rice. The next morning, when some of us went outside to await the arrival of the truck, a small crowd of polite but curious people gathered around us and began to talk. When Commissioner Lord walked out of the house and started putting on his shoes, one of the officials engaged him in serious political conversation, speaking in a loud voice. This dialogue was obviously for the benefit of the local people.

"What does freedom mean to you?" the official asked.

"Freedom in my country means that I can do whatever I choose, subject to the laws of the country," answered Commissioner Lord.

"But we have that same kind of freedom also," responded the official. He was right, of course. In any country, no matter how repressive it may be, its citizens are free to do what is not forbidden by law. Lord instantly saw his mistake and tried to recover by the use of a personal illustration. He couldn't have chosen a worse one.

"In my country, I am free to eat so much food that I can get this fat," he said, holding his oversized Salvation Army tunic out from his body to show how much weight he had lost. A man five and a half feet tall, he had entered captivity weighing 250 pounds. He was now less than half his previous weight, and his worn-out tunic hung on his thin body like a tent.

"Too much, too much. That is too much food to eat," chanted the growing crowd.

"Yes, it is too much to eat," conceded Commissioner Lord. "But in my country, I am free to eat too much food if I wish." Looking at the Communist official, you could almost see it coming.

"No man has the right to eat that much food when there are hungry people in the world!" screamed the official. The crowd went wild with shouts and applause. The great debate had ended, and guess who had won!

Commissioner Lord was crestfallen. Instantly, he knew that he had made a serious blunder. I had never seen the Communists outmaneuver him before. He could verbally slug it out with the best of them. Even with his very life at stake, he had stood toe to toe with The Tiger and given a good account of himself, never backing down on any issue until The Tiger brought out the gun.

"But Commissioner, the Communists are the materialists. Why did you use a materialistic argument when you knew our best weapon against them was a nonmaterial one?" I asked him later.

"Larry, I wasn't thinking about what I was doing until it was too late," Lord confessed. Immediately, I regretted what I had said. More than anyone else in our group, the commissioner displayed outstanding qualities of leadership and a solid grasp of the realities of our situation. No one was his equal in courage, audacity, and resourcefulness when it came to dealing with the Communists. No one else could have done the job as well as he did. No one else would have wanted to try; the job was too dangerous, too demanding, fraught with too many headaches.

On occasion, Lord could be difficult to get along with. He could be petty, and his feelings were easily hurt. After a personal squabble with someone, he might not speak to him for days, but he always forgave him in the end. Having lost a son in the Pacific theater in World War II, he did hate all things Japanese: "Do I look like a Japanese?" he would thunder to the occasional new guard who might try to speak Japanese to him.

For Commissioner Lord the price of integrity was high. British to the core, he upheld his country's proudest traditions by skill, courage, and fair play. I don't know how we could have gotten along without him. I would like to think that his experience in North Korea was his finest hour.

When we first came back to Manpo, we did not recognize it; there were so few buildings left standing that the familiar landmarks were gone. Our Russian-made truck moved through the city and carried us to a narrow valley about three miles to the southwest. Climbing out of the truck, we saw that we were surrounded by a series of strange-looking buildings. Farther up the valley, the whole area was an anthill of feverish activity with prisoners carrying dirt from one place to another. Bishop Cooper walked up to greet us about this time. He had made the trip from An-dong with the earlier group.

"We have struck rock bottom this time," he whispered.

"Don't tell the others," Commissioner Lord advised.

"Bishop, how could this place be any worse than what we've already been through?" I asked.

"Have you ever had to bow to a machine gun tower before?" the Bishop asked blandly.

"What is this place?" Commissioner Lord asked.

"It is some kind of prison for North Korean civilian criminals," Bishop Cooper replied.

"Commissioner, what does that sign say?" I asked, pointing to a sign in Korean by the side of the road. It read "*Kyo wha so.*"

"It says, 'A Place of Culture or Learning.' It looks as though we are going to be reeducated," Lord replied.

14. THE PLACE OF LEARNING

AN officer and some guards appeared on the scene and ordered us to follow them. Walking farther up the valley, we had a closer view of the teeming activity that we had seen on our arrival. What we saw was not reassuring. Groups of ragged, hollow-eyed men were running about carrying dirt and gravel, whipped along by screaming guards. The dirt and gravel were being dug from the side of the mountain, placed in straw bags, and then carried to other areas by men who looked so weak that they could hardly walk. Our considerable experience in such matters told us that a great many of these men would not be alive much longer; that October day in 1951 warned us that winter was not far away, a time when many would die.

Bishop Cooper was right about having to bow to the machine gun tower. About halfway up the valley, we found ourselves standing directly opposite a tower located on one side of the mountain. All prisoners whose business took them past this point in either direction were required to stop, turn toward the tower, bow low, scream out the nature of their business, and ask permission to pass. The two-man machine gun crew in the tower would sometimes pay very little attention to those who came and went. At other times, they would question the hapless prisoner for several minutes, even if it was obvious from the sack of dirt he carried that he was on official business.

The officer ordered us to stop as we approached the tower. "Don't ever come here without a guard," he warned us. In this exposed position, you found yourself looking right into the muzzle of a mounted machine gun. Our escort then shouted at the two men in the tower to announce our business. Just why he made an exception in our case, we never knew, but his order was one that we were happy to follow.

Farther up the valley we came to a long, low building half buried in the mountainside. That was to be our home for the present. It would be difficult to decide what part of it was the most depressing. On entering the building, one was greeted by the smell of mold, indicating the presence of dampness. Water entered the building in two ways: through the roof when it rained, and continously by seepage from the mountain. The dugout was dark and drafty at all times; there was no heat of any kind.

For several days we had no idea what was going to happen to us. Apparently the authorities were content to keep us in the dark concerning their real intentions for us. Their intentions for the poor North Korean "criminals" in this Place of Learning were obvious. At first, we were deathly afraid that they might try to reeducate us as well. We had already seen and heard enough to know that Communist reeducation was a devastating experience. Fortunately for us, the Communists later told us, we were considered incorrigible, incapable of being made to see the truth.

As it turned out, prison inmates were busy at that very moment preparing a dugout for us in the adjacent valley. After ten days inside the main prison compound, we were moved half a mile to our new home.

I suspect what the authorities really meant by "preparation" was that its former occupants were being moved out. When we arrived, the room was so dirty that we found it necessary to clean it before we could move in. Our new quarters consisted of one long, low building dug into the side of a mountain with two heated floors running side by side the length of the building. The two heated floors were separated by a depressed walkway that provided access. Although there was no privacy, the two separate heated floors did make it possible to divide the men and women. A stove fueled by coal dust was located in the middle of the walkway. Ilian Kijikoff took on the job of permanent fireman. He liked his work so well that he would not let anyone else near the stove. We carried the coal-dust fuel in straw bags from the main prison compound. Within a few weeks we were covered with the very fine coal dust that was given off when the stove was stoked. We had no way to keep clean after the nearby stream froze over for the winter.

We realized from the first night in our new home that it was very drafty. After complaining to the authorities, we were soon given large straw mats to install on the two ends and the one outside wall. The room was so dark that we could not see well enough to move about even in the daytime without the aid of a small oil lamp.

Those of us who had been resourceful enough to wear our old winter clothing underneath our summer wear when we left An-dong were glad we had done so. We had been promised more winter clothing as soon as we arrived at our new location, but it did not arrive until December. In the meantime, many in the group were soon suffering from the cold.

Our first priority was to prepare a winter wood supply for cooking food in the kitchen, a procedure that also heated our floors. This proved difficult, since the 500 North Korean civilian prisoners located in the valley next to ours at the Place of Learning also required fuel and had already scoured the area for two or three miles in every direction. We were obliged to travel as far as five to seven miles to obtain our fuel. Once the wood was cut, we had to carry or drag it back to our camp. The distance made only two trips per day possible.

Our most serious problem in trudging across the mountains in search of fuel was our footwear. We had been given new tennis shoes at An-dong during the summer, but mine were so small that I had cut out the toes for extra room and they were still so tight-fitting that I could not wear the much-needed padded socks with them. When he became aware of the situation, our helpful guard told us that we could obtain large straw sandals from the main prison compound, where the prisoners made straw footgear. It might seem that shoes made from rice straw would be unsuitable for use in below-zero weather, but we never had any trouble with them unless we were unlucky enough to step into a thermal spring hidden underneath the snow and ice. Once our feet were wet, we could not remain outside for very long. Inside our dugout, we removed our shoes and padded socks and placed them underneath the straw mat on which we slept. Next to the heated floor, they would usually dry during the night.

There were no deaths among our group in Manpo that winter; our weaker ones were already gone. The North Korean civilian prisoners at the Place of Learning were not so fortunate. One morning I had been taken by the guard to the main camp to carry rations. While waiting near the commandant's office, I heard two officers talking outside. "How many deaths have we had this month?" one of them asked.

"We have had twenty-eight so far," the other responded. Suddenly, they both stopped talking and looked in my direction to see if I had understood. I tried to show no reaction. One gets quite good at playing such poker-faced games when one's own safety may depend upon it.

Our basic grain ration was cut for a brief period from the usual daily 600 grams per person to 450. (Fortunately for us, this temporary reduction did not occur in the wintertime, when vegetables would have been in very short supply.) When we protested, we were informed that we were eating on a par with the criminal prisoners at the Place of Learning.[1]

I was frightened only one time by North Korean civilians at a propaganda-hate show in the city of Manpo. Several of us were taken by the guard one day to a political meeting. On our arrival in front of a partly bombed out building, we noted a rather large group of North Korean men and women standing nearby. When the activities finally began, the program consisted of inflammatory speeches by various officials concerning the ill-bred Americans. On occasion, ear-piercing screams could be heard coming from the large crowd as they were aroused to a fever pitch by the rhetoric of the speakers. It was all very carefully orchestrated by those in charge. By that time our own guard had been augmented by several other men in uniform. Even so, when the crowd surged in our direction at one point in a fiery speech, our guards had to struggle to hold them back. Whether we were ever in any real danger, I could not be certain.

The "Hour of Hate" (right out of George Orwell's 1984) concluded, and we began our journey back to our camp with our lone guard. It was about noon, and the temperature was quite warm. Coming to a tree by the side of the road, the guard told us to sit down and rest for a few minutes. Looking back, we noted some of the crowd from the hate session drifting in our direction. We decided that it might not be prudent to remain under the tree and urged the guard to move on. "Don't worry," he said, as he contined to relax and smoke his cigarette. We could only hope that the crowd would pass right on by us, but they had other plans. They stopped, turned off the road, and were soon talking with us and offering us cigarettes. There was even some laughter mixed with their questions, and they were in no hurry to leave. It was difficult to evaluate the degree of danger we were in, but we were reasonably certain that the North Korean authorities had the situation under control at all times.[2]

One spring morning in 1952, we were ordered to go to the main compound of the Place of Learning to witness a People's Court in action. The North Korean civilian prisoners were already in place and seated on the cold ground when we arrived. We were marched up to the others and ordered to sit down also. Soon the proceedings began— not the trial, but the proceedings.

First, one of the local prisoner-leaders—easily identified by his near-normal weight, his warm clothing, and his black armband— walked to the front and began telling stories and jokes about the ill-bred Americans. He finished his act by singing a solo depicting the heroic struggle of the North Korean people against the Americans. "I have done badly," he remarked in mock humility at the end of his song. That is a Korean idiom reserved only for those times when you are really sorry for your actions. Instantly the crowd began cheering and applauding. "Please sing some more for us," the other prisoners shouted. That was part of the well-rehearsed plan, we concluded.

When the prisoner-leader had finished his performance, his subordinates clamored to get in on the act to prove their loyalty to the motherland and their hate for America. "This is all automatic," Father Crosbie whispered to me. "The Communist authorities can sit back and let the prisoners run the propaganda show. They don't have to do anything." Sure enough, the show went on for two hours. It could have gone on all day; there were still junior group leaders who had not been given an opportunity to go on stage. (Incidentally, all the prisoner-leaders wore a black armband to identify them, but their extra physical weight made that practice unnecessary. You could have walked through that prison blindfolded with ordinary bathroom scales and correctly identified the prisoner-leaders.)

At the conclusion of the entertainment portion, the so-called trial got under way. Apparently a North Korean civilian had tried to escape from the camp and had been recaptured. The trial, we were told, was to determine his punishment. A line of chairs and tables had been set up in front of the group to accommodate the judges. There was a prosecutor representing the state and a counsel for the defense. The defendant would have to stand throughout the entire proceeding.

The prosecutor arose and read aloud the charges against the defendant and then took his seat. At that point an amazing thing happened. Three well-dressed men, who had been standing in the background, walked to the center of the stage. They were introduced as witnesses. For the next forty-five minutes they proceeded to lecture, quote from well-known Communist leaders, read poetry, and sing propaganda songs. A recurring theme was, "This man [the defendant] is trying to act like an American"—a very serious charge.

The prosecutor arose and asked for a five-year sentence; the counsel for the defense proposed two years. The judges voted and handed down the sentence: two extra years in addition to the sentence the man was then serving. Only about five minutes had elapsed from the time the witnesses finished their presentation to the final sentencing by the judges.

We were preparing to leave when the three witnesses approached us with broad smiles. "What do you think of a People's Court?" they asked enthusiastically. We were confused about their official title as "witnesses."

"Did you know the defendant?" Kris asked.

"No," they answered.

"Then you saw him try to escape?" Kris asked, pressing the issue.

"No, we have never seen the defendant before."

"Then how can you be witnesses for the defendant when you don't know him?" Kris continued.

"Oh, we are witnesses for the people. We represent the people. The defendant had his representative. He doesn't need another one." There were no witnesses for the defense. When they saw our look of amazement, they volunteered more information.

"This afternoon we are going to Kanggye to another People's Court there. We came from a trial in Sinuiji two days ago. That is our business. We represent the people at People's Courts wherever we go."

What we had just observed terrified us as much as anything we had seen in North Korea. In this country there were professional witnesses whose job had nothing to do with justice; they were paid propaganda hacks. They served no useful function as far as the trial was concerned—and neither did anyone else; the outcome was known in advance.

Having gone through the winter without being able to bathe, we decided in the spring of 1952 to do something about it. What we were planning was audacious in the extreme and could not have succeeded without the aid of one of the boys in the French group whose mother was half Korean and half French. The guards had always assumed that Mansang Hoang was loyal to them and would tell them whatever went on in the camp. In order for our plan to work, it would be necessary to use Mansang to confuse the guards.

There was a storehouse containing several fifty-five gallon-barrels located next to our dugout. Our plan was to steal one of these barrels at night and hide it. The next day Mansang would inform the guards that we had heard noises in the night coming from the storehouse. When the guards went to inventory the number of barrels, Mansang would lend a hand to confuse the count. That is exactly what happened. The barrels were not stacked very well, so the guards sent Mansang to help count some of those in the rear of the storeroom. "How many barrels can you see, Mansang?" the guards asked. "There are nine back here," Mansang called out. In fact, there were only eight. "That is correct," the guards confirmed as they locked the doors to the storehouse and went on their way. The first phase of the plan had worked.

The second phase would not begin for at least two weeks, giving the guards a little time to forget about the incident. We had a very decent guard at that time who took every Thursday off, so we planned the next phase of the project to begin early Thursday morning. Everything was made ready in advance. At five o'clock that morning we dug up the barrel, cut it in two with a chisel that we had managed to liberate, set the halves in place on stones, and promptly lighted a fire. Long wooden poles and straw mats had been procured in advance to install around the barrel for privacy. Our plan was for all work to be completed before the arrival of the guard at nine o'clock. He was a new guard, so we knew that he would not question the new bathhouse. When our old guard returned the next day, we told him that his substitute had arranged for the bathhouse. We knew from experience that the guards never checked with each other about such things. No one ever questioned us concerning that bathhouse. It was used at least once a day for the remainder of our stay there.

The authorities had operated a small factory in the valley next to our dugout before our arrival. Soon after we arrived, they took down the building and carried it to another place. They simply cut off the electric lines that had run to the original site and left them lying on the ground. When we discovered by checking them against one another that the lines were still live, we organized another project. Early one morning we restrung the two electric lines on our side of the valley, complete with wooden poles. We then brought the lines into our dugout, installed two makeshift sockets, and awaited the next phase of the operation.

We did not have to wait long. At one of my interrogations with Blondie, I found a light bulb in a desk and brought it back to our house in my pocket. Father Crosbie and I devised a method to move the light bulb back and forth between the kitchen and the main living room whenever we wished. We guarded that precious light bulb with our lives, because we knew that we would not find a replacement.

We were all interrogated by Blondie during our stay in Manpo. A very well-read and knowledgeable person, he knew the tricks of his trade, but he was not vicious—at least not with us. His interrogations covered America's so-called use of germ warfare against North Korea and similar propaganda, using customary Communist logic. He asked many questions about life in America and the place of religion in our society. When he disagreed, he was not shy in expressing his opposition.

I got the impression from his searching questions that he was really trying to understand the American viewpoint on many subjects, but his extensive training in Marxist-Leninist theory compelled him to see all of reality in the light of "class struggle." After one particularly long and exhausting session, he pushed his chair back from his desk, took a deep breath and announced wistfully, "Well, Larry, I'm afraid that you and I do not speak the same language."[3]

But Blondie's grasp of the English language was, indeed, excellent. During all my interrogations, only once did I use a word that he did not understand. The surprising thing is that the word was not an unusual or big one: he asked me to explain what "valid" meant. This seemed very strange to me, and I wondered about it later. I concluded, perhaps with a little prejudice, that in the Communist world all orders coming down from the top were, by definition, valid; those coming from below were not. Hence, the word was not really needed.

I was very surprised years later when Blondie, whose real name is Gregory Kuzmitch, defected to the West. It may well be that even in Manpo, North Korea, in 1951 and 1952, he had questions about the Communist system; that would in part explain his relatively benign interrogation sessions with us. I'm certain that the Russian Internal Security Police (now KGB) had trained him in the art of terrorizing his prisoners during interrogation when necessary. For some reason, he chose not to use that part of his training on us.

At one particularly interesting interrogation I finally mustered enough courage to ask Blondie a question that I had been afraid to ask of my North Korean interrogators ever since my death cell experiences in Pyongyang: "Why do the Communists change the definition of words like peace, freedom, democracy, truth, and justice?"

"Of course we changed their definition. Don't forget that in the English language those words developed their meanings in the Western world. Therefore, they reinforce the traditions and values of the Western world. Do you think we would be foolish enough to use those words with your meanings so that they reinforce your traditions and values? We have changed the meanings of such words so that they now reinforce and support the class struggle, the kind of world that we are trying to build." That was as clear an insight into the Communists' concept of truth as I had ever heard.

On one occasion, Blondie asked me what I had heard from home. I told him that I had heard nothing.

"Don't you get letters from America?" he asked.

"No, I have never received a single letter from anyone since I have been in North Korea. I haven't been able to write any either."[4]

"I'm sorry to hear that. I understand that you had not been married long when you were captured."

"Yes, and I'm worried about my wife. The last time I saw her she was not well."

"Do you think your wife might be in a family way?" he inquired. His choice of words seemed unusual; I had not heard the expression "in a family way" in years, and I wondered where he had learned his English. Most Europeans and Orientals that I had met had learned their English from the British, but Blondie's accent was neither typically British nor American.

In time, I found that I did not dread walking the three miles into Manpo and facing Blondie's interrogations. The schedule was usually such that I was interrogated about three hours in the morning and then, following a break for lunch, two or three more hours in the afternoon. What we all wanted more than anything else was some news from the outside world, especially news concerning the peace talks to end the war. Blondie did not tell us everything that we wanted to know, and his opinions were biased, but he did sketch out for us the bare outlines of the course of the war from its beginning. The North Koreans had never done that for us. They always wanted to keep us in the dark as much as possible.[5]

We were provided with some diversions during the spring and summer of 1952, even occasional trips to Manpo to bathe in the Yalu River and to view Russian movies at the local theater. Though of poor quality and heavily laden with propaganda, they did provide us a welcome relief from our everyday boredom.

During our stay at Manpo, we were told by several local people that some older German prisoners, both men and woman, had lived there the year before and that several had died; these prisoners, they said, were from a place in Wonsan. A large German Benedictine monastery was known to have existed in the North Korean city of Wonsan since long before World War II. While Germany and Japan were allies, the Benedictines were allowed to continue their work, but with the coming of the Russians into North Korea in 1945, the status of these German citizens changed. When the Korean War broke out, the Benedictines were apparently arrested by the North Korean authorities, and some were charged with serious crimes.

According to our local informants, the Benedictines had resided in the same dugout that we were living in. We looked carefully for signs of the graves of those who might have died but did not find any for a long time. Then one day when Father Crosbie and I were sitting near our house, something suddenly caught my eye. I saw five small pine trees of equal height in a cleared area where there were no other trees; they were arranged to form a cross, one tree for each of the four points and one in the center. The trees were two feet tall and marked an area of approximately ten by twenty feet. We felt sure we had found the graves of the Benedictines.

One night during the summer of 1952 as we sat outside in the darkness, we noticed that the roof of a nearby Korean farmhouse was on fire. Running the quarter-mile to the house, we climbed up on the burning roof and, with the use of long poles, succeeded in pushing the burning straw to the ground. The fire was soon extinguished, and except for the loss of a bit of straw, there was no damage. In fighting the fire, however, I had come too near the edge of the roof and had fallen to the ground, injuring my left ankle severely. I was in so much pain for a time that I could only crawl out of the way and watch. I could not bear any weight on my left ankle and had to be half-carried back to our dugout.

The next morning as I lay on the floor in our room, I heard Commissioner Lord shout from the outside, "We have visitors!" The next moment, the door was opened to admit the commandant of the Place of Learning, followed by a smiling and bowing old man and woman carrying a basket of vegetables. The commandant gave them permission to speak. "We are sorry that you injured yourself in fighting the fire at our house last evening," the old man said, bowing low. "We hope that you will soon recover. Would you please accept these unworthy gifts as a token of our appreciation for what you did?"

It was truly a touching moment for me. I didn't want to accept the gifts, because I knew how little those people had. At the same time, I knew the Korean custom in such matters: to have refused the gifts, for whatever reason, would have been to insult them. The old man and woman beamed as I expressed my gratitude for what they had given me. Even the commandant smiled. The old people would not have dared visit me without his permission. The commandant had brought along a medic to look at my ankle. After he gave me some aspirin, they left.

We saw a little evidence of the war from time to time. Occasionally, we could see the contrails of large numbers of aircraft moving north directly over the Yalu River and continuing out of sight. A lesser number, three to six contrails, could often be seen following; these would begin a wide turn to the right or left as they neared the border separating North Korea and Manchuria and would then disappear to the south. We theorized that the Communist aircraft were operating from air bases in Manchuria, where they would be beyond the reach of American attack from the air.[6]

On one occasion we saw a flight of some nine F-84 Thunderjets move in from the south at very low altitude and attack a target near Manpo with rockets and machine guns. The attack was conducted in single file over an area near our camp. The aircraft flew by us in shallow dives, so close that I could see a bright red band painted just behind the air intake on the nose. There was quite a bit of large-caliber antiaircraft fire exploding in the area. After all the planes had made a pass at the target, they disappeared to the south.

We were treated quite often to the rain of flack from exploding antiaircraft fire directed at American aircraft. That was one of our worries at that time. Once the American planes had departed southward and the firing had stopped, we could hear a low buzzing sound for perhaps thirty seconds as shrapnel rained down; at times it could be heard striking the ground. During this critical period no one moved. In spite of our fears, however, no one in our group was ever struck by it.

When we left the Place of Learning at Manpo on August 13, 1952, we were elated. The rumor was that we were to be turned over to the Chinese in Pyoktong. We all believed that we would receive more food and medical attention if we were placed under Chinese control. For some reason we had suspected all summer that we might be moving, so we had not bothered to stockpile a large supply of fuel for the winter.

The authorities arrived at our dugout with about a dozen prisoners before we had boarded the truck that took us to our new home. We soon saw that they had come to take anything of value that we had accumulated during our stay—and they knew exactly where to look. Pulling down the straw ceiling, they found numerous axes, sickles, nails, digging tools, and copper wire. There was so much that we were afraid some of the prisoners would be injured by falling objects. To our surprise, the officials made no comment whatsoever when they discovered our treasures.

It was on this occasion that we saw some of the allegedly criminal North Korean civilians for the last time. Many were what we would today call "prisoners of conscience"; they were there because of their beliefs. We had seen some of these same men the year before when we had first arrived at the Place of Learning. In the interval they had all gone downhill in weight and general health; some who had been in good condition were now skin and bones. We had mistakenly assumed that Americans died in such vast numbers at Hanjang-ni because they were inherently weaker. In the Place of Learning, we learned that starvation and death are not race-conscious. The authorities watched us very closely as we prepared to leave; even so, we were able to slip some food to one of the prisoners. Unless his sentence was nearly served already, however, I am afraid that he did not make it.

The emaciated condition of these men struck us particularly hard when we remembered a speech delivered at the People's Trial. One of the judges had stood up and addressed the group following the sentencing of the defendant. I suspect that his words were intended for those of us from the free world more than the 500 citizens of North Korea who were also prisoners. "We are a very humane country. In fact, we are one of the most humane countries in the world. In America, it is common practice to sentence people to fifty, sixty, or even a hundred years in prison. That is disgraceful. Here, the maximum sentence is ten years; rarely is it over seven. Two years is the average of those serving time here. The ill-bred Americans have much to learn."

Knowing how the North Koreans really treated their prisoners, Kris observed, "A three-year sentence in this place would be a life sentence for anyone."

"Then why bother to send anyone here if his sentence is for five years?" I asked. We had, in fact, met such a prisoner.

"This is the Place of Learning, remember?" Kris replied. "Think what it teaches the other prisoners to watch a man slowly die here."

We were very happy to be leaving Manpo and the Place of Learning for good.

15. LIFE AT UJANG

TRAVELING to the southwest, we were stopped by some Chinese officials in the village of Ujang. Apparently it had been the intention of our North Korean officer to take us farther, but the Chinese objected for some reason. They seemed to have great authority in some of the internal matters of North Korea. We waited in Ujang for three days while the various officials tried to work out the problem. Finally, on August 16, 1952, we were moved three miles out of the village to five Korean houses located by a small stream. We were told that the Chinese had refused to accept control of our group because they had not been informed about the presence of women and children.

Nevertheless, the Chinese agreed to supply us with food, and we had plenty to eat as a result. We had all the rice we could eat every day. With our ration of flour we were able to make steamed bread in our rice pots. There were always vegetables and bean oil as well. The following winter we were actually supplied with more pork than we were able to eat. Fat pheasants were part of our ration from time to time during the cold weather. We were able to trade some of our extra rice for the valuable soybeans that we had come to depend upon. There were issues of clothing, blankets, soap, toothbrushes, combs, and mirrors. We were lucky here; we had known misery, starvation, and deprivation, but at Ujang we were better off than most of the local Korean civilians. They had every reason to be jealous and hostile toward us, but they were friendly despite their suffering.

Even their farm animals were hungry. Dogs in the neighborhood were so hungry that they would gulp down your bar of soap if you weren't careful. Nor could you casually put down a piece of cloth that had been used in the kitchen: if the cloth had any oil on it, the dogs would devour it in a second.

We were free to go to the nearby mountains in search of wood for fuel. Although we were restricted to our own immediate area, it would be debatable whether the local citizens had any more freedom of movement that we did. They told us, in fact, that they were required to obtain permission from the authorities to travel out of their own area. The villages and private homes were still off-limits to us. If we were observed talking to someone for too long on the public road, Three Star, our commandant, would walk out and break it up.

In the mountains, however, where we were able to talk to the local people for hours at a time, we made a concerted but not very successful effort to learn about the war. The trouble was that the residents did not know anything: "They keep us in the dark about the war," they said.

"What do the newspapers and radio say?" we asked.

"They are as good as nothing. But we are worried. Do you think that this war is as big as the one you fought a few years ago?" We assumed that they were referring to World War II. "Is this a big war between Russia and America?" they eagerly inquired.

Observing the contrails of jet aircraft, we were able to determine more about the war than the ordinary citizen in North Korea could learn from the newspaper and radio. For example, when we saw as many as forty aircraft cross the international border separating North Korea from Manchuria, we were sure that they belonged to the Communists. Proof that our theory was correct was provided in a few seconds by the appearance from the south of nine to twelve more contrails that behaved differently: when they reached the Yalu River, they made a wide turn and flew back in a southward direction. Such actions indicated to us that the war was limited to Korea. The conclusion could also be drawn that the United States was still fighting in South Korea and very probably had control of the air over North Korea. The Communist aircraft were based in Manchuria to avoid being attacked on the ground.[1]

Father Crosbie began keeping a diary here for the first time. He had talked about it earlier but had been afraid of how our captors would react. For several months beginning in the fall of 1952, however, Father Crosbie talked with members of the group about our experiences in North Korea and put them down on paper. I remember seeing him on many occasions talking with individuals and in groups. In late fall, Father Crosbie decided that in order to write after dark he needed a light of some kind for the room. The Koreans introduced us to a knot that grew on pine trees wherever a branch had been cut off. These pine knots could be easily lighted because of their high resin content, and they burned for a long time.

We spent several days walking the mountains collecting these knots before we had a sufficient supply. I then helped Father Crosbie construct a miniature inset fireplace in the corner wall of our room, connected to the outside by a small flue to carry away the smoke. Three Star, our commandant, was very unhappy with our project, but as he didn't say much about it for a few weeks, Father Crosbie worked on his diary day and night. After several warnings, Three Star finally ordered the small fireplace removed, but by that time Father Crosbie had completed most of his important writing project.

17 Dec

1952

Death claimed its last victim from our group at Ujang. Ilian Kijikoff had been failing for some weeks and could no longer eat as much as he should. He was known to us non-Russians as "Quartermaster," after the job that he had been given in Kosan some two years earlier. In that very responsible position of looking after our food ration, he was always fair and honest. He died peacefully on December 17, 1952.

The North Koreans had grown tired of the war by that time. Interrogations were not being conducted very often, and when they were, it was usually a half-hearted kind of exercise. I remember my last interrogation. The young officer who sat down in front of me appeared nervous as he cleared his throat. I could tell that the young man behind the makeshift desk was lacking in experience, but I had to guess that he also had little stomach for what he was trying to do. Perhaps a certain number of interrogations were required of him before he could be promoted.

After forty-five minutes, he paused as though to collect his thoughts. It must have been obvious, even to him, that he was not getting anywhere. I don't know what made me do it—it was certainly not planned—but all at once I began speaking without even knowing what I was going to say. "I am now thirty years old, and for all I know I may die in this country. At the moment, that doesn't seem terribly important to me. Even if I should return to my homeland very soon, my life is now about half over. But I wouldn't trade my memories of my life for your future in this God-forsaken country." Immediately, I was shocked at what I had said. Such talk was very dangerous. I would not have dared to speak like that to The Tiger or any other North Korean Communist a few months earlier.

The interrogator sat looking at me for a moment, his face frozen. Then his eyes dropped, and he got up and left the room, leaving me alone with the guard. After we had waited for a few minutes, the guard told me to return to my room. My interrogation was over. That young interrogator remained in the area for several days, but he never spoke to me again.

When it was all over, I was sorry for what I had said. After all, he was not a man like The Tiger or Burp-gun Charlie; this young man didn't fit the carefully designed mold of that repressive society. I had judged, correctly as it turned out, that my interrogator was a decent person. The only time in my entire prison experience when I verbally hit back at the other side without fear, I picked on someone who was also a victim of the system.

Then I remembered an instance that demonstrated to me the true priorities of Communism. A few months earlier Commissioner Lord had participated in a heated discussion with a Communist official about the care of the elderly. Lord expressed his strong view that society should look after the elderly. The official shot back, "We don't concern ourselves with the elderly, one way or the other. Communism is a young man's game." My young interrogator, I suspect, had become jaded at playing the young man's game. For the first time I had won the war of words, but it was a hollow victory.

The Communists of North Korea allowed no competition from any other ideology. Religion of any kind was forbidden. Anyone who practiced the Christian faith, for example, was regarded as disloyal to the state. Yet the Communists at Ujang, aware that we were going home soon, did two things for us to try to win our favor: they gave us all we could eat so that we wouldn't look starved when we were displayed to the world press, and they told us that we had religious freedom—but only among ourselves. It was the final irony: as prisoners we were not only supplied with more food than the ordinary North Korean citizens enjoyed but we were now given a degree of religious freedom that they were denied.

I had been obliged to learn to pray with my eyes wide open in the death cell in Pyongyang. Under The Tiger's regime, too, we had had to worship on the inside; such was his hatred of religion. At An-dong there had been both Protestant and Catholic religious activity between the missionaries and the American prisoners. In fact, we felt that our religious presence among the POWs was the main reason we were separated from them. "You are working against what we are trying to do," the North Koreans told us when we were removed from the POW camp at An-dong. After that, we had often conducted worship services but only in a very discreet manner.

Once we had been given permission by the Communists at Ujang, we Protestants began conducting worship services outside our hut each Sunday morning. The Catholics would similarly meet and say the Rosary together. Our worship services were observed by North Korean civilians at Ujang as they walked on the public road past our houses. A few of them would stop, turn in our direction and stand motionless and at attention during the entire religious observance. As we stood up at the conclusion of the service, they might give a low bow or perhaps make the sign of the cross and then move off. In time, there were as many as six North Koreans observing our worship.

One Sunday morning, Three Star and the village leader caught on to what was happening and stopped the civilians from making these demonstrations. In a country like North Korea, a Christian or any other religious person must face the obvious: to bear the name is to bear the burden.

But some of the people were not to be denied. The next Sunday morning as we concluded our worship service, we happened to look up to the mountain just north of our village and saw a solitary North Korean rise to his feet and bow low in our direction. The next Sunday there were three North Koreans observing our worship. One made the sign of the cross before going on his way. We were thus observed at each of our worship services until we departed North Korea. It was significant, however, that no matter how many of the local people watched us from various mountain locations, each one always sat alone. They would probably have been arrested if two or more of them had met together.

In talking with some of the North Korean Christians as we walked the nearby mountains in search of firewood, we asked them about their religious faith. Their answer was always the same, as though they had it memorized: "It is good to believe as a Christian in the heart, but it is not good to tell anyone about your faith or to practice it openly." Knowing only that much about a country is enough to convince any unwilling resident that he is living in the land of death—every kind of death.

Perhaps this is the reason why Psalm 27:13 became our favorite Bible passage: "I had fainted, unless I had believed to see the goodness of the Lord in the land of the living." The phrase "The Land of the Living" (with capital letters) thus became a symbol for all that we valued.

Both the Chinese and North Korean officials who visited us from time to time predicted as early as January 1953 that we would be released soon, and during early 1953 we got some information about the progress of the peace talks at Panmunjom for the first time. The officials told us that the peace talks were being held up by the prisoner-of-war issue: "The Americans have threatened to kill many of our prisoners in South Korea if they try to return to our country after the war," said one. We then knew the answer: many North Korean and

Chinese soldiers who were being held by the United Nations in South Korea did not want to return home. Their refusal would have been a great loss of face for the Communists.[2]

It came as no surprise to us when an official came to our camp in March and engaged Bishop Cooper, Monsignor Quinlan, and Commissioner Lord in conversation. One of the officials measured their noses, ears, fingers, and toes—the traditional method used by Korean police for identification purposes before the advent of modern fingerprinting techniques.

Soon our group began to dwindle. The English left on March 21, bound for Pyongyang, according to the authorities. The French followed on March 30. Lotte Gliese, our lone German, was questioned about her connection with the French. She had, in fact, taken refuge in the French consulate in Seoul in the early days of the war, and finally she was included in the French group and departed for Pyongyang with them.

We Americans thought we would be last to leave, but it didn't quite work out that way. On the morning of April 20 the door of our house was suddenly thrown open, and a voice shouted in Korean, "*Esa ha gessa*" (let's move). We seven in the American group departed, leaving behind the Australian Father Crosbie and the Turks and Russians. We thought it would be only a matter to time before Father Crosbie followed us, but we were not so sure about the others, who were actually stateless people without a government to inquire about them. The Russians and the Turks were in tears as we drove off. "Please tell everyone you see that we are here," they cried. Sagid walked down the road about a quarter-mile in the direction of our intended travel in order to be the very last to say goodbye to us.

16. THE JOURNEY HOME

ON arriving in Pyongyang, we found a city totally destroyed. We were quartered in two rooms in a tunnel, one of many in that area which had been dug under a mountain. Our hosts were headquarters personnel of the North Korean People's Army. The members of this unit and their families were living in other rooms in that same tunnel. The entire complex was supplied with electricity, but there were no switches for turning off the lights. We slept on wooden beds with mattresses that weren't too bad.

In Pyongyang we were measured for new clothing, given hot baths every day, and served nourishing food. The diet mainstay was caviar, jam, and bread—as much as we could eat. On several occasions the North Koreans commented on our extreme caution and noted that we did not speak unless spoken to. It was a learned response on our part and one that we were reluctant to give up. The North Koreans assigned a major to be with us at all times and to look after our every need. He had another function as well: he slept in the same room with Kris, Father Booth, Danny, and me in an effort to determine the cause of our hostility to the North Korean government. The major kept making inquiries about us and asking why we didn't talk very much: "Are you angry? Why don't you talk to me?" "I won't hurt you, no matter what you say." But we were in no mood to jeopardize our situation by being really candid with the Communists for the first time in three years. They even tried to ply us with alcohol to loosen our tongues. A few of them got drunk, but they got nothing from us.

But the major was persistent. One night in our room, his conversation droned on until the early hours of the morning. Danny and I were the only ones responding to the major; Kris and Father Booth had gone to sleep. Finally, Danny unloaded on the major. He told of the Death March, the shootings, the beatings, the starvation diet, the lack of medicine and clothing, and all the other outrages we had suffered. "Civilized people don't act like this," he summed up. True to his word, the major listened without trying to argue or blame someone else.

The next day we were decked out in our new clothes which had been made with wool cloth from Czechoslovakia. Suits, dresses, and overcoats were all cut from exactly the same cloth. We were then invited to follow an officer who had come to our room. On emerging from our tunnel, we were greeted by the sight of a long table covered with military blankets on which had been placed fruits, nuts, and strong rice wine. We were urged to eat and drink as much as we wished; an official served up large glasses of wine and encouraged us to drink. No one had to tell us—we knew we were being baited. We ate the fruit and nuts but steered clear of the rice wine. It was obvious that they were trying to get propaganda statements from us by getting us drunk.

Then a large bus pulled up behind us and a group of about twenty people carrying cameras of all types unloaded from the bus and moved toward us. They too tried to engage us in conversation, but we were not very friendly to them either. After we had waited around about an hour, rebuffing repeated attempts to entice us with rice wine, an officer approached a speaker's lectern at one end of the long table. He introduced a general in the North Korean People's Army, who was standing behind him. Cameras began to roll as the general swaggered to the lectern.

The general spoke in Korean, and his remarks were translated by an officer standing at his side. "In accordance with the very humane policy of the government of the Korean People's Democratic Republic," he said in part, "you are being released to your homeland today." The general paused and looked directly at the seven American prisoners. At that moment the cameras turned to focus on us. We stood motionless. No one in the American group said or did anything to indicate that we had even heard the news that we were going home. Slowly the cameras that had been focused on us stopped whirring.

The general would try one more time. All cameras again swung in his direction and were turned on. "You Americans are going home. Don't you understand? You will be seeing your families soon. Aren't you happy that you are going home?" The cameras came back to us but were quickly turned off when we did not respond in the appropriate manner. The general abruptly turned on his heel and stormed off. His departure was so sudden that even the interpreter had to suppress a laugh of embarrassment.

With the general gone, the members of the "foreign press corps" moved up to talk to us. They were all from Soviet-block countries, and it was obvious what they wanted.

The seven tired Americans, on their way to the U.S., have just landed at
Tempelhof Airport, West Berlin, on May 12, 1953, after a flight from
Moscow. Left to right are Father William Booth, Dr. Kris Jensen, Larry
Zellers, Helen Rosser, Bertha Smith, Nell Dyer, and Danny Dans.

"You do not seem to be happy that you are going home," one said
to me.

"Oh, I'm happy all right. I'm just not going to celebrate until I am
out of this country," I said.

Another reporter asked me, "Aren't you grateful to the North
Korean People's government for your very humane treatment? After
all, you have been treated in accordance with the principles of human-
ism [sic]." No one answered.

Standing next to us wearing familiar arm bands was a group of three or four people: "We are from the Red Cross of the Korean People's Government. Is there anything we can do to help you?"

"We are all right now, thank you. We have never seen you before. Where were you when we really needed you?" Kris asked irreverently. One of the men managed a weak smile in response.

"What do you think about your very good treatment?" another asked. More silence. Some of the press corps were beginning to show signs of embarrassment. Then one of them asked a question that broke the logjam.

"Isn't there anything for which you can thank the Korean People's Government?"

Nell fielded that question handily. "Yes, as a matter of fact, there is. I thank the North Korean government that I am still alive. Knowing how little they value life in this country, I feel fortunate that I still have mine." There were some embarrassed smiles from the foreign press corps.

"Have you been treated badly?" one asked.

"Yes," was her terse one-word answer.

"We found out about that major who did some bad things to you in 1950, and we punished him severely," a North Korean officer shouted. "He was given Korean money worth sixty-seven thousand dollars to provide transportation and food for you, but he took it. He is a very bad man! He stole it from you and from us! He was court-martialed and sentenced to two years in prison. We are now reviewing his case. What he did was so bad that we may increase his punishment."

"Do you mean that a review board can increase the punishment after he has been sentenced the first time?" I asked. I knew that this could not be done in America.

"Yes, we can do that in our country," he replied.

"But we didn't know all these bad things were happening to you," another officer joined in.

"You didn't know, and you didn't care," Danny said, summing it all up.

There was an embarrassing silence. Then the members of the foreign press corps moved slowly toward their bus, ending the press conference. The next day a Peking radio broadcast monitored in Tokyo reported that the seven Americans being released from North Korea had thanked their hosts for their very humane treatment. The press had made up the appropriate words when it couldn't get them from us.

A North Korean military doctor accompanied us by truck across the Yalu River to Antung, China. He must have been carefully selected for the job, because his manners were impeccable. Approaching the international bridge at Sinuiju, the doctor removed all signs of rank and insignia. "It is the rule," he said. We carried nothing, so going through North Korean customs was no problem. Arriving at the train station in Antung on April 30, 1953, we left the truck and, with our escort, walked into a small room where representatives of the Russian government were waiting for us.

The doctor stopped short at this point; we waited to see what he would do next. Drawing up to his full height and then giving us a low bow, our North Korean escort said simply, "Go in peace," the traditional Korean parting. We responded in kind. He turned and departed.

We turned around and saw two smiling and well-dressed Russians. "Hello, we represent the Russian government. You are being transferred to our care. We are happy to see you. Are you all right?"

"We are fine. Thank you for your help," Kris responded.

It was difficult for us to believe that we were really free of North Korean control. Our bodies were free, but our minds could not make the adjustment. We were afraid that something unfortunate would happen in the world political situation, and we would be returned to North Korea.

The night train trip to Mukden was uneventful. In response to our questions, the Russians told us that we would not be released through Hong Kong, as we had supposed. Instead, we would be taken to Moscow by the Trans-Siberian Railway. There we would be turned over to the American ambassador, who would arrange for our transportation back to the United States. We could not understand the need to make a long journey across Russia when we could have been released in Hong Kong.

The two Russians who were traveling with us were not alone. There were Chinese officials in our coach as well, but they stayed completely in the background. We were so excited that we did not sleep very much on the trip. Food was brought to us on the train, but we were not very hungry.

When we arrived in Mukden on May Day, the Russians and their Chinese hosts took us to a hotel because no other trains would run that holiday. Danny, Father Booth, Kris, and I were given rooms, and the three women were located in another.

"Now you will need some toilet articles," one of the Russians said. In a short time some shopkeepers arrived with various wares for sale.

"But we don't have any money. How can we buy these things?" we asked.

"I will pay for them," volunteered our Russian host.

"But how much will we be allowed to spend?" Kris asked.

"Buy what you will need. You will be traveling across Russia, so you will need quite a few things."

After making our purchases, we were asked whether we would like to see some of the city. We were then driven around to various points of interest in two old American automobiles. On one or two occasions we were permitted to leave the car for a better view, but only if there were no Chinese around. It was a festive May Day occasion, and Chinese were almost everywhere. There were parades, which we were allowed to view from behind the safety of a high wall that had been built around a park.

Leaving Mukden, the next day, we were taken by train to the border town of Manchu-Li and transferred to another coach for the short trip to Otpor, Russia. There the Russian representatives from the embassy in Peking took their leave, after introducing us to a young lady from the Russian Intourist Agency. Our polite new hostess gave us some very disturbing information: we were no longer to be escorted. We had been under guard for so long that we were frightened at the prospect of wandering across Russia on our own. When we expressed our concern, she took us on board our train and introduced us to an old man and woman who operated a tea and sandwich shop in the rear car. "If you have any trouble, get in touch with them. They will look after you," she reassured us. After giving us credit vouchers for use in the dining car and a thousand rubles, she said, "You can spend this wherever you like. You can even buy food from vendors who come to the train."

Once under way, our greatest problem was overeating in the dining car. The Russians there knew who we were and insisted that we eat everything on the menu. I was struck by the capacity of the Russians to drink vodka, which they mixed with everything. Looking out of the window of the train, I saw vast forests far removed from towns or roads. Near Novosibirsk, I noted that the forests had been leveled for many miles. The great distances between towns and the lack of roads in the countryside made a great impression on me. The double-track railway was, at that time, the only way to travel in vast regions of Russia.

The long train ride gave us plenty of time to think and to contemplate our new lives. We also wondered about conditions in North Korea and about our POW friends who were still there.[1]

I had suffered from night blindness during our second and third winters in captivity, caused by insufficient vitamin A. The condition could vary from simple "tunnel vision," where I could see only a small circle, to total darkness: when it was very bad, I could not see anything at night, even with a full moon. When we were taken anywhere in the winter at night, I had had to be led by the hand. The total calories in our rations at Ujang had been more than sufficient, but the diet was still not balanced. With the very good food that I received at Pyongyang and also on the train, however, my night blindness disappeared while we were en route to Moscow. It never returned.

"Hello, I'm Chip Bohlen. I'm happy to see you," said the man with the smiling face as we detrained in Moscow on May 11, 1953. It was Ambassador Charles E. Bohlen, but the name meant nothing to us until some of his staff told us who he was. After being checked into a hotel in the center of Moscow, just overlooking the tomb of Lenin, we were given a little time to freshen up and rest.

The ambassador had planned a luncheon and reception at the embassy in our honor. Before we left our hotel Ambassador Bohlen warned us to remember that we were in Moscow—not America. Even though we would soon be in the American Embassy, he went on, we were not completely free. Further, the international press corps would be at the reception and would certainly want to ask us about our treatment in North Korea. On that particular subject we were to be very careful, he cautioned. Because negotiations were still going on at Panmunjom to end the Korean War and bring about the return of American prisoners (the signing of the armistice was more than two months away at this time), our answers to such questions could affect those negotiations and the safety of our prisoners in some way. "So remember," he concluded, "you are still in a Communist country. You are not free yet."

When we arrived at the reception, each member of the press came running to us armed with pencil and notebook. I fielded a few questions at first but later withdrew from the group to a corner of the room. There I was soon joined by a very pretty and delightful young American lady named Cissy who worked at the embassy. She spoke with the most beautiful and cultured southern accent that I had ever heard. Soon we were joined by Ambassador Bohlen, whom I had noticed moving about the large reception room from one group to another.

"Larry, why aren't you over there talking to the press?" he asked.

"They seem to be doing all right without me. Anyway I'll do my talking when I finally reach freedom," I replied.

I had an opportunity at the luncheon to ask an American diplomatic official why we American, British, and French civilian prisoners were not released through Panmunjom. I was told that the Communists wanted to release us as far away from the free world press at Panmunjom as possible.

Following the luncheon, we spent the afternoon seeing Moscow in two American Embassy staff cars with Father Georges Bissonnette as our guide. Father Bissonnette, an American, was authorized to serve as a priest to American diplomatic personnel in Moscow under an agreement with the Russian government.

That night in our hotel one of our Russian guides briefed us on our planned activities for the following day. When he had finished, Kris asked him a question. "Do I have permission to get up at six o'clock and visit Lenin's Mausoleum?" Our hotel overlooked Red Square, and the mausoleum was located just across the street.

"Of course, but it is closed. We do not know when it will be open to the public again," the guide replied. We already knew from Ambassador Bohlen that following Stalin's death in March of that year, the Russians had begun preparing his body for public viewing in the Lenin Mausoleum.

"Well, I would like to visit the outside of the mausoleum anyway, if that would be all right," Kris said.

"Of course that would be all right. But since it is closed, why do you want to go?" the guide asked.

"I have a few things I would like to say to Uncle Joe," Kris said. Rightly or wrongly, we prisoners had always blamed Joseph Stalin for the Korean War and our subsequent capture by the North Koreans.

On hearing Kris's answer, the guide turned without saying a word and walked out the door, leaving us alone in the room.

The next day, a U.S. Air Force C-54 transport was permitted to fly to Moscow to take us to Tempelhof Airport in West Germany. We were told that Ambassador Bohlen had made a request to the Russians for that flight and that such a procedure was very unusual. Flying across Russia to West Berlin, I wondered how it would feel to be really free once again. I thought that freedom would come in West Berlin, but I was wrong. Again we were warned by American officials to be careful of what we said to the press.

A Pan American Boeing Stratocruiser flew us to Frankfurt on May 12, 1953, where we were to remain for an hour before our departure for the United States. I left the plane with Father Booth and walked to the parking area, away from the reporters who were waiting in the air terminal. At last, I would be free. The North Koreans could not get to me there, I thought. I was wrong again. I had to agree with the official advice not to talk about treatment in North Korea; what we might say could have an adverse effect on the peace negotiations and the safety of our POW friends who remained in North Korean prisons. It struck me that in a perverse sort of way those North Koreans were still preventing me from exercising the right of free speech; I was not able to say what I wished.

My thoughts went back to what I had said to a member of the Communist press in Pyongyang, that I would wait until I was out of North Korea to celebrate. I had found that I had to wait until I was out of China, and then out of Moscow.

For a few minutes I stood on the parking ramp at Frankfurt airport considering my new situation. Then it came to me: I might not yet be able to celebrate free speech, but I could celebrate life in the free world—the Land of the Living—and that was enough.

POSTSCRIPT

FATHER Crosbie followed the American group across Russia to Moscow about two weeks later. The Turks and the Russians had to wait for almost another year for their release. When they arrived at Panmunjom in March 1954, they had added an extra member: Dimitri and Mary, a Russian prisoner, were the proud parents of a new son. Those who are still living now reside either in the United States or in Turkey. None chose to go to the Soviet Union.

Sadly, the South Korean politicians who were prisoners with us have never returned. There have been unconfirmed rumors over the years that some of them have since died in captivity in North Korea.

The surviving American military prisoners of war were returned to freedom after the Korean War armistice was signed on July 27, 1953. Approximately 250 military men of the original 756 that I had known in prison were returned. I see some of these men—now known as the Tiger Group—at annual reunions of former POWs of the Korean War. Most of those who came back are still alive, although some are members of the walking wounded in one way or another. Every person in that group makes me proud, but some also make me sad. Some do not have much of a future, as we count time. Patched up and held together with prayers and tranquilizers, they await only that time beyond time when they will be made whole again for the last time.

My friend Mr. Cho Dong Yun, from the school where I taught in Kaesong, managed to survive by hiding for weeks under the floor of a storage shed at his home. When he had come to me on June 28, 1950, after American aircraft had attacked North Korean transport outside of Kaesong, I had told him to go home and stay out of sight.

After a very brief vacation with his family in the summer of 1953, Kris Jensen went back to Korea to make a six-week study of conditions there for the Rockefeller Foundation. He later returned to Korea with his family and again plunged into his work with customary abandon, never sparing himself or his health. He died suddenly of a heart attack on November 20, 1956, during the move from one busy appointment to another. Until the very end he was very much in control of his life and very certain, as he always was, that he was exactly where he was supposed to be.

Imagine my surprise when in June of 1988 I received a call at my home from Bill Evans, Jr. In prison, Bill Evans, Sr., had often told me about his Korean wife and son, but I did not know whether they had survived the North Korean occupation; after Bill died in captivity, I thought it unlikely that we would ever know. When Bill, Jr., called, we arranged a meeting at the Dallas–Fort Worth airport on July 9, 1988, and, as he awaited flight connections, spent three hours at a nearby McDonald's. Bill lives with his wife in Stratford, Connecticut, and teaches at Fairfield University. He has erected a small memorial to his father in Japan, where his mother now lives. Bill knew that his father had failed to survive his North Korean imprisonment, but he did not know the circumstances, date, or place of death. I was saddened yet honored that I was able to tell him what he had waited thirty-eight years to hear.

A few weeks after my return from captivity I received a letter from the wife of Walter Eltringham, that unselfish man who gave his meager food ration to others and probably died as a result. She was having difficulty collecting Walter's life insurance. The problem was resolved when I wrote the insurance company, giving the date and place of Walter's death.

Sagid Salahudtin, the young Turkish boy to whom I taught physics and geometry in prison, came to the United States after his release and continued his mathematics and science studies. He is now a scientist and lives with his family in the Washington, D.C., area.

The chauffeur for the American missionary women in Kaesong also survived. It was No Sun-sang who drove the automobile to the prison where all of us would be arrested. We had not realized what that very polite young man from the Secret Police was up to when he came to our house. He was so clever that he had talked us into gladly driving our personal cars to our own imprisonment.

George Blake, British vice-consul in Seoul at the time of the Communist attack, was released with the other English nationals in 1953. It was in 1961 that he was convicted of espionage by a British court and sentenced to forty-two years in prison, the longest sentence ever given a British national for spying in peacetime. Some suggested that the forty-two-year sentence was the result of simple arithmetic: one year in prison for the life of each Western agent Blake had compromised. In the press, Blake was reported to have said that he came to an overwhelming belief that the Soviet Union deserved to triumph. When Blondie—Gregory Kuzmitch, our Russian interrogator at Manpo—defected to the United States, he reportedly told the CIA that Blake revealed no British secrets in his interrogations in 1951 but that he did show some indication of weak loyalty to the West. On October 22, 1966, Blake escaped from his Wormwood Scrubs prison cell and was secretly spirited out of England to East Berlin. He was given the Order of Lenin by the Soviet government and now lives in Russia on a lifetime pension; he is occasionally seen in Moscow by members of the Western press.

Frances returned to the United States in the fall of 1950 but received no information about my being a prisoner until January 25, 1952. During all the years I was gone she never lost confidence that I was still alive and would one day be released. At the time we were reunited, Frances was very ill and not expected to recover. She finally regained her health after many months of struggle, expert medical help, and the prayers of friends. I returned to my seminary education, enrolling at Drew University in Madison, New Jersey, and graduated in 1956 with a Master of Divinity degree. After being commissioned a chaplain in the U.S. Air Force, I was stationed in Yokota Air Force Base, Japan. There Frances and I established a home and adopted two Amerasian girls from an orphanage near Yokohama. They are now American citizens; one is married to an Air Force pilot, and both are living happily in the United States. Since I retired from the Air Force in 1975, Frances and I have been enjoying life in Weatherford, Texas. Frances likes gardening and has a special interest in ecology. My hobbies include reading, jogging, and amateur radio.

Prisoners tend to fantasize about what their lives will be like when they are released, often creating future problems for themselves with unrealistic expectations. After the first blush of freedom wears off, some find ordinary routine life hard to manage. "Joy at the first moments of freedom has to last returning prisoners of war for a long time."[1] For me, the joy has lasted. In 1962 I did go through a brief period when I found it difficult to become motivated about anything, but that soon passed and never returned. My nightmares are no longer serious, although they were for a time. Once or twice a month I still dream that I am in North Korean captivity; I am aware in those dreams that I have been there before, and some of the same guards are there with me, but they are the peaceful ones—The Tiger is never present. Occasionally I dream of being taken to the various places in North Korea where we once barely existed, only now I am given good food and generally well looked after. But always in these dreams there is one unresolved problem: I cannot go home!

It is almost four decades since I returned from Communist imprisonment. All my bitterness toward those who caused me pain is gone. But not so toward the Communist system—a society that places a high value on those who are prepared to commit any moral outrage in support of human engineering on a grand scale. Communist societies in the traditional sense are able to exist only through the employment of overwhelming forces of repression and high walls, the Berlin Wall having been the most obvious.

The monolithic structure of the Communist world has crumbled in Eastern Europe. That is great news! But the lessons of history are not always learned, nor are they always remembered. There are still totalitarian bureaucracies in the world, trying to create a new type of mankind. Their efforts to design a heaven on earth by naked force always result in a hell instead, as millions in Eastern Europe can now testify.

Communist societies in the old traditional mold provided us with a model for controlling great numbers of people, but they were never good places to live. Experts agree that nowhere is that old, discredited, repressive mold more in evidence than in present-day Communist North Korea.

Most of the men and women who were with us in North Korea are now gone. Many who are still alive have long since forgotten their acts of kindness to help other people in desperate circumstances. I saw Father Philip Crosbie, the Australian priest, in Seoul on February 4, 1987, our first meeting in thirty-four years. He is still serving there as a missionary. I asked him whether he remembered sharing his yellow jacket with me on the train trip from Pyongyang to Manpo in September 1950. "No," he replied. Memory lapse is an admirable quality in people who know what it really means to share. That's the way it should be.

NOTES

1. FIRST ENCOUNTER

1. Fehrenbach, *This Kind of War*, p. 55.
2. Goulden, *Korea*, p. 42.
3. Blair, *The Forgotten War*, p. 54.
4. Jackson, *Air War over Korea*, pp. 16-17.

2. ENTER, THE SECRET POLICE

1. Those who would raid our houses were more polite and devious than the Japanese were to Agnes Keith when they invaded her home in Borneo in 1942. There the Japanese told her that they could take anything they wanted to help Japan fight the war. This included alcoholic drinks, cigarettes, and silk stockings. (Keith, *Three Came Home*, p. 34).
2. Keegan, *The Face of Battle*, p. 302.

3. DEATH CELL IN PYONGYANG

1. Fehrenbach, *This Kind of War*, p. 61.
2. MacArthur, *Reminiscences*, pp. 373-74.
3. Ibid.
4. Some of my interrogators appeared to be following the lead of the Chinese Communists, who tried to reeducate their opposition. Like one of their victims, Nien Cheng, I was also considered a member of the hated bourgeois class. Her interrogators told her, "The bourgeois class is our enemy. We hope to reeducate most of its members and make them labor for their food. Those who resist and oppose us will certainly be eliminated" (quoted in Nien Cheng, *Life and Death in Shanghai*, p. 226).
5. Deane, *I Should Have Died*, p. 16.

4. DEADLY DIALOGUE

1. Deane, *I Should Have Died*, p. 52.
2. In the Hanoi Hilton prison in North Vietnam where Robinson Risner was held from 1965 to 1973 during the Vietnam War, he was subjected to the intense pain of physical torture many times. In the end, they broke him: "I had done what I thought I would never do—agree to talk" (Risner, *The Passing of the*

Night, pp. 88-89). It is unreasonable to expect American prisoners to withstand the pressures of interrogation under all conditions. "The simple fact is that it is virtually impossible for anyone to resist a determined interrogator" (Barker, *Prisoners of War,* p. 75).

3. The North Koreans and later the North Vietnamese were very good at using propaganda aimed at impressing the outside world. The Japanese in World War II were less successful (Keith, *Three Came Home,* pp. 177-79).

4. The North Vietnamese also used religion to further their propaganda aims. In 1967, American POWs were permitted to attend Mass celebrated by a Catholic priest from Hanoi. They discovered later that they had been secretly photographed for propaganda purposes (Hubbell, *P.O.W.,* pp. 374-76).

5. THE SCHOOLHOUSE

1. White, *The Captives of Korea,* p. 30.
2. MacArthur, *Reminiscences,* p. 418.
3. Deane, *I Should Have Died,* p. 8.

6. NIGHT TRAIN TO MANPO

1. Fehrenbach, *This Kind of War,* p. 97.
2. Ibid., p. 259. There were many such instances during World War II of allied POWs being killed or wounded in attacks by friendly forces, all caused by Japan's refusal to mark their POW ships properly. The Blairs describe a similar situation with the sinking by an American submarine of the Japanese vessel *Kachidoki Maru,* loaded with 600 British POWs (Blair and Blair, *Return from the River Kwai,* pp. 167-75).

7. AUTUMN ON THE YALU

1. Keith, *Three Came Home,* pp. 269-77.
2. Pincher, *Traitors,* p. 24.
3. Wright, *Spy Catcher,* p. 169.
4. Hastings, *The Korean War,* p. 329.
5. Deane, *I Should Have Died,* p. 101.
6. Cookridge, *George Blake,* p. 101.
7. There are varying opinions concerning the date of Blake's conversion to Communism during his imprisonment. Pincher has a different theory altogether: "It is now certain that Blake had committed himself to Communism long before the Korean War" (*Traitors,* p. 157).
8. Cookridge, *George Blake,* p. 101.
9. Bourke, *The Springing of George Blake,* p. 222.
10. Pincher, *Traitors,* p. 164.
11. According to Clay Blair, (*The Korean War,* p. 370) and others, the nearest elements of the United Nations forces invading North Korea were farther away from us at that time than we thought, making it very unlikely that we would have been able to link up.
12. Fehrenbach, *This Kind of War,* p. 276. The issuance of that order gave

rise to even more fear, suspicion, and paranoia in the North Korean Army and provided a climate in which anything could happen. The ramifications of that directive were not lost on the officer who would very soon lead us on the Death March.

13. The Tiger's first speech was typical of those of all North Korean Communists concerning their reason for holding us: it was ideological. We didn't possess the correct political thinking to be allowed to wander about freely. By contrast, a Japanese commanding officer in Borneo in World War II told his British civilian prisoners that the causes for their confinement were racial and punitive: "You are a fourth-class nation now. Therefore your treatment will be fourth-class, and you will live and eat as coolies. In the past you have had proudery and arrogance! You will get over it now!" (quoted in Keith, *Three Came Home*, p. 44).

8. THE DEATH MARCH BEGINS

1. Dean, *General Dean's Story*, p. 187.
2. Blair, *The Forgotten War*, p. 139.
3. Deane, *I Should Have Died*, p. 41.
4. Crosbie, *March till They Die*, p. 43.
5. Stokesbury, *A Short History of the Korean War*, p. 21.
6. Falk, *Bataan*, pp. 56-66. Our Death March in Korea of 110 to 120 miles was longer than the one on Bataan. We had cold to worry about without shelter and adequate clothing; they had extreme heat and lack of water. Had we been well fed and otherwise in good health, we could have walked that distance in the eight days allowed without any trouble. We were fed—however inadequately—along the route of the march, but like those American and Filipino prisoners on Bataan, we were almost starved when the march began.

According to the Japanese plan, which was badly flawed, the greatest distance that POW's would be required to move on Bataan was no more than nineteen miles, with food being provided only at the conclusion of the march (Toland, *But Not in Shame*, pp. 335-36).

7. The problem of trying to fit the the new realities of modern American life into a military tradition that dates back to the master-serf relationship in medieval Europe is very adequately addressed by Fehrenbach. He demonstrates how the performance of American soldiers, who at first fought so badly in Korea, were finally trained to do their job: "The problem is not that Americans are soft but that they simply will not face what war is all about until they have their teeth kicked in" (*This Kind of War*, p. 438).

8. Quoted in Glines, *Jimmy Doolittle*, p. 182.

9. THE FOURTH DAY AND BEYOND

1. Blair, *The Forgotten War*, pp. 109-10.
2. Hunter, *Brainwashing*, p. 253.
3. Falk, *Bataan*, pp. 236-37.
4. POWs don't often have much to laugh about. The notable exceptions were the Italians, many of whom were happy to be captured by the Americans in World War II. Morison (*Sicily-Salerno-Anzio*, 9:90) cites an example of some

Italian soldiers who were captured during the battle for Licata in the Mediterranean. Knowing that they were being sent to the United States, they joked with the American soldiers about their good fortune.

By way of contrast, American submariners who rescued Japanese crewmen from sinking ships found the behavior of those prisoners very unpredictable. Although some would volunteer military information on their own, many were suicidal and dangerous, requiring constant watching (Lockwood and Adamson, *Zoomies, Subs, and Zeros,* p. 192).

10. WINTER AT HANJANG-NI

1. By contrast, the Communist POW workers in UN prison camps in South Korea, closely supervised by the International Red Cross, were fed a balanced diet of 2,800 calories per day, and all prisoners had access to the adequate services of a field hospital (White, *The Captives of Korea,* pp. 117-19, 135-40).

2. Ibid., p. 95.

3. Albert Biderman, *March to Calumny,* p. 159.

4. White, *The Captives of Korea,* p. 96.

5. Ibid., p. 88.

6. Keith, *Three Came Home,* pp. 61-62.

7. Deane, *I Was a Captive in Korea,* p. 149.

8. Fehrenbach, *This Kind of War,* p. 463.

9. Lawton, *Some Survived,* p. 208.

10. Arthur, *Deliverance at Los Baños,* pp. 145-47.

11. See Alexander, *Korea,* p. 253.

12. Hunter, *Brainwashing,* p. 255.

13. We in North Korea were certainly better off in this instance than were the American POWs in North Vietnam for whom the Communists brought in a local clergyman to conduct a Christmas Day religious service in Hanoi in 1968: "A 'Reverend pastor' who was introduced as 'Chairman of the Evangelical Church of Hanoi' was offering a homily in which he likened 'the beloved and respected leader, Ho Chi Minh' to Jesus Christ, and Lyndon Johnson to Herod, the baby killer" (Hubbell, *P.O.W.,* p. 466).

11. CHANGE OF COMMAND

1. Harkins, *Blackburn's Headhunters,* p. 129.

2. Keith, *Three Came Home,* p. 112.

3. Ibid., p. 57.

4. Ibid., p. 111.

12. DIGNITY AT AN-DONG

1. Hunt and Norling, *Behind Japanese Lines,* p. 37.

2. Blair, *Beyond Courage,* p. 6.

3. Ibid., pp. 52-105. I had the honor of getting to know Clem Summersill in the early 1960s at Stead Air Force Base, Nevada, where we had both been assigned as instructors at the Air Force Survival School.

4. Biderman, *March to Calumny*, p. 90.

5. There is confirmation that a U.S. Air Force bombing attack on the bridge at Linchiang, China—just across the Yalu River from Chunggangjin, North Korea—did occur on March 31, 1951 (Futrell, *The United States Air Force in Korea*, p. 321).

6. The problem of trying to obtain adequate intelligence on enemy strength would continue to plague the American military command in Korea. "The intelligence estimate on Nov. 1 [1950] was that there were about 60,000 Chinese in North Korea. Actually, at that point in Chinese deployment, there were about 180,000" (Middleton, *Crossroads of Modern Warfare*, p. 195).

7. Fifteen years after the Korean War, the Viet Cong used the same technique of breaking down the rank structure of American POWs in order to divide them and make them easier to control (Grant, *Survivors*, p. 126).

8. A valid difference of opinion does exist concerning the wisdom of taking moderate exercise when one is almost starving to death. I voted in favor of daily exercise. Nien Cheng, a Chinese woman who spent six and a half years in a small prison cell in Shanghai at the height of the Communist Cultural Revolution, discovered the value of physical exercise: "I managed to exercise each day and after a few months recovered my physical strength somewhat, as well as my feeling of well-being" (*Life and Death in Shanghai*, p. 203).

9. White, *The Captives of Korea*, p. 330.

13. A CHANGE FOR THE BETTER

1. The women in our group were probably subjected to less sexual harassment than were their British counterparts under the Japanese in Borneo during World War II. There, Agnes Keith found herself charged with slander by the Japanese commander when she complained that a guard had tried to rape her (Keith, *Three Came Home*, pp. 150-64). On the other hand, the Japanese in control of Keith's camp demonstrated a degree of kindness to a very old woman prisoner that would have been unthinkable among the North Koreans who were in charge of us: they permitted an ailing Catholic nun, Mother Bernardine, to leave the camp and return to her convent because the food there was better. (ibid., p. 106).

14. THE PLACE OF LEARNING

1. Following World War II, when the Japanese almost starved all their prisoners, the Geneva Convention was revised to state that the ration given to prisoners in wartime must be sufficient and that the "habitual diet" of those prisoners must be taken into consideration (White, *The Captives of Korea*, p. 77). This definition is complicated by the simple fact that an American or other Westerner will starve and die on a diet that an Oriental can live on for a very long time. Yet it would be naive to expect a belligerent country to feed enemy prisoners better than its own citizens (Fehrenbach, *This Kind of War*, pp. 462-63).

2. In North Vietnam, some of the worst treatment that many of the American POWs received from civilians occurred not when they were captured but at staged hate-propaganda parades in Hanoi; there the blindfolded and handcuffed POWs were fair game for anyone who had a grudge to settle

(Hubbell, *P.O.W.*, pp. 183-99). The treatment of American POWs by civilians of the belligerent nation has varied. Allied airmen were sometimes lynched by angry mobs of German civilians in World War II. Robinson Risner's treatment after he was shot down in North Vietnam was relatively restrained, although he had to be protected from some old ladies who were trying to hit him with sticks (Risner, *The Passing of the Night*, p. 10). Similarly, Dave Booker, the U.S. Marine Corps pilot in our group, found himself surrounded by enraged North Korean women who tried to get to him but were restrained by guards (Clarke, *Journey through Shadow*, p. 246). Mo Baker, U.S. Air Force pilot, told me of his reception after being shot down in North Vietnam in 1967; his experience was more brutal: his leg, which had sustained a compound fracture, was twisted completely around by laughing civilians (personal interview, 1987).

3. Blondie was trying to do what he was paid to do: make a convert. The Communist ideology of the 1950s considered every man, woman, and child in the free world a potential convert, and specified that where possible, the enemy was to be converted rather than killed. In a perverse sort of way, this viewpoint, especially during the early part of our imprisonment, may have been the main reason that any of us were allowed to survive.

By contrast, the propaganda dynamic behind the conquest of Asia by the Japanese was race: "Asia for the Asiatics," and "the Japanese East Asia Co-Prosperity Sphere." Outsiders from the West could have no part in their new order. The Aryanism of the Nazis similarly limited the acceptance of their doctrine to citizens of Germany and its allies (Fehrenbach, *This Kind of War*, p. 470).

4. The North Koreans "manipulated the flow of the prisoners' mail" (Kinkead, *In Every War but One*, p. 117). That could mean that a prisoner got little mail or none at all—as was my case. In our group almost no one received any mail.

5. Whereas we in North Korea were given no information from the free world, the POWs in North Vietnam were given lots of it (Grant, *Survivors*, pp. 176-88). I think the reason is obvious: the news coming from America during the Vietnam War was so depressing to POWs that it served the purposes of their interrogators.

6. The tactics of Chinese and North Korean pilots in operating combat missions into North Korea from safe bases in Manchuria contined until the signing of the armistice on July 27, 1953 (Jackson, *Air War over Korea*, pp. 152-53).

15. LIFE AT UJANG

1. Russian pilots also flew combat missions over North Korea while operating from their Manchurian sanctuary, but they were withdrawn before the end of the war (Jackson, *Air War over Korea*, p. 153).

2. In early 1953, the Communists at the peace table were opposing voluntary repatriation of POWs, because they knew that many of their own prisoners in South Korea would not return unless forced to do so (Rees, *Korea*, p. 380). They finally abandoned their position on voluntary repatriation on March 30, 1953, thereby making an armistice possible (Fehrenbach, *This Kind of War*, p. 643).

16. THE JOURNEY HOME

1. Many American POWs would not gain their freedom until after the signing of the armistice on July 27, 1953 (Blair, *The Forgotten War*, p. 975). Even then, the internal war and the bloodletting in North Korea did not end: a short time after the signing of the armistice, Radio Pyongyang announced the execution of ten senior officials in the Kim Il Sung government (Rees, *Korea, the Limited War*, p. 450).

POSTSCRIPT

1. Barker, *Prisoners of War*, p. 4.

SELECTED BIBLIOGRAPHY

Alexander, Bevin. *Korea: The First War We Lost.* New York: Hypocrene Books, 1986.

Arthur, Anthony. *Deliverance at Los Baños.* New York: St. Martin's Press, 1985.

Barker, A.J. *Prisoners of War.* New York: Universe Books, 1975.

Biderman, Albert D. *March to Calumny.* New York: Macmillan, 1963.

Blair, Clay, Jr. *Beyond Courage.* New York: David McKay, 1955.

Blair, Clay. *The Forgotten War.* New York: Times Books, 1987.

Blair, Joan, and Clay Blair, Jr. *Return from the River Kwai.* New York: Simon & Schuster, 1979.

Bourke, Sean. *The Springing of George Blake.* London: Mayflower Books, 1971.

Cheng, Nien. *Life and Death in Shanghai.* New York: Grove Press, 1986.

Clarke, Conley. *Journey through Shadow.* Charlotte, N.C.: Heritage, 1988.

Cookridge, E.H. *George Blake: Double Agent.* New York: Ballantine Books, 1970.

Crosbie, Philip. *March till They Die.* 1955; ltd. ed rpt. Dublin Ireland, 1985.

Dean, William F. *General Dean's Story.* New York: Viking Press, 1954.

Deane, Philip. *I Should Have Died.* New York: Atheneum, 1977.

––––––. *I Was a Captive in Korea.* New York: Norton, 1953.

Falk, Stanley. *Bataan: The March of Death.* New York: Norton, 1962.

Fehrenbach, T.R. *This Kind of War.* New York: Macmillan, 1963.

Futrell, Robert. *The United States Air Force in Korea, 1950-1953.* Washington, D.C.: Office of Air Force History, 1983.

Glines, Carroll. *Jimmy Doolittle: Master of the Calculated Risk.* New York: Van Nostrand Reinhold, 1980.

Goulden, Joseph. *Korea: The Untold Story of the War.* New York: McGraw-Hill, 1982.

Grant, Zalin. *Survivors.* New York: Berkley Books, 1985.

Harkins, Philip. *Blackburn's Headhunters.* New York: Norton, 1955.

Hastings, Max. *The Korean War.* New York: Simon & Schuster, 1987.

Hubbell, John G. *P.O.W.* New York: Reader's Digest, 1976.

Hunt, Ray C., and Bernard Norling. *Behind Japanese Lines.* Lexington: University Press of Kentucky, 1986.

Hunter, Edward. *Brainwashing: The Story of the Men Who Defied It.* New York: Farrar, Straus & Cudahy, 1956.

Jackson, Robert. *Air War over Korea.* New York: Scribner, 1973.

Keegan, John. *The Face of Battle.* London: Penguin Books, 1978.

Keith, Agnes Newton. *Three Came Home.* Boston: Little, Brown, 1947.

Kinkead, Eugene. *In Every War but One.* New York: Norton, 1959.

Lawton, Manny. *Some Survived.* Chapel Hill, N.C.: Algonquin, 1984.

Lockwood, Charles A., and Hans Christian Adamson. *Zoomies, Subs, and Zeros.* New York: Greenberg, 1956.

MacArthur, Douglas. *Reminiscences.* New York: Fawcett Books, 1964.

Middleton, Drew. *Crossroads of Modern Warfare.* Garden City, N.Y.: Doubleday, 1983.

Morison, Samuel Eliot. *Sicily-Salerno-Anzio,* vol. 9. Boston: Little, Brown, 1975.

Pincher, Chapman. *Traitors.* New York: Penguin Books, 1988.

Rees, David. *Korea: The Limited War.* New York: St. Martin's Press, 1964.

Risner, Robinson. *The Passing of the Night.* New York: Ballantine Books, 1973.

Stokesbury, James L. *A Short History of the Korean War.* New York: Morrow, 1988.

Toland, John. *But Not in Shame.* New York: Random House, 1961.

White, William. *The Captives of Korea.* New York: Scribner, 1957.

Wright, Peter. *Spy Catcher.* New York: Viking Penguin, 1987.

INDEX

Acheson, Dean, 7-8
aircraft, American: B-26 Invader, 8-9, 18;
C-87, 11; B-29 Superfortress, 51-52,
157-58, 222 n 5; navy dive bomber, 52;
F-51 Mustang, 52, 62, 121; Ballanca, 96;
F-80 Shooting Star, 137, 158; F4U-1
Corsair, 158, 170; F-84 Thunderjet, 197;
C-54 Skymaster, 212; Boeing
Stratocruiser, 212
American Embassy, 1, 211
American government, 7-8
American prisoners. *See* prisoners,
civilian; prisoners of war, military
(POWs)
American unpreparedness, 94, 100
Anderson, Rev. L.P., 3, 8, 29, 30, 31
Andersonville prison, 138
An-dong, North Korea, 176, 202; site of
UN burials, xi, 166; civilians and POWs
fraternize in, 158-59; work details, 178
Antung, China, 208
armistice, Korean War, 211, 214
Ashiya Air Force Base, Japan, 9
Australian prisoners, 56
Austrian prisoners, 56

Baranski, Cpl. Alphonse (POW), 81, 82
Bataan Death March: compared to
Korean, 102, 118
Beatrix, Mother (French civilian
prisoner): assisted on Death March,
101; disappears, 107
Belgium, 7
beriberi, 136; treated with soy beans,
148-49
Berlin, 182
Berlin Wall, 217
Bissonnette, Father Georges, 212
Black Dragon Society, 95
Black Watch, 57
Blake, George (British diplomatic
prisoner): knows Russian language,
62; early life, 72; betrays West, 73;
wife's reaction, 74; raids turnip field,

83; escapes temporarily, 84; meetings
with, 140; interrogated by Blondie, 183;
arrest and defection, 215-16
Blondie (Russian interrogator):
identified, 73, 183, 194; interrogates
Zellers, 193-95; gives news of peace
talks, 195, 223 n 5; defects to America,
216
Bohlen, Charles E., 211, 212
Booker, Capt. Dave (POW), 158, 170
Book of Common Prayer, 137
books from Russia, 176-77
Boose, Col. Donald W., Jr., xii
Booth, Father William (American civilian
prisoner), 53, 205, 209; on Death
March, 116; punished, 142; at
Frankfurt, 212
Boysen, Dr. Alexander (POW): on Death
March, 101; visits at Hanjang-ni, 140-41;
advises daily exercise, 165; cares for ill
and wounded, 165, 172
Brannon, Rev. Lyman, 146, 147, 148
Buchenwald Prison, 118, 175
Bulteau, Father Joseph (French Catholic
missionary prisoner), 130
burial sites, 124-25, 129, 155, 166
Burp-gun Charlie, 122, 184, 201
Byrne, Bishop Patrick (American Catholic
missionary prisoner): at Pyongyang,
53; on Death March, 97, 111, 112;
becomes ill, 119; sent to hospital, 128;
death of, 129

Cadars, Father Joseph (French Catholic
missionary prisoner), 130
Camp Red Cloud, Korea, xi
Canada, 46
Canavan, Father Frank (Irish Catholic
missionary prisoner): on Death March,
93; sent to hospital, 128; death of,
129-30
Catholic prayer books, 137
Chanteloupe, Maurice (French journalist
prisoner), 56